When I'm 64

A Story of Love and Resilience

Lauren Levis

Published by Inkshares, Inc., Oakland, California
www.inkshares.com

Edited by Dawn Raffel
Cover design by Lisa Levis
Cover Photo: Lauren Gibson Photography
Interior design by Kevin G. Summers

ISBN: 9781947848214
eISBN: 9781947848221
LCCN: 2017956969

First edition

Printed in the United States of America

INTRODUCTION

ALL THAT I know about truth and love took me a long time to comprehend, yet the bulk of it came to me in a single flash, the moment I first held my daughter. Seeing her sweet face close to mine, the same face that I had dreamt about since I was a small girl first toying with the idea of motherhood, made me something larger than a single person. I became a part of an incredible story, the start of which had been set in motion a lifetime before.

This book pays homage to my father, a complex and, at times, heart-wrenching story of a man's life. He was a man in search of himself when he got lost in addiction, a lover who lost his family while wrapped up in the arms of another woman, and a lonely old man left to live on his own when his luck finally ran out. Fighting for survival every step of the way, he endured a tormented childhood, abused at the hands of practically every adult who came his way. Emerging mostly unscathed, he became an air traffic control operator who had a problem with authority and a penchant for trouble. He found himself directionless and running with the wrong crowd. Searching for something better, he began to try his hand playing different parts. He was a hippie, a drug addict, a prisoner, a chef, a teacher, a husband, and a father. It was in this last role where he truly achieved what he had been searching for the whole time: the ability to love and to be loved.

My relationship with my father wasn't a typical one. He wasn't my protector and provider; I couldn't turn to him when someone or something was giving me a hard time. Rather, he was my larger-than-life storyteller, constantly there to remind me that no matter what life had to throw at me, he had already survived something much worse. He spent hours recounting life's lessons, hoping against hope that even a single piece of information he shared would suffice for me to consider a difficult lesson already learned and save me from the pain he had endured.

When I first held my daughter, I felt the surge of love that he must've felt when he looked into my eyes, and suddenly I understood what he had tried to do for me. In some ways, it was too late. I realized the only way I could go on was to record his painful existence, sharing his life for the world to see. While these stories are important for me, I hope that in seeing his trials, tribulations, and mistakes unfold, you too may find the will to keep fighting for yourself, against all odds.

His story doesn't begin with me or with the loving gaze of a mother on her firstborn child; it goes back to a cabin in the hills of Appalachia. That was where he learned his first and most important lesson—how to survive in the worst of circumstances—and developed his knack for hiding, even in the midst of a crowded room.

I've been looking for the best way to tell this story for many years, and when my father and I began discussing sharing his life story, it became clear almost immediately that the most appropriate voice for this story was his own. While I physically put the words onto the paper, these are his experiences and, most importantly, his journey. This is the point where I leave you and let my father tell his amazing story of love and survival once and for all.

For my mother, whose stability, unwavering support, and unconditional love allowed for a happy ending.

A CHANGE IS GONNA COME

WHEN I REFLECT on my childhood, looking to see if there was any one thing that made me the way I am, there is one day in particular that I return to. I was four years old, sitting on a log in the woods. I was hiding for the day, and I thought I had a pretty good spot picked out. That is, until I heard the screams. I heard my Uncle Jim shouting and my mother, Cecile, screaming for dear life; I also heard her brother Tommy, or maybe it was actually her brother Hill, running after them. Some of the details have gotten lost, but the picture that I can see is crystal clear: Jim coming into the clearing, dragging my mother by her hair. Jim had a gun.

He pointed it straight at me and said, "I'll shoot anyone who tries to stop me."

I stood frozen in the clearing, unable to move. The next twenty minutes aren't as clear to me, but I remember the gist of what happened. Jim beat and raped my mother, while I watched. I stood there as he leaned the gun against a tree, mere feet away from me. I could have saved her. I could have stopped him. I could have saved us right then and there. Instead, I did nothing but stand there. What was wrong with me? Why didn't I stop him?

When he was done, Jim grabbed his gun and looked at me. His eyes seemed to scream at me that I was a failure, worthless and powerless just like my mother. I felt my lower lip quiver and the tears started to stream faster and faster down my face. I used my fists to wipe away my tears when I felt a hand on my chin. My mother stood before me, her eyelid swollen shut and blood trickling from a cut on the side of her mouth. Her eyes had a different message. Instead of pain, I saw fire.

"Put your chin up. You don't let nothing that bastard does make you cry. You hear me? Crying doesn't do any good except to get your shirt wet. You be brave now. We're still alive, aren't we?" she said, grabbing my hand.

She squeezed it as we walked back toward the cabin. With her chin held high and her eyes straight ahead, Cecile showed me how to survive, one foot in front of the other, pushing on through her pain.

On September 20, 1946, on a beautiful clear morning, I was born to Cecile Belle Jordan and John Herbert Wagner Jr., in Fairfax County, Virginia. I was their first child and would prove to be the last living thing that their damned union ever produced. We lived not far from the hospital for the first few months of my life, but we quickly relocated back to Cecile's family home in North Carolina, where I would spend the formative years of my youth.

Running water and electricity are both conveniences that existed long before 1946, both things that many people cannot imagine life without, but these were pleasures that the hill folk in Borea County, North Carolina, still did not have access to. That doesn't mean that we didn't bathe or cook; we just had to do things differently. This was one of the first lessons I learned as a child. I was different—different from my friends whose families weren't as harsh, different from my cousins, and different from everyone I knew. I watched as other children got called in to wash up for supper. I, on the other hand, never got called to come in, and I avoided going home like the plague.

I lived in a log cabin with nine of my cousins and all of their parents. We gave new meaning to the term "close family." You can't get much closer than sleeping in piles, everyone on top of each other, in a small cabin with dirt floors, no electricity, and a lack of running water. We would walk to the river and fetch buckets of fresh water to bring home to boil for dinner and also to fill the washbasin. Each week, my mother would walk several miles into town to purchase food to feed all of us, a single five-pound sack of flour and sometimes a link of sausage. It's easy to see how the youngest and smallest of the children would get left without much food. It was survival of the fittest, and at that point, I was certainly not the most fit.

Franklin D. Roosevelt had been president for more than twelve years and was in the midst of ending World War II and leading the country out of the Great Depression when he passed away, leaving Harry Truman in office in 1945. The western world was already on an upswing by the time I was born, but you wouldn't have known by what went on in Appalachia; we were all still pretty depressed. Clothes were hand-me-downs, and you were lucky if you got a single pair of shoes to last you for the year.

My mother, Cecile Belle, was a hardworking girl of eighteen when she brought me into this world, maybe an adult by legal standards, but she hadn't had the life experience of a typical adult. I cannot say for certain whether she resented me or not; I can only say that it sure seemed like it. The easiest way to explain my relationship with my mother is to attempt to understand her relationships with her family before I was introduced to the scene.

Rape, incest, and abuse were just a few of the defining characteristics of Cecile's upbringing as a Jordan in North Carolina. My mother was born into a family with six children. Three boys, two sisters, and herself. Her brothers were all older and seemed to have been born bad. Jim, Tommy, and Hill still lived in the cabin with us when I was growing up there, all those years later. They had added some of their own wives and children to the brood, but none of them could afford their own place. That was how we all ended up in that cabin together, fighting for our lives.

Jim and Tommy tortured their sister throughout her childhood. There simply was not much else for them to do, and while he was better, Hill was no saint either. Jim was the ringleader, the spitting image of their father, an abusive alcoholic who instilled twisted ideals in his children, especially the boys. Tommy was your typical sidekick, always there to chide and tease, and occasionally to twist the knife in a little deeper. With two brothers with a serious mean streak, there wasn't much Hill could do to avoid being painted with the same brush. He had a soft spot for his sister, but if he let it show too often, he would quickly become the target of Jim's aggressions.

Cecile was a beautiful girl, and she was the only one of them with the brains and work ethic to leave the countryside. Beginning at age fourteen, she would commute out of the hills for work and actually had managed to build a potential future for herself. She tried to rise above the madness of her brother Jim, striving to leave his brutality behind. Jim beat his siblings, his young wife, and their children unmercifully for any reason that presented itself. He would have them pick switches off the trees or use any other item he could get his hands on to inflict pain. If the physical abuse wasn't bad enough, sexual abuse was also not uncommon, and Jim made sure that Cecile knew that she was not better than him or the woods in which they lived. He beat her down in every way imaginable, which was the main reason she left home for Virginia, where she met John Herbert.

I wish I could say things got better for Cecile when I was born, but my father was a womanizing drunk and had not planned to ever have a family. He was a traveling trucker and would leave for weeks on end with no word as to when he would return or for how long. When he did come home, it was to berate my mother and beat her. With a new baby, Cecile needed help, even if it was the worst kind of help. She packed our few things, grabbed me, and returned to the scene of what must have been a grisly childhood for her, only to begin to leave me vulnerable to the kinds of torture she herself had already survived.

After our return, Cecile again began leaving for work outside the area, and this did nothing but anger Jim more. He just could not understand what she did not get the first time. If leaving before had done nothing to better her, what did she think was going to happen now? Not only was she back drawing on the family's few resources, but she had brought with her yet another screaming mouth to feed. The only difference was that he now had me to take his anger and aggressions out on in Cecile's absence. I was the youngest and by far the smallest of the nine cousins who lived in the cabin, and therefore the easiest to catch. I would get beat from the minute Jim woke until Cecile returned from work. He would then turn his hatred toward her. You must be wondering why she left me there, seeing how I looked when she came home. You could also wonder why Tommy and Hill didn't stand up to Jim, either. I can't answer those questions. This was the only life any of them had ever known, and they had all survived it, as would I.

My mother did make one major attempt to see that I was safe during her absences. While she was working in town, she met a nice family who seemed trustworthy. Somehow, she arranged for me to stay in the safety of their home during the day. She would get to come visit me on her breaks, and she knew I was tucked safely away from Jim's violent hands. It was strange to be a part of someone else's home and see how they all functioned without hurting one another. In the mornings, I would arrive around breakfast time and get to feel a part of something that wasn't so deranged. They had their own children and they actually let me play with them. This was the only place that I was not being used as a human punching bag.

Eventually, the family approached Cecile after I had been staying with them for about a year. They wanted to know if they could adopt me. My mother never took me to their home again. Looking back, I wonder how my life would have unfolded had she given me to them, but part of me feels it really couldn't have been that different. To be honest, I believe that some people are born with suffering in their blood, and no matter how the circumstances change they will still be drawn to tragedy.

As I got older, I got a little bit smarter. I would leave when my mother left for work in the morning and try to stay hidden until she came home. This worked at times, but other times it just made Jim angrier when I did come back. As a child, it was very difficult to figure out what I had done wrong. I got beat when I stayed. I got beat when I left. I got beat when I was good. I really got beat when I was bad. You can't expect to learn right from wrong if all of your consequences and rewards are the same. You lose the ability to differentiate between what is a deserved punishment and what will happen if you behave well. There was no consistency, no way to develop a sense of morality in such a hostile environment.

The thing about living in an abusive environment is that you can never rest; if you let your guard down for even an instant, it can come back to bite you. When I came home in the evenings I would approach the cabin slowly, hoping that Jim would be asleep. Some days I was lucky, but luck isn't something to be counted on. One unlucky night, as I came close to the back door, I heard him moving around followed by a terrible screeching sound. Turning the corner, I registered that Jim had my pet opossum in his hands. While opossums aren't typical house pets, we had to make due with the animals that lived around us. This opossum wasn't afraid of me and he would sometimes follow me around in the evenings. That night, Jim seemed to be waiting for me to come home, and maybe if I hadn't been there he would have let that opossum live. Jim told me to stand against the back wall of the cabin facing the woods. He took the opossum over to the tree where I picked my switches and proceeded to nail the opossum to the trunk. He made me watch as he skinned the opossum my only friend in the woods, alive.

I made conscious choices to make friends away from home, but even that was difficult because I never wanted anyone to know where I came from and how little we had. There was one place where you did not need much money to play or fit in, and it was on the dunes on the side of the roads. Local kids would take anything they could get their hands on and play "trucker" by rolling their toy trucks up and down the large brown dirt piles on the side of the road. I would sit and watch the kids play most days since I did not have a truck of my own.

I can't remember if I finally got the truck for my birthday or Christmas, or maybe even just because somebody had a bit of extra cash. Whatever the case, I got a truck of my own. A twenty-five-cent plastic truck with wheels that did not spin, but they were wheels nonetheless. The very next day I woke early, excited to take my truck down to the dunes. Finally, I was going to be able to play. I rolled my truck up to the top of the dune and started to make my first pass when one of the older kids snatched it out of my hands.

"Give that back!" I shouted at him, but he just kept on running.

At the top of hill, he placed my truck at the end of a line of similarly pitiful excuses for toy trucks. There were other smaller kids gathered around, whining for the big boys to give their toys back. I watched as he pulled out his BB gun and began firing away. He shot all of the trucks, including mine, full of hundreds of tiny holes. He laughed as he threw the remains back to their distraught owners.

Crushed, I grabbed my truck and ran home. For the life of me, I cannot figure out why I thought that would be a good solution to the problem. I ran through the front door, crying as I came in. My mother was home, despite the fact that it was the middle of the day and she should have been at work. She asked me what happened and I told her all about the boys with the BB guns and what they had done to my truck. She listened and I could see the fury rising up in her eyes.

Within the span of five minutes my mother had dressed me in one of my cousins' dresses. She marched me, dressed like a girl, down to the dunes where all the other boys were still playing. If I had thought she was going to help me in a normal maternal sort of a way, I had thought wrong.

"Which one of you turned my boy into a sissy, crying baby?" Cecile shouted.

The boys took one look at her and they all took off running before she could get to them. Their fear of her wasn't enough to keep them from laughing at me on their way or reminding me of the incident every time I went down to the dunes. Eventually, I stopped going there, too.

John Herbert, my father, had not been around much, but apparently one of his usual routes changed and brought him through our neck of the woods. It must've occurred to him that he had an estranged wife and son, so John drove over to our cabin and found me home alone. Rather than wait for my mother to come home, John Herbert decided to pull me up into the front seat of his rig and set off to make his round of deliveries. Seeing my dad pull into the area in front of the cabin brought a strange mix of emotions. While I was happy to see him, life had taught me to be wary of adults, especially those I was related to.

That week I got to see the country from the front seat of my dad's big rig. I practiced being invisible. If I could just keep from bothering him, maybe he would let me stay and I could cash in my ticket out of the woods. I felt an odd sort of pressure that if I behaved a certain way, I could convince Dad that my mother and I were worth saving. On the second night of my trip, my father was talking to some of his trucking buddies while we were all stopped for a bit of a break at a diner. And me, I had developed a lot of questions in my time away from home.

"How far can the truck go?" I asked excitedly. "How fast can you drive it? Have you ever been in a race?"

No response.

"Dad, why is the front red and the back silver? Did you have to paint it yourself?" I wondered aloud, walking the length of the truck.

As I got closer to my dad, he finally seemed to hear my questions and looked down at me. As I opened my mouth again, he picked me up and tossed me to the side.

"Christ, shut up already," he jeered.

He turned away quickly, laughing with his buddies. I landed hard on my chin, and the impact drove my eyetooth far up into my gums, lodging at an unnatural angle. Not that I had much to smile about before, but that was when I began to make sure my teeth were covered whenever I had to crack a smile for a picture. One more thing for me to be ashamed about. Overall, I must have been too much trouble for him, too, because he dropped me back off at my mother's house a week later. I did get a pretty good ass-kicking out of it, which I'm sure I deserved since my mother had been so close to being rid of me and I'd blown it.

Cecille Belle Jordan and John Herbert Wagner Sr.—
Fairfax, Virginia, 1946

I'LL NEVER SMILE AGAIN

DAYS TURNED INTO weeks, and weeks turned into months. The months turned into years and we were still living in the woods with Jim, Tommy, Hill, and the gang. Around the time I was seven my mother started seeing someone new: Frank Hardee. Frank was not a bad man—not a good one either, mind you, but at least he didn't have it in for me like Jim. He was hardworking and loved my mother, so I really couldn't have asked for much more. When Frank got out of the Navy, he and his brother Leroy began working in the booming Miami construction business down in South Florida. I am not sure exactly how it came to be, but the decision was made that my mother and I would move with Frank down to Miami.

When we first got to Florida, I found a new feeling replacing the fear that dwelled in the pit of my stomach. It was light, airy, and springy. I had never felt anything like this before; it was so new I had a hard time defining it. Over time, I learned it was called hope. For the first time, I did not have Jim lurking in the shadows of my mind. I could sleep without wondering what I would wake up to, and my mother seemed happy, almost. Mom and Frank got along well enough, but I couldn't help feeling that there was something keeping them apart.

Since I had never experienced a regular childhood and, with that, the feelings of love and safety, I began to believe that what was keeping my mother and Frank apart was me. Here they were, young and in love with their whole lives ahead of them, but then there was me. My existence was a constant reminder of the dark days in the woods, of the beatings, the hurt, and the pain that she experienced. I represented everything that Cecile was trying to leave behind but couldn't because I was always going to be there. I tried to disappear, to ask for nothing, to require nothing, but that would only last for a few hours and then someone would remember me.

Abuse is one of the evils of this world that's effects last much longer than the actual event. What I didn't understand at the time—and still don't truly believe even now—was that those beatings and the violence were not my fault. The family I lived with early in life knew no other way to function. They had all been abused and, therefore, all became abusers. It would be up to me to decide whether or not I would continue the cycle of violence as I got older.

Growing up in the Miami area was infinitely better than life in the woods in so many ways. There was more to do, more people to see, and many more places for me to go. Money was an issue again, but at least Frank had a decent job. On the first day of school in our new town of Dania, I was enrolled in second grade. My mother decided to walk me in and fill out all the forms that go along with starting at a new school. Getting up that morning, I realized all I had to wear was my hand-me-down overalls from one of my older cousins in the woods.

Cecile told me it was fine and to hurry up so she could still get to work on time. As we walked through the front door of the Dania school in my overalls and two-year-old shoes with holes in the soles, everyone stopped what they were doing and stared. The clothes the other children were wearing shocked us. They didn't look a thing like the children who lived in the woods. This is when I first realized we were in a city now and that the backwoods were a very different place. Here I was again, different from everyone around me, starting off on the wrong foot.

A few weeks later, my Uncle Hill came down to visit. Frank, Hill, his girlfriend, and my mother went out for drinks at the local bar. They were having a good time out together, drinking and dancing until about one o'clock in the morning, when Frank went to the bar and asked for another drink.

"No, sir. You've had quite enough," the bartender replied.

"Who do you think you are, telling me what I can and can't drink?" Frank roared, teetering back and forth on the balls of his feet.

The bartender grinned. "I think I'm the one running this place, and you can take what I say or you can get the hell out of here."

Frank turned away from the bar, long enough for the bartender to reach over and grab his empty glass, and that's when Frank turned around swinging. He clocked the bartender clear across his jaw. He must not have hit him very hard because the bartender was still standing. The bartender reached back over the bar and shoved Frank. He fell backward, tripping over a stool and hitting his head against one of the tables.

My mother was just a few stools away and was watching this whole interaction. She reached down and pulled her high-heeled shoe off her foot. Brandishing her weapon, she charged the bartender, knocking him in the head again and again until he hit the floor, unconscious. She grabbed Frank and, with the help of Hill, got him out to the car, and together they all left for home.

They came in and were all excitedly discussing the fight. I had been asleep, but with my room right off of the living room I always woke up when someone came home. My Uncle Hill was trying to keep the mood light and was doing a few simple hand tricks with razor blades. He'd pull them out of his pocket, take the paper off the blade, and then place them in his mouth and pretend to chew on them without ever cutting himself. I was watching this from my bedroom; I had pushed the door open a little more than a crack and had a decent view. My mother was putting on a pot of coffee when she noticed me in the doorway. She came to me to tell me to go back to sleep when Frank saw us talking.

"Bring him out. Let the boy watch Hill's tricks," Frank slurred.

"No, Frank. He needs to be in bed," she replied, and she began to close the door.

That was more than Frank could handle. He exploded out of his chair, came barreling into the bedroom, and pulled me through the doorway so I could watch the tricks. My mother tried to grab me and pull me back into the room, and that's when all hell broke loose.

Frank shoved my mother hard back through the kitchen, knocking her down. Then he grabbed me and pushed me past my mother. He went to the closet and pulled out a .22 caliber rifle and carried it to me. He held it pointed in my direction, which made my mother go crazy. She ran at him, and he reached back and hit her in the face, knocking her into a little chair in the corner of the room. He smacked her in the face with the backside of his hand and used the rifle butt to settle her down good.

Hill jumped up from the couch and grabbed Frank. "You better cool it," he said.

Frank waited for Hill to release him and then lunged at my mother again, hitting her on the right side of her face. Hill pulled Frank back and threw him back into the wall. Frank still had the rifle in his hand and turned slowly away from Hill. He came over to the chair where I was sitting and threw the rifle to me. It hit me in the chest and landed on my lap.

"Pick up the rifle." Frank's voice was calm and steady. "You point that at your mother."

I stood, shaking, and began to lift the tip of the rifle. Hill lunged past Frank and grabbed the gun away from me. He shoved Frank down onto the couch and began to yell, swinging the gun back and forth through the room.

"That's gonna be enough, goddammit!"

"That bitch had no right to do what she did at that bar—that was my fight to fight. No woman pushes me around!" Frank shouted back.

I was still standing frozen in the room where Hill had taken the gun from me, when I felt my mother pick me up. She walked me into the bedroom and laid me down. She pulled back the covers and got into the bed next to me. Lying there in the dark, her arms draped around me, she fell asleep almost instantly.

The next morning, Frank was gone. As I carefully walked toward the kitchen, I heard my mother cooking. She was making biscuits and sausage gravy, my favorite.

As I entered the kitchen, she pulled me into her for a flash of a hug and said, "Sit down, John boy, and pay attention. You're gonna need to learn how to cook sooner or later."

That morning was the first of daily cooking lessons. Over the course of the next few weeks, Cecile showed me how to make collards with ham hocks, how to properly fry chicken, and how to make her creamy cheese sauce for macaroni and cheese.

Cecile was looking for a new job when she found out that she was pregnant with my brother, her and Frank's first child, Anthony. In an attempt to make ends meet and be home more often, Cecile started to work in a small restaurant near our house. She cooked home-style Southern soul food and sold chewing tobacco, cigarettes, gum, and candy to the local working men. Cecile would take me with her to work on days when I didn't have to go to school, and it was here that I truly learned to cook.

Cooking became an outlet. A way that I could be close to my mother without having to talk to her or expect anything from her that she couldn't give. I watched the way she moved about the kitchen with confidence, something that I never saw in her anywhere else. She knew the recipes and the steps to make a meal that would be both delicious and filling for the men who came into her kitchen. When Cecile cooked, she was a different person, maybe the person she would have been had she not had such a hard upbringing. I followed her instructions in the kitchen and became a pretty good little cook myself. I had no idea at the time that these skills would be the most important tools that Cecile would leave me with.

Of course, even the kitchen could not protect me from everything my mother put me through. I guess I began to over-step my bounds while I was working with her. I felt as if I had the run of that convenience store for a time and prided myself on being able to provide my few would-be friends from school with things from the store.

Without any money, getting stuff from the store consisted of me slipping a few pieces of candy or gum into my pockets when no one was looking. The next day I would take whatever I had gotten to school and give it to other kids. I still was not popular, but at least kids would talk to me when I came to school in the mornings. The next thing I knew, some of the kids started making requests for particular items. It started with candy and gum and gradually grew over time into more expensive items, like whole candy bars and then even more big-ticket items.

I must have been about nine years old when I started lifting cigarettes for the kids at school. It wasn't a large town, so the school had a bunch of mixed-aged kids all in one building. A lot of the kids I tried to impress were older than me, and they all wanted to smoke. I had to steal packs more often in order to meet their demands, and the store manager began to notice things were missing. He did not suspect me, but he definitely put some pressure on my mother to pay more attention to the counter while she was cooking. I did not find out about these conversations until later, when it was too late.

Unaware that Cecile was paying more attention to the counter, I didn't try to conceal what I was taking any more than usual. One evening I slipped a pack of Lucky Strike cigarettes into my waistband and headed toward the door.

"What you got there, you little shit?" Cecile exclaimed.

I felt her on me before I reached the door. She hit me in the back of the head with a crystal ashtray that had been sitting next to the stove. Stars blurred my vision and I felt my knees go slack. Crumpled on the floor, I endured a severe beating while she searched my pockets. She also found a candy bar and two packs of gum.

"You thief! Did I teach you to take things that weren't yours?" she screamed as the blows continued to rain down on me. I was not capable of speech at this point, so I did not attempt to respond. I think that only added fuel to her fury.

"Well, you're gonna learn now," was the last thing I remember hearing.

The next morning, I woke to get ready for school, careful to choose clothes that would cover my fresh bruises. I needn't have wasted my time, though; I was not going to school. I was to spend the entire day at the store with my mother. She did not speak to me on the walk to the store, so I knew it was going to be bad. Usually, the quieter she was, the more she was thinking, and thinking led to the worst kinds of punishments.

As I walked in the front door, there was a stool parked next the counter. Right near the cigarette display. I hesitantly walked toward the kitchen and was shoved in the direction of the stool.

"You want to steal? You want to smoke? Well, now you can smoke all you want. Sit there on that stool," Cecile barked as she grabbed a pack of cigarettes and a container of dip from the counter.

Cecile packed one into my lip and handed me a cigarette and a lighter. Now the cigarettes I stole were never for me, but she couldn't know that. I chose not to tell her because I knew it wouldn't do me any good. I tried to light the cigarette, and finally she snatched it from me and lit it herself. She shoved it back at me and commanded me to inhale.

I choked out the exhalation while she watched with a smug look on her face. I pulled down the cigarette and was ready to stub it out when she handed me another one.

"Light it off the first one. This'll teach you not to smoke anymore," Cecile said.

The rest of the day continued on like this. I got more and more dizzy as the number of cigarettes continued to climb. The only time I did not have a cigarette in my mouth or a dip in my lip that day was when my head was in the bucket next to me because I was throwing up. As soon as I would regain my composure enough to pick up my head, she would shove more cigarettes in my direction. On and on it went until closing time. I wouldn't even look at another cigarette until ten years later.

The years wore on, and things were mostly the same. I would go to school—now mainly friendless as the freebies from the store disappeared—keep to myself, come home, and cook at the store. Most people I met wouldn't even see me. I had gotten so good at hiding in plain sight. I had one friend though, my little brother, Tony. While he grew up in the same house as me, his experiences were a world apart. He never lived in the woods; he never had to experience the brutalities I witnessed on a daily basis. Not only that, but Tony had a father, one who lived with him and saw him every day. I guess looking back, I can admit it: I was jealous of Tony, but he is the only person who can even begin to understand what I went through. Tony had a lot of breathing problems and as a result wasn't really allowed to be by himself. With my mom and Frank working all the time, I was left in charge of him fairly often, and he followed me around pretty much everywhere I went for a few years.

On Sundays, my mother would send us on our way to church with a dime each, which we were to put in the collection plate during the service. We'd wait down at the end of the street for the bus to come and head straight for the back. After a few stops, we'd slink down behind the seats so that when we got to the church stop the driver wouldn't see us. Now that bus driver saw us get on, so he must've known that we hadn't gotten off when we were supposed to, but we just thought we were so slick. Instead of church, we'd hop off at a park and spend the morning playing and climbing trees, always careful not to get too dirty or rip our clothes.

One Sunday morning, I climbed up extra high into my favorite tree and got the idea to swing from branch to branch, like Tarzan. I stood on the sturdiest branch, leaned out, jumped, and landed on a nearby branch. Then I swung back and forth to get some momentum and jumped for the next branch. Around and around the tree I went, flying farther in between branches each time. I paused on a sturdy log to catch my breath and noticed Tony dangling from the limb in front of me.

"Tony! Get back over here!" I yelled. When had he gotten out there?

"I can't, John. I'm stuck!" he shrieked, his little legs dangling beneath him.

Deep breaths. "Okay, okay. Listen. Swing back a little and as you come forward, use your legs to help move you to the next branch. That one has a limb beneath it, and I'll be able to help you get down," I instructed.

I watched as Tony struggled to swing his legs back with any real force. Back and forth and back and forth he swayed without ever really going anywhere. I looked out toward the branch and saw that his fingers were starting to lose their grip.

"I'm slipping!" he screamed.

In slow motion I saw his fingers pull away from the branch and Tony let out an ear-piercing scream as he went crashing to the ground beneath the tree. I scrambled down from the large limb and ran to him. I looked him over, and aside from the tears he appeared to be okay. That was, until he rolled over and I saw the sickening angle of his arm. I helped him stand up, and his arm was hanging limply beside him.

Think! What should I do? I knew we needed help, but I also knew we weren't at church like we were supposed to be. I checked the time and realized church should've been over by this point anyway. Maybe I could just say that we went to the park after church. I told Tony to follow me to the drugstore, where I knew there was a pay phone. I pulled out my dime, popped it into the phone, and rang my mother's number. Angry isn't the word I would use to describe her reaction. Infuriated was more like it.

"I hope you're joking. How could you let him get hurt?" she spat into the phone.

"He, uh, was just climbing the tree and slipped," I mumbled.

"Why weren't you two boys at church?" she demanded.

"We were done with church so we went to the park after," I said.

"I'm coming to get you. Don't either one of you move until I get there." She slammed the phone down.

As I hung the phone up on my end, I put my finger into the change return. The pay phone said phone calls were five cents. I had used a dime, so there should've been five cents change. The return was empty. I thought and thought about that five cents the whole time we waited for our mother to arrive. I thought about the candy I could've bought and maybe even the fountain soda that those few cents could have afforded me.

I heard her enter the store before I saw her. "Where are my boys?" she asked the clerk behind the register.

I turned as he was gesturing in our direction. Her big blue eyes were actually filled with concern as they settled on Tony's arm. She scooped him up as she looked over at me.

"Let's go, John boy," she said.

We were standing, waiting for the bus, and she genuinely seemed to be taking this one okay. I looked up at her and said, "Mom, how come that pay phone didn't give me my change? I put in ten cents and it didn't give me my five back."

It took her only a few seconds to figure out what I was talking about and only a few more to backhand me across the face. "You lying little coward!" she bellowed. "Ya'll didn't go to church! You been playing in that park the entire time or else you wouldn't have had that dime in your pocket still. Oh, you're gonna pay for this one!"

Busted. The stupid dime. We were so close to pulling it off, but that missing five cents just burned a hole right through my pocket. She stewed about our little caper the entire thirty-minute bus ride home. By the time she got Frank's belt from its hook in the bedroom, I knew she was right. I was going to pay, and it was going to be with the skin off my back.

John Wagner Jr. School Photo—approximately 1956, age 10

MACK THE KNIFE

EVERY ONCE IN a while, we would get a phone call from Hill, an update on how everyone in the woods was doing in our absence. He was always the one to keep in touch, as he was closest to my mother. When one day our phone rang and it was Tommy on the phone, we knew this call would be different from the rest.

The night before, Jim, Tommy, and Hill had gone out to get a bottle of moonshine and brought it back to Tommy's house to drink. It was strong and they were getting hammered pretty fast. Well, at least two of them were. Jim and Tommy were downing the bottle, and Hill was not getting his fair share. He started arguing with Jim for more. I would never have argued with Jim, no matter what the problem was, but I guess it was different for Hill, who had been fighting with him since they were kids. Jim refused Hill time and time again, which only made Hill angrier. Things were escalating quickly, and Tommy started to get nervous. Like the rest of us, he knew what Jim was capable of. What Tommy did not know was that Hill had a knife.

Maybe Hill was sick of being pushed around by his brother, or maybe he just really wanted a drink. But whatever the reason, a scuffle began and Hill stabbed Jim in the thigh. Tommy tried to step between them, but there was no stopping it; Jim deftly grabbed the knife and spun Hill around into a headlock. Jim dragged the knife across Hill's throat while Tommy screamed for him to stop.

Hill didn't die right away. He also didn't stop asking for the moonshine. Blood was gushing from the wound on his neck, and he clamped his hand over it to try and slow the bleeding.

"Give me a swig. I have to kill the pain," Hill wheezed.

"Sure, it's right here," Jim said, laughing.

He placed the bottle just out of Hill's reach on the bedroom floor. Hill pulled himself up a little and started to drag his body across the floor toward the bottle. Just as he got close enough to reach it, Jim moved the bottle a few feet farther toward the living room.

"Come on, Hill. It's right here. I thought you wanted some," Jim taunted.

Hill dragged himself the next few feet only to watch Jim move the bottle again. This continued for quite some time. Jim forced his dying brother to drag his body out of the bedroom across the living room floor and then back into the bedroom, where he finally died. He never got a last taste of that moonshine.

Tommy was pretty freaked out by now, and he didn't know what to do with himself. He took off out the front door of the house and just started running down the street. He must have been pretty drunk, or perhaps it was just sheer exhaustion that overtook him, but Tommy slipped and fell into one of the drainage ditches on the side of the road.

Early the next morning, a trucker was headed down the old country road that Tommy had chosen to flee on. The man driving the truck looked out his window and saw a man, lying face down in the ditch, covered from head to toe in blood.

Fearing the worst, the trucker radioed for the police and hopped out of the truck to see if the man was breathing. As the truck driver's hand clamped down onto Tommy's neck, Tommy awoke with a start.

Dazed, Tommy looked around and, meeting the trucker's gaze, said, "I hope you called the police, because I think we killed my brother."

The police arrived and took Tommy to the house where he claimed his dead brother's body was. Of course, in a normal murder, if there is such a thing, you would expect the murderer to leave the scene and possibly attempted to dispose of the body. But when the cops pulled up to the house, they were faced with Jim, still wearing his bloody clothes, smoking a cigarette, and finishing up the bottle of moonshine on the front porch. The police pushed past him, entered the house, and discovered Hill's body lying right where he had died on the bedroom floor. They cuffed Jim on the porch, who was still smiling as they put him into the back of the police car.

Anyone who knew Jim was glad that he was finally behind bars. I hate to say it, but Jim got out quickly. I was too young to remember how exactly that came to be; all I knew is that he was on the prowl again. Maybe it was just the time in between his arrest and the court date, or maybe the cops didn't care that Jim killed his brother because at least there was one less Jordan to worry about. Either way, Jim was out for the time being, but he had crossed a line; he had murdered another human being, and for him, there was no going back.

Jim was married and had several children of his own. His wife went by Elvira, as she was very tall and had long black hair—bearing a striking resemblance the famous character played by Cassandra Peterson. Elvira and their three children were still living in the cabin when Jim was released after Hill's murder. There was absolutely no evidence of an affair, but it was very real to Jim nonetheless. Eventually, Jim became so consumed with his obsession that he confronted her.

Jim pulled out his shotgun and repeated his allegations that he believed his wife had been cheating. She pleaded with Jim to put the gun down, that the children were home and they should not see him like this, but he did not listen—he never did. Jim pulled the trigger and shot his wife in the head in front of their three children. As the story goes, Jim quickly regretted his decision to kill his wife and proceeded to drop to his hands and knees and attempted to dig the bullet from her brain. It was too late, of course; she was already dead. This time, Jim was arrested and was not released. He died in prison many years later. A dark chapter in our family history was finally put to rest.

Jim Jordan under arrest for the murder of Hill Jordan

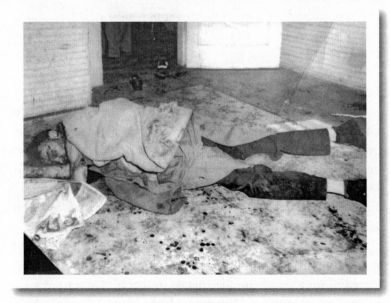

Police Crime Scene Photo – Hill Jordan, deceased

ANOTHER ONE BITES THE DUST

MY MOTHER EVENTUALLY grew tired of Frank and his drinking. She was an alcoholic herself, but she didn't like to put up with that behavior from anyone else. Their interactions grew less frequent as Frank rarely came home without his brother, Leroy. Frank and Leroy worked construction together and would be home in time for supper most nights. I didn't notice it right away, but Leroy began coming to our house earlier than Frank to spend time with Cecile alone. Eventually, Frank stopped coming home altogether. It wasn't long before Leroy moved in with us and Frank moved out.

Now this wasn't a big deal for me; I had never had my real father at home and Frank never really cared about me one way or another. This brother swap was truthfully a much bigger deal for Tony, since his father had just become his uncle and his Uncle Leroy became the man of the house raising him. It was almost like we were back in the woods where the lines between siblings and lovers had blurred the first time.

Tony was having many of the same feelings that I felt about not belonging or fitting in, and he began to withdraw to a crowd of rough-and-tumble friends in school. He started staying out past supper and left me with the brunt of my mother's rage. The beatings became more frequent as Cecile drank more and would get angry that Tony had not come home for dinner. I began to yearn to leave the family house and move out on my own. Not that I had any idea how I would make it, but I knew that I couldn't live like this anymore.

High school was nearing a close for me, and I decided to enlist in the Air Force once school was finished. While I wasn't out yet, I could see the light at the end of the tunnel. Senior year was probably the best school year of my life. It was 1964 and summer was approaching. It was hot in Miami and things were heating up all over the country, as kids broke free from the molds that society had placed them in. A few weeks before school was out, I did the boldest thing I had ever done and asked a girl to prom. Aside from my insecurities about the scarring on my back from the beatings and the eyetooth that was still lodged in my gums, I also had my height to worry about. At seventeen, I still stood only at four feet eleven inches. The malnutrition from poverty had taken its toll. Getting up the courage to ask Beverly Wolf to prom took all of the audacity I had and then some. Surprisingly, she accepted. I worked hard to get ready for prom and even managed to get my hands on an old suit so that I could look presentable when I picked her up.

Beverly and I arrived at the Fontainebleau Hotel in Miami, Florida, dressed to the nines and ready for a great night out. In addition to being senior prom, this was my first date, so I was understandably nervous. I sat in the backseat with her and idled between wiping my sweaty palms on my suit pants and swallowing hard. Finally, Beverly looked at me and asked if I had ever kissed a girl. I shook my head. She leaned in, and I planted a quick peck on the side of her mouth. She giggled and said, "It's more like this." Beverly grabbed my face with both hands and stuck her tongue as far down my throat as she could. It was as close to heaven as I had ever been. She pulled back with a silly grin on her face and said, "Let's go."

She hopped out of the car while I tried to regain some small measure of composure.

We walked into the hotel and it was beautiful, ready for us all. Any time I had ever gone anywhere with my mother, we either stayed with family or in a motel. The Fontainebleau was beyond my wildest dreams of opulence and sat poised to become one of the hottest destinations in the world. The band was just getting ready to start as I headed over to the punch bowl to get drinks for me and Beverly. What we didn't realize was that the band we were about to see would help shape the music world for years to come. Diana Ross and The Supremes took the stage. They played their only hit up until that point, "Where Did Our Love Go," and quickly started another song. "Baby Love" was about to take the country by storm, but the South Broward High School class of 1964 got a first peek at their moneymaker.

After prom, there wasn't much left in the way of school for us. Graduation day was right around the corner, and a few days prior to the ceremony, I was given a white cap and gown to wear. From the moment that gown touched my hands, I loved it. Aside from any obvious connotations associated with the end of adolescence and the beginning of my adult life, I especially liked it because not only was it brand-new, it was pure and white. When I walked in the front door after picking up my gown, my mother was sitting in her armchair waiting for me.

"Let me see it," she demanded, standing.

I admit I was extremely nervous as I handed it to her. I was so absolutely terrified that she was going to do something to it. It wouldn't have been the first time that she ruined something important to me, but this one was going to hurt more than most. As I braced myself for her wrath, she quietly studied the gown and her face took on a somber look.

"What is it, Momma?" I whispered. She looked at me, and I saw her eyes were filling with tears. She held the gown for a few more minutes while she cried.

"Do you think I could try it on, John boy?" my mother asked.

"Sure, but why would you want to do that?" I asked her. I was extremely puzzled by this side of my mother. I had never seen her cry before.

She didn't answer right away. Instead, she carefully unwrapped the gown and began to put it on. She struggled with the zipper so I stepped over to help her. As she placed the cap on top of her head, Cecile turned to face me.

"Get the camera, John boy. This is the only time I've ever worn one of these. Graduation wasn't something I got to do. By the time I was old enough to graduate high school, I was already pregnant with you and married to John Herbert. This is the proudest day of my life, my boy. We're graduating!"

Cecille Belle Jordan wearing John's cap and gown—June 1964

ZOOT SUITS AND PARACHUTES

ON JUNE 22, 1964, I signed my enlistment papers to join the Air Force. Without any money, college was not an option for me, but I knew that something better than life with my family was out there. I shipped out in the summer before my eighteenth birthday. I boarded a plane for the first time in my life and said goodbye to my mother. The airplane touched down at the Boron Air Force base in California, where I was about to collide with the cultural revolution that was taking the world by storm.

Most people look at college as the best years of their life, as a time that they could let loose and find out who they really were. That was the opportunity that the Air Force presented to me. Here I was, surrounded for the first time with other boys my age who didn't know what had happened in my home, nor did they care. Many of us were from poor and dysfunctional families, and it was truly a coming-of-age experience.

The first day we lined up to be assigned to our bunks. The general walked up and down the lines of new recruits, sizing us up for our placements. He got to me and looked right over my head.

"John Wagner? John Wagner?" he said.

"Down here, sir," I responded bashfully.

It took him a minute to figure out what to make of this five-foot-tall boy of seventeen standing in front of him, but to his credit he didn't much hesitate. I was assigned to air traffic control, since I did not meet the height requirements for training to become a pilot. Next came our bunk assignments. The military beds on base had a pullout bottom half that extended down, depending on the height of its occupant. My bed was missing the extension, but that wouldn't affect me much, or so they thought.

When I first reported for duty and started getting to know the other new recruits, there was a change almost immediately. For the first time, I fit in. I may have been short, but everyone wore the same clothes and we all got the same pay. I felt equal in some ways to the other men who enlisted that summer. I don't know if it was the standard three meals per day, the fresh California air, or my new-found freedom that did it, but I grew to be five feet eleven by the end of that first year.

In addition to the liberty I found in not having to constantly look over my shoulder, the Air Force provided me with many things that had been missing from my life. First, there was structure. I had to be up, dressed, and reporting for training by six in the morning. For the rest of the day, we ran through a series of routines. Chores were first, followed by breakfast. Everyone reported for basic training in the morning and then went off to lunch at noon. In the afternoon, we had specific training for our particular assignments and then some free time before dinner. For most people, this would have been considered rigid and maybe a bit too much, but I was thriving. I knew what was expected of me and I also knew the consequences.

At home, one of the biggest problems I faced was that I was playing by my mother's rules, and she often didn't tell me what they were until after I broke one. By never knowing what I was supposed to do, I was a victim to her whimsy. Punishments were handed out depending on her mood, not on my actions. When you have no control over how you are disciplined, you begin to lose interest in doing the right thing. If you are treated the same for good and bad behavior, it really does not matter what you choose.

Not only did I love the Air Force, I was also falling in love with California. The summer of '64 was a time of change for everyone. The civil rights movement was in full swing, and musically there was an explosion in the making. While the Beatles had broken open the scene, there were now bands like The Doors, Led Zeppelin, Jimi Hendrix, The Grateful Dead, and Cream rocking my generation on the underground circuit. There is nothing that can quite compare to the freedom you feel on a warm, sunny California day with rock and roll as the background music of your life. We listened to the radio as we worked under the glare of the sun; I had never felt more alive.

The Vietnam War was at the forefront of the country's concerns, and here I was, willingly enlisted in the military. Air Force training began to speed up as the demand for more and more soldiers forced all branches of the military to send young boys of eighteen overseas to fight in a war that they were nowhere near prepared for. As I began to love California more and more, I realized my ship-out date was approaching faster than I had anticipated. I did my best to stay focused on my training in air traffic control, but with so many other activities for me to explore, I was having a difficult time even thinking about the safety of pilots and planes in the sky.

For one, I was making a paycheck and I had finally saved up enough money to buy myself a car. I had wanted a Chevrolet for years, and for the first time I was in a position to be able to get myself something that I wanted. I marched down to a local dealership with my uniform on and made sure that my shoes were perfectly shined. Like a typical eighteen-year-old boy, I was impulsive by nature. I bought a car on a whim, in cash, and drove it back to the base. Now I had a toy to play with on weekend leave.

I began to prepare for my deployment. I knew I would be stationed for a brief time in the Philippines before moving into the heart of the war in the Vietnam. Two weeks before I was to leave, I was granted a weekend leave. As a last chance at fun, I borrowed a buddy and put him in my car, and we took off to explore the area around Edwards Air Force Base. Driving along the highway, I saw all sorts of people from all over the country traveling together. I found their free-spirited nature so appealing that I spent most of my weekend driving around and taking in as much of the area as I could before I had to leave.

Instead of returning to the base that Sunday night, my life took a sharp right turn. On my way back to the base, I was fiddling with the radio and generally just goofing off in the car with my friend. We were cruising fast with the windows down, the wind blowing back our hair. It was one of those moments in time where things almost seem to move in slow motion. We were laughing and carrying on while, unbeknown to us, an eighteen-wheeler was approaching from the opposite direction with a driver who was also not paying attention. As I turned to speak with my buddy, my car slowly edged over the center line, into the lane of oncoming traffic. At sixty miles per hour, my car collided head-on with the eighteen-wheeler. Without a seat belt, the impact sent my body flying out onto the side of the road.

STATE OF CALIFORNIA—HIGHWAY TRANSPORTATION AGENCY EDMUND G. BROWN, Governor

DEPARTMENT OF CALIFORNIA HIGHWAY PATROL
35068 Barstow Road
Barstow, California
  92311

November 3, 1965

P 407237
Geary

JOHN HERBERT WAGNER
BOX 1323 750 RADRON
BORON AFS, CALIFORNIA

Dear Sir:

A complaint has been filed against you in the ___JUSTICE___
_____Court of_____BARSTOW_____Judicial District,
alleging violation(s) of Section(s)_____
                              21650
of the Vehicle Code, to wit:_____
 failure to drive on right half of roadway not in passing
_____
_____
_____offense(s).

This is a result of an investigation of the accident or
incident in which you were involved on__November 2, 1965__.
You may avoid a warrant for your arrest by contacting the
above-named Court, which is located at_301 E. Mt. View_
_Barstow, California_____on or before_November 19, 1965_
between the hours of_8:00 a.m._ and _5:00 p.m._ to answer to
this charge.

Do NOT communicate with the California Highway Patrol, as
this matter is now under the jurisdiction of the Court.

Yours very truly,

BRADFORD M. CRITTENDEN
Commissioner

By _A. G. Strom_

A. G. STROM, Captain
Commander
Barstow Area

cc: Barstow Court

CHP FORM 239 REV 5 (6 62)

Department of California Highway Patrol—
Court Summons for the accident with the eighteen-wheeler.

DAZED AND CONFUSED

WHEN I AWOKE, I had no recollection of the circumstances that led to me lying in a hospital bed at the base. Because I was a card-carrying Air Force man, the first responders sent me straight to the Edwards Medical Center, probably the choice that saved my life. My skull was crushed and some of my face had been left behind on the road. I suffered multiple fractures over the rest of my body and was beyond lucky to be breathing on my own. My passenger had been wearing his seat belt, so his injuries weren't nearly as extensive.

The most gifted surgeons in the world were military doctors, and yet another stroke of luck landed me in the care of one of the world's best plastic surgeons to reconstruct my head and face. The doctors decided that what was left of my teeth wasn't enough to warrant putting in individual fake teeth. They pulled my remaining teeth and fit me with full upper and lower dentures. They couldn't know my history of hating my teeth, but those doctors gave me a gift—the gift of a smile that I was not afraid to show. It took several weeks, almost a full month, before I was able to move around much and have my abilities reevaluated. While most of my motor functioning was intact and I would be able to walk, talk, and eat without assistance, I had suffered a traumatic brain injury. The portion of my brain that formed short-term memories was permanently impaired. I would be able to function normally in society, or as close to normal as most people functioned during the sixties, but I would have trouble recalling new information.

Needless to say, I missed my deployment date. Rather than shipping out for Vietnam where my chances of survival could have been much lower than in sunny California, a near-fatal car crash may have saved my life. It turns out that having your skull crushed and your cognitive abilities called into question qualifies you for discharge from the military, with or without having met your two-year enlistment agreement. The Air Force set me loose on America without another thought; they had bigger fish to fry.

Without the structure that the Air Force had provided me, I stumbled around, trying to find out what was next for me. As much as I loved California, it wasn't my home and I really didn't know many people out there. Without a place to live and someone cooking my meals, I couldn't manage to stay. I returned to Florida to get my bearings, hoping to find freedom again soon. I moved in with my mother, Leroy, and Tony, but I couldn't handle the stifling environment. I had gotten a taste of life in the Air Force, and going back home wasn't a sustainable option for me.

While I was trying to collect myself, I didn't realize that 1965 marked the year that a hundred thousand Cubans would also seek refuge in Miami. Where there had been a mostly white and African American population, the influx of refugees changed the complexion of the city overnight. The Miami metro area was brimming with people looking to make a quick buck, and there were nowhere near enough job opportunities to satisfy the demand. I was a poor candidate to potential employers flooded with cheap labor.

I still had the desire to rise above my poor upbringing, and I found myself surrounded by a new and burgeoning industry in Miami: drug trafficking.

As the rise of the hippie movement had more and more people clamoring for all kinds of illicit drugs, Miami turned into one of the major ports from Latin America. Law enforcement struggled to keep up. Marijuana, cocaine, and later heroin would come in on the underside of boats and planes. The kilos coming in were measurable only in the thousands.

The major problem that the cops faced was that they had nowhere near the resources that the drug lords had. With the amount of money that was coming into Miami, a sort of economic revolution began. The drug dealers were able to purchase the fastest boats, the fastest planes, and the most armed forces to make sure that the drugs made it out of the harbor and into the living rooms of millions of Americans nationwide.

Where did I fit in? Well, I was somewhere between a casual user and a dealer. When I first came back from California, I started going out with Tony and his friends. Mixing myself back into the community, I ran into an old schoolmate, Corey Kearns, who had never left home. Corey's father was the Florida state senator at the time, right out of Hollywood, Florida. Corey and I were both looking for the same things: a way to make money and a name for ourselves that had nothing to do with our families. We became fast friends.

When Corey graduated high school, two years before me, he decided that he did not want to follow in his father's footsteps into politics. As a matter of fact, Corey decided to try and destroy his father's footsteps and do everything in his power to make sure people knew they were nothing alike. I never knew what Corey's father did to him to make him feel this way, and I really didn't care. We all had our own crosses to bear. Plus, I was too busy enjoying myself; living with Corey had turned into a lot of fun. A lot of trouble, but a lot of fun.

When the Cubans took over the drug trade in South Florida, they were looking for an in with the local politicians. While they couldn't touch Corey's father, Corey offered them the protections that they needed. Even though he had tried to get rid of his father's influence, Corey still had great connections with law enforcement. Regardless of their personal relationship, his dad still had to maintain his image, and that included the image of a perfect family. Because of this, Corey was able to get away with almost anything.

Being a kid with a lot of money and connections in a small area can get boring unless you find a hobby. Luckily, Corey had one; it was fast cars and faster motorcycles. During the day we would ride around Miami Beach with the top down on his convertibles, looking for something to get into. At night we would race. Now I am not talking the *Fast and the Furious* or anything, but Corey had a few Ferraris that we would race on the residential streets. Corey would start up the cars, and our crew of fifteen would take turns racing to the end of the block.

The first night, I was one of the drivers and I got behind the wheel of a Ferrari. Luxury cars are typically quiet, but Corey had his mufflers removed and glass back duel exhaust systems installed for maximum volume. Anyway, I started the car and checked the neighboring houses to make sure the windows were all still in place; the sound of those cars getting revved up was near glass-shattering. Pushing the pedal to the floor, I was at the end of the street before I even realized I was moving. I turned to laugh with Corey, who was driving the other car, and instead I was face-to-face with a police officer.

"What are you going to do without the car, Corey?" another cop asked as he yanked my friend out of the car.

"I don't care what you do with it. I'll get another one."

"Your father is not going to be happy about this, Corey. Why don't you just go home, and we'll forget this ever happened," said the officer.

"That sounds good to . . ." I tried to respond but Corey was quicker.

"Screw you, and screw my father, too."

And so it went. We were booked and taken down to the Miami-Dade police headquarters. This was my first experience in a police station, but it certainly would not be the last. We sat in the holding cell for about twenty minutes. The cops were on the phone the whole time we were there. I can't be sure, but I'm fairly certain they got in more trouble than we did for picking us up. The first officer looked pissed as he approached the cell. He did not say a word as he released us. We got off scot-free and walked out to the two Ferraris waiting in the parking lot. Life was good.

Running with Corey was proving beneficial, not only to my bank account but also to my love life. Somewhere in the midst of the cars, the sun, and the fun, I met MaryAnn. I was out at a dance hall with Corey and the gang when I saw a beautiful blonde making a scene on the dance floor. It was like my eyes were a spotlight and they kept turning to find her. I had some courage by this point, so I asked her to dance. She blew me off three times in a row. By the end of the night, I must have done something right because she walked over to me on her way out the door.

"Here's my number for being so persistent," she said. "Give me a call sometime."

I couldn't find the words to respond, so instead I ripped a piece off the napkin she'd handed me and scribbled down my number in return. As I gave it to her, she turned with a smile twinkling at the edges of her eyes and walked out into the night. Corey and I stayed for a little while longer, but we eventually headed home alone that night as well.

The next morning the phone rang. MaryAnn was on the other end.

"John, I'm at the gas station by the dance hall. When I got home last night, my father beat the shit out of me for having been out all night. Would you be able to come pick me up?" she asked.

What was I supposed to do? I knew my fair share about ass kicking, and I also knew about not wanting to go home. My heart was thudding out of my chest for this girl, and I made a snap decision that would drive the rest of my life.

"I'll be right there," was my reply.

I picked up MaryAnn and brought her back to Corey's, and we moved forward from there. As we got to know each other, it was clear that we got along well enough and, my God, was she beautiful. Everyone gave me another look when I had her on my arm. I felt like a man when I was with her. She could party as well as I could, and I found that while we had common affinity for coke, she was really more into barbiturates. Luckily for her, I had a direct connection to any drug available in the Miami area.

Corey had moved up a bit in the drug world and was able to rent a house right out on the Hollywood Beach boardwalk, smack in the heart of the action. In order to get this house, all Corey had to do was help his connections make sure the importers wouldn't get busted at the port. He had a shortwave radio that he would use to listen to the boat captains coming in from Columbia. The boats would shoot around the backside of Cuba and wait for the call that the port was clear, that the cops were busy somewhere else. Since Corey knew so many people, he was able to get his hands on a police PB radio as well. He would use both sets to coordinate the location of the cops so that the drugs could make landfall undetected. Myself and the other fifteen people in our band of idiots would haul ass down to the marina to meet the ships coming in and help them unload the product. Coke, pot, and heroin would come in packed in duffel bags or on skids that floated behind the speedboats. This was actually the easiest way for them to get the drugs in because, in the rare case that the cops were on to them, they would be able to cut the line and not get busted with anything on board.

The speedboats would pull in and unload while we heard the police boats chugging in slowly behind them. We would sling the black bags into the back of vans and floor it out of the marina. Sometimes we made deliveries to local dealers, but mostly we brought the stash back to Corey's, where we cut it up for resale. Having such a connection was ideal for me. I got to use for free most of the time and had all the power that comes with a house full of drugs.

You would think that the cops would be able to figure out this little operation pretty quickly, and you'd be right, which is where Corey's family ties came in handy. No one wanted to bust the senator's son; that could be very bad for their career. Rather than let him get busted, the local cops decided it would be in their best interest to let him know that they were planning a raid on his house. With that warning, we would have at least a day or two to make sure we could get rid of all the stuff we had hidden before they came through to search.

The quickest way for us to get rid of our stash was to send word out to the local dealers that we were having a fire sale; in other words, come get your weight cheap, before the cops get it. The garage sale was born. The first few times, this worked like a charm. We would sell off our pot, and whatever else was lying around, in large orders only, no nickeling and diming allowed. We usually moved twenty-five-pound duffel bags at pretty close to wholesale prices. Then the group of us would head out to party for a few weeks while things cooled down in Miami. We'd all pile into an old school bus and ride away together.

Corey's grandfather had been a big businessman, and one of the ways he spent his money was on pieces of real estate that he thought would be worth something someday. He owned patches of land all over the South. Most had never amounted to anything but swamp or farmland. What these plots afforded us, though, was priceless. They were a great place to escape, and since they were scattered, we never had to go to the same location twice in a row. Our bus would roll up packed to the gills with drugs and people ready for a good time.

All of us would get our stuff together and head off to one of these acreages in a secluded area. We would set up camp, sometimes in preexisting cabins, other times in tents, and a few times even in rented motel rooms close by the land. We would get high, blast music, and rock out every night. Some of the best times we ever had were at these reserves where there was no outside influence on us—we could just be ourselves.

Before the garage sales, each of us would pack up our own bags, including what we intended to keep for our personal stash, and wait to finish moving the large quantities out. Afterward, we'd take off together; the plan was the same every time. We had pulled this off multiple times and maybe we got lazy, but the last time we didn't make it out of the house before the cops kicked the doors in. Obviously, the crew was nervous while we waited for the search to be completed, but we thought everything would be okay since we had gotten rid of all of the major weight a few hours before. We sat around together, waiting for the all clear, but instead I got hit in the back by a cop.

I'll never know if it was just a mistake or if MaryAnn hid the bag herself for the money it could bring in, but somehow one of those twenty-five-pound bags of weed was found mixed in with my bags to go out to the colony.

"John Wagner, you are under arrest for possession of marijuana with the intent to distribute. You have the right to remain silent. Anything you say can and will be used against you in a court of law. You have the right to an attorney . . ." the officer said as he slammed cuffs on my wrists.

"It's not mine—" I started to explain.

"Right, of course not. Maybe you can tell me why this letter addressed to you from your girlfriend is in this bag, then?" the cop retorted.

That was a great question. MaryAnn had written me that letter a few weeks before when she had gone upstate to visit a friend in northern Florida. She had come back just in time for the garage sale. Did she set me up? Was she trying to steal from Corey? Twenty-five pounds was equivalent to about $25,000 at that time, which was a huge infringement on Corey's hospitality, and it looked like I had done it.

I sat in a prison, awaiting trial for close to a month. No one posted bail for me, since Corey put the word out that I had tried to steal from him. Corey hadn't been at the house the day I was arrested. He tended to be the first one out on raid days; he had the most to lose. I had ridden to the precinct with the duffel bag full of pot on the seat next to me, so you can imagine my surprise when I showed up for arraignment and discovered I was charged with possession of one pound of marijuana. I tried to call Corey, but he wasn't taking my calls. He was sure I was guilty of stealing from him and really didn't care whether it was one pound or twenty-five.

When the day of my trial arrived, I headed into court. I had heard from MaryAnn that the cops had only entered one pound of pot into evidence. The bag itself and the other twenty-four pounds were nowhere to be found. I didn't have much going for me, but I made sure my lawyer knew about the missing evidence.

As the trial began, my lawyer made a motion to dismiss the case.

"On what grounds?" the judge asked incredulously.

"On the grounds that there is no evidence against my client. When he was arrested, there were twenty-five pounds of marijuana in the duffel bag, yet the charges filed reference only one pound seized. No one in their right mind would claim to have more drugs in their possession, unless they were telling the truth."

Pausing, I watched the judge's face closely as he absorbed this information. He began to rifle through the paperwork in front of him. Finally, he looked up.

"Can the prosecution produce the bag in question? Where is the evidence?" the judge demanded.

"The bag that contained the marijuana was misplaced at police headquarters, Your Honor."

The judge shook his head in disbelief. The case against me was dismissed. While Corey wasn't in the courtroom, word of my victory definitely reached him. I had hoped that he would now know that I hadn't stolen from him. While he believed that the police stole twenty-four pounds of pot for themselves, he was not so sure that I hadn't planned to take it to the colony and sell it for my own profit. He didn't do anything to me, but I also wasn't one of his favorite people anymore. It was the beginning of the end of my ride with Corey.

SOMEBODY TO LOVE

GETTING PROCESSED INTO the criminal justice system for the first time can be a very scary experience. It certainly made me think about how lucky I was to get out without serving jail time. Perhaps it should have occurred to me to change my ways before I got trapped, but I assigned too much weight to fate and luck and not much to myself. Most of my life had been out of my control, and I had learned that things happened to me, not *because* of me. My actions never had real links to consequences, so why should the connection between punishment and my choices be made now?

Corey did not let me back into his inner circle. I had to pay for a lot of things that used to come for free. One of those things was the drugs MaryAnn and I were using. MaryAnn was seriously hooked on barbiturates and liked to have as many pills around as possible. Without the free drugs, money began to ratchet up the tension between us. In addition to my suspected betrayal, the added stress of being broke didn't bring us closer.

MaryAnn moved upstate and began staying with a different group of friends. After a few weeks, she called and asked me to come up and join her. When I got there, I realized the town was buzzing with talk of a large concert being staged in the area. There were rumors that a lot of big names were converging for a show. Excitedly, I realized this must be why she called me. As I walked into the apartment where I was supposed to find MaryAnn, I was met by several men I didn't recognize. I pushed past them and tried to see into the bedroom, but the shades were drawn and it was very dark. I could barely make it out, but I thought I saw the shape of at least one person lying on the bed.

"MaryAnn, are you in there?" I called.

She did not stir, but the man leaning on the edge of the bed did. As he got up, he knocked a full bag of pills onto the floor. That woke her a little.

She lifted her head, "John, is that you? Did you bring me anything good?" She dreamily smiled as she drifted back onto her pillow and fell back asleep.

"What did you give her, man?" I shoved the guy back out of the room. It was then that I noticed a slip dress on the floor. I turned and realized that she was naked under the covers.

The guy laughed as he walked out. "I gave her only what she asked for."

I tried to gather MaryAnn up and get her out of the house, but she was just too high. The concert went on without us. We spent the next three days in that bedroom with MaryAnn only waking up to swallow more pills. I wish I could say that I didn't join her, that I waited for her to wake up and then swore off drugs forever. That would be a lie, though. We really made quite the pair, each one of us more messed up than the other.

When we eventually returned to Miami, we were less welcome than we had been before. The circle was closing in and people were starting to get paranoid. Dealing with a group of fifteen avid drug users can be exhausting. You never knew which version of people you were going to meet up with. Corey was getting sick of everyone using him and started pushing people away. What he didn't realize was that he was just making them more desperate, thereby making himself more of a target.

MaryAnn and I needed money, and we needed it fast. I really wanted to get out of the area for a while, but it was going to take some money to do that. We came up with a plan to rob one of our dealers who we knew always kept a lot of cash on hand. The plan was to send MaryAnn in first to distract everyone and get the party started. Then I would show up, take the cash, and make up some excuse about heading out early. She would stay a little bit after me, and then eventually she would leave and meet me.

Our ill-conceived plan actually went smoothly, and we made out with about $5,000. After MaryAnn came home, we decided that she should go ahead to New Jersey, where she had a few relatives on her mom's side. Things were too tight for me to leave with her, and it would have been obvious if we both took off at exactly the same time, so she went on ahead of me and was supposed to call when she was set up.

A few weeks went by and I followed MaryAnn up to New Jersey. Since she had the cash and I was fairly certain a lot of it would have been spent by the time I got there, I needed another way to bankroll my trip. I went to talk to my mother and Tony about my plans to leave Florida. My mother didn't think it was a good idea to follow a woman anywhere, but her opinion really wasn't that important to me. Since meeting MaryAnn, my mother's influence on my life had diminished significantly. Tony actually surprised me with his response. He asked me to meet him the following morning before I left.

When I showed up at the house, Tony was waiting outside on the covered porch, smoking a cigarette. In front of him on the table was a small suitcase.

"If you make it to New Jersey without opening the case, you'll be happy with what you find." He laughed, taking a deep pull of his cigarette. He pushed the briefcase across the table to me.

Looking at Tony, I realized he had really grown up in the last few years. The sickly little boy who used to follow me around everywhere was practically unrecognizable in this hardened teen sitting in front of me. I was not used to this side of my brother, but I decided to take him up on his offer and I took the case.

Several busses later, I met up with MaryAnn in New Jersey, staying with some family members. MaryAnn and I waited for everyone else to go to bed, and then sat down to open the case together after everyone else had gone to bed. What we found inside was enough drugs to make a name for ourselves in the area. Of course, we decided to use most of the drugs ourselves and sold just enough to get by. This was our pattern: get high and then worry about money and consequences later.

Without an actual home to call our own, MaryAnn and I floated around, staying with friends and transplants in the area. Before coming to Florida to stay with her father, MaryAnn was born and raised in New Jersey, so she still had a few friends we could lean on. We tried out a few living situations, both in New York City and near the beach at the Jersey Shore. While Miami was a city, New York was a whole different ball of wax. There were just too many people in too small a space for us to stay there for any length of time.

After moving in with a couple friends near the beach, I decided that MaryAnn and I should be married. With us constantly bouncing around, I wanted people to know that she was with me, permanently. I know that this is going to sound terrible, but I do not really remember anything that led up to our engagement. The details of this time have been lost to drugs and the lies we told ourselves. The more times you tell a story, the more times the details change to suit your agenda. What actually happened, I can't recall, and I bet if you were to find and ask MaryAnn, she wouldn't be able to tell you much herself.

I do know that we were married in New Jersey because that is where most of her family was from. Tony and my mother both came up for the wedding. They drove up in my mother's green camper van, which had seats and a table and a place to sleep. They were there for the ceremony but left quickly after that. MaryAnn and I looked good at our wedding, but we were on a slippery slope of drug use that was beginning to take a serious toll.

After the wedding, we moved into a house in the north end of Long Branch, New Jersey, with a few people MaryAnn knew. There was a restaurant nearby where I was able work a few nights a week to try and bring in some cash. The truth is I just couldn't work fast enough to bring in the kind of money we needed to support our habits. Because we no longer lived in an area that was bringing in drugs off the boats, the quality of what we were getting was lower and the price tag was higher. We had to pay more to get less at a time when neither of us was truly capable of working very often; we were just too messed up to be reliable.

That's when we met Joe. Joe was a local heroin dealer who enjoyed hanging out with his clients. A lot of dealers would meet you, quickly exchange drugs and money, and be on their way, but Joe wasn't like that. He liked to hang out and watch people get high off his stuff. I always enjoyed a speedy high myself, but it was easier to just stick to what MaryAnn wanted, and MaryAnn had advanced from pricey pills to the more affordable heroin. Many nights after working at the restaurant, I would come home and find Joe at my apartment with

MaryAnn. Joe would keep her company and keep her high while I was out working, and then I could take over. I would lace one up for myself and another for her, and we would drift off together.

In the middle of our mad little world, there was something that was beginning to show itself, a fairly large bump. MaryAnn was pregnant. I was not sure how I was supposed to feel about the prospect of becoming a new dad, but I knew I was not ready. I also knew that, contrary to what MaryAnn told me, she was definitely still getting high all the time. She didn't seem interested in stopping her drug use and I knew that I was not ready to stop, so we continued on. Things were mostly the same as before she got pregnant, but I did notice that MaryAnn and Joe were acting stranger and stranger when I came home. He barely looked at me and eventually he showed up less and less when I was there. I guess my guard should have been up, but I was more concerned with getting high than with whatever was bothering him. I had enough of my own problems to contend with.

Barbiturates and sleeping pills had kept MaryAnn busy in Florida over the years, but they just weren't worth the money in Jersey. They cost more than heroin, and they certainly did not get you nearly as high. When something is free and you don't have to consider getting more, drug addiction can be easy, even fun at times. If you never have to have a craving that you can't relieve, then all of the ugly things that people do to get drugs never happen to you. It is easy to trick yourself into thinking you are just getting high, just having fun, when everything you could want is at your disposal. When the constant supply is removed and you have to worry about getting some, and then where you're going to get some more, that's when the claws come out. That is when the drugs win—in the middle of the night when you run out.

MaryAnn was out of heroin. There was nothing to shoot in the apartment and she was starting to freak; she was getting itchy and bitchy, the worst combination. Crawling around the floor, she was looking for a dropped bag, a speck that she could convince herself would stop the dull ache that was forming in her bones. Eventually, she just couldn't take it anymore. She was pacing, holding herself, and then she stopped.

"John, I need you to go out," was all she said.

I got up from where I had been lying on our bed and looked at her. I really saw her that night and she was not looking good. Skinny around her face, pale, and beginning to waste away, aside from the large belly—she scared me. Those scrawny legs and arms sticking out from her enlarged center made her look like the addict she had become. Despite how far we'd come from the fun-loving kids eyeing each other up in a crowded dance hall, I still loved her and I wanted to make her feel better. We both knew what the beginning stages of withdrawal felt like. I just could not bear to watch that tiny bloated frame shake any harder than it already was. I pulled on a pair of pants and headed out to score.

Joe didn't pick up. He did not return any of my calls, which meant that he was in for the night. I was going to have to do one of my least favorite things—try and score on the street. Long Branch is not a particularly seedy town, unless you want it to be. There are drug addicts and dealers in every town, in every county, in every state of this country, and Long Branch is no different. Decent people go to bed and then the rest of us come out to play. I walked down Broadway and looked for the shadiest of the shady characters lurking on the street. That is the only way to cop the best heroin. Eventually, I saw my mark.

"You holding, man?" I asked a guy lurking around the corner of Siperstein's Paint Warehouse.

"What are you looking for?" he replied.

"Just a dime." I tried to get a read on this guy, but there was not enough time. He had me on the ground in seconds. He pinned his knee into my back as he threw my arms behind my back. The cuffs were on in seconds.

"Sir, you are under arrest for possession of heroin with intent to distribute. You have the right to remain silent. You have the right . . ."

I had the right to get screwed, apparently. The man I had chosen to approach was an undercover cop. Just getting me for trying to buy heroin would have been too easy. He decided that I really looked like a good guy to a take a big fall, and he jammed a large wad of baggies into my pocket as his partner material-ized from around the corner. His partner was in uniform. I was charged with attempting to sell heroin to a uniformed police officer, not the crime that I had, in fact, committed.

In that holding cell, I experienced one of the most painful few days that I have ever lived through, which is really saying something. In the cell with no drugs there was only one thing for my body to experience: withdrawal from all the substances that I had been pumping into it for years. I shook, I screamed, and I puked. I would lie on the floor panting as the shakes seized me. One moment in particular sticks out for me as the lowest point. I had my head in the toilet bowl and was attempt-ing to suffocate myself with the toilet water. Of course, my instincts kicked in and my body pulled back at the last possible second, forcing me to draw in another ragged breath. I looked over at the cop on duty and saw him laughing at me. I couldn't even kill myself properly.

MaryAnn bailed me out. I had gotten lucky when I had been arrested in Florida, and I couldn't shake the feeling that this time would be different. The judge assigned to hear my case had a reputation for nailing people hard in drug cases, especially if they had any priors. Pair that with my numbskull of a public defender and the odds were definitely not stacked in my favor.

As the trial approached, MaryAnn was getting close to delivering. She looked about ready to burst and I kept my distance from her. I was working extra shifts to put money aside for the baby, but every time I would come home, MaryAnn would be up in our room with Joe, rocked out of her mind. I couldn't bear the thought of using again myself—the withdrawal had just been too painful. I dulled my anxieties with alcohol, but I could feel the distance between us growing with each passing day. MaryAnn's nerves were fried; she was all jitters, almost like something huge was about to go down. The baby coming was a big deal, and in normal circumstances pregnant mothers are nervous, but this felt like more than that. The tension was palpable and hung around us in a haze.

After work one night I came home and saw that MaryAnn was breathing heavily and sweating a lot. I woke her up and realized that the bed was soaking wet. Her water had broken. I ran around the room, trying to get together a bag of things she might need at the hospital, but I had no idea what to grab. I was not ready for this baby, and neither was she. Fathers were allowed in the delivery room, but certainly not expected, so I took a place in the waiting room with MaryAnn's family. They knew something was not right with us; they had suspected our drug use since I first started dating MaryAnn. We hid my arrest from them, but our lies were beginning to be more than we could hide.

Brian Wagner was born on December 3, 1971. I went in to see MaryAnn after she delivered and the baby was safely tucked into the nursery. The nurses were very concerned that both MaryAnn and the baby had tested positive for heroin and marijuana, and they were not allowing anyone to see Brian. When I approached the bedside, I could see that MaryAnn was in pain. I began to run my hand over her hair and she started to cry.

"There is something wrong with the baby," she said. "He doesn't look right."

I held my breath while I waited for more. "The doctor said that all the heroin we did had lasting effects. Sometimes too much heroin can make babies' hair come out kinky."

"So, what, he has curly hair?" I asked, relieved that it was not worse.

"And his skin is darker than it should be. That can happen sometimes, too."

"Well, that's all right honey. I'm sure he's beautiful," was all I replied. I did not care what Brian looked like as long as he was going to be okay.

My court date was scheduled for two days later. I left MaryAnn at the hospital holding our dark-skinned, kinky-haired son and went to trial. Her story explaining Brian's looks really didn't add up, but I had so many other things on my mind. What Brian looked like wasn't going to change my being there for him. I was determined to do a better job than my absentee father had done for me. I had to figure out a way to be there for him and MaryAnn, and I knew that I would need to do something drastic if I didn't want to land in prison.

Desperate, I decided that maybe if I was brutally honest with the judge, something I had never really been with anyone, he might take pity on me. My public defender didn't have much of a defense planned anyway, so I tried my hand at explaining that if I'd had heroin in my pocket, I would not have been out at all that night in the first place. All I needed was a bag or two for my wife and myself, and if I'd had it in my pocket I would have stayed at home. Next, I attempted to appeal to the justice system by admitting to my past transgressions so that they might find me more credible. I explained to the judge that I had not been trying to sell heroin.

"I have sold cocaine, marijuana, LSD, pills, and a few other things. I have never sold heroin in my lifetime. My wife likes to do it too much," I swore under oath.

I will never know if the judge believed me or not. Part of me thinks he knew I was telling the truth about not selling the drugs that night, but he thought that I was still guilty enough to go to prison. Just because I did not have possession with intent to distribute on that night did not mean that I had never committed that crime. Maybe I shouldn't have been quite so honest with the court that day, or maybe it would not have mattered either way. The judge was pretty sure that I was serious degenerate and would only further blight society by being allowed to rejoin it any time soon. The fact that I had a son waiting for me at home who had been born addicted to heroin did not seem to soften any hearts for me either.

THE SOUND OF SILENCE

I WAS SENTENCED to serve two five- to seven-year sentences and a three- to five-year sentence, to run consecutively in Trenton State Penitentiary. The judge decreed that I was a menace to society and I was "not going to get away with it." Often, sentences like this run concurrently to shorten the time in prison. While I had never served any time, my record wasn't exactly clear. The charges of reckless driving from the accident in California were at the top of this list, followed by the noted bookings for the Ferrari racing. Lastly, there was the arrest for possession with intent to distribute marijuana, despite the fact that the charges had been dropped. None of this could really be held against me, but it only helped cement the judge's belief that I was in need of some serious rehabilitation in jail. He did not want to have to think about anyone seeing me for years.

In jail, I was assigned a new public defender to handle my appeals. This guy seemed to have more experience than the lawyer representing me at the trial, and we decided to appeal on the grounds that the sentence was cruel and unusual for a nonviolent crime. After several tries, we won and I was granted the opportunity to serve my three sentences concurrently. That sounds like I got lucky, but please keep in mind that this is the state penitentiary we are talking about. Even spending one day, much less five to seven years, is not a lucky situation to be in.

When I first arrived for processing, they took everything I had on me and placed it all in a small box. They then led me through a series of checks, including a physical exam to make sure I was healthy enough to be kept with the other inmates. This was not a county jail; here there would be hardened criminals, rapists, murderers, and child molesters. I must've looked like a scared little kid, and on paper I was, but little did they know my Uncle Jim was a rapist, child molester, and murderer all in one, and I had already survived him.

The penitentiary was much like I expected it to be. There were rows of cells in each block with a rather large area in the center where inmates played all sorts of card games. As I walked in and headed toward my new home for the next five years, everyone stopped playing and started shouting, "Fresh meat!" I kept my head down, avoided direct eye contact, and began the transformation back to my old invisible self.

The first few days, everyone asked what I was in for. Now this could have been just a question, but I knew that what they were really trying to figure out was whether or not I was hard. If I told them I was in for a drug charge, I was afraid they would think I was not tough enough and that I could be easily taken advantage of. That is the principle concern when you first arrive in jail, whether or not someone else can have you. I knew that I was tough enough to handle myself, and I also knew that I could take a beating if it was going to be handed out, so instead of answering questions, I decided to keep to myself and try to make as small of an impression as possible. I would need to figure out how things worked if I was going to survive the next five years.

The library at the prison was a place where I could go and usually not meet too much trouble. So that's what I did. I went to the library and tried to find books that could keep me occupied and quiet for as long a time as possible. Two of the books I discovered there were *Light on Yoga* and the *Tibetan Book of the Dead*. The way these books were written was unlike anything I had read in school. I had to read and reread each section in order to fully understand their meaning. I threw myself into the study of Tibetan yoga with a zeal that I had lacked for much else in my life. I would read, meditate, and then try to figure out what the hell I was going to do for the next half a decade in jail.

When MaryAnn and I had visited New York City a few years earlier, I'd discovered a little yoga studio that followed the teachings of a man named Swami Vishnu-Devananda. He had been born in India in the 1930s and studied under Swami Sivananda. Together, they had opened several ashrams in the Western world. Reading through the yoga sutras gave me the idea to start writing to the Swami. It's not like I had much else to do, other than get myself into trouble, so letter writing became my safe haven.

I wrote to Vishnu-Devananda and explained the entirety of what had landed me in my current predicament: wrongly imprisoned in a dangerous state penitentiary. It was a long letter—several pages, if I remember correctly—and I sent it straight to his ashram in the Bahamas. I waited for his response, eagerly hoping to hear my name called as the mailbag came around each day. The promptness of his response surprised me. In just a few weeks, I was holding his reply in my hand. I opened the letter eagerly, with both of my books nearby in case I needed to reference anything he might say. I was met by the shortest note I have ever received. It consisted of only two words: "Do nothing."

At the time I had no idea what this meant. Do nothing? What could he mean, just sit there and do nothing? I wrote to him again and proposed several meanings that his letter could have intended for me to glean. Again, I received a letter in just a few weeks. Again, he responded to me with "Do nothing." What to do with this advice, I truly wasn't sure. For the first year or so, I did exactly what the Swami advised; I did nothing. I stayed in my cell and meditated as much as possible and asked for guidance from the powers that be.

TANGLED UP IN BLUE

EVENTUALLY, I GOT extremely lonely. While I had never known real love, I had never experienced the solitude that I felt in prison. I had succeeded in truly isolating myself from my fellow prisoners. None of them really cared about me anymore, and for the most part I was left alone. I did not have a cellmate—only block mates—so my interactions with others were restricted to the times we were allowed in the common areas during the day.

When you are as lonely as I was, you have a lot of time to really think about things. There is not much to distract you from yourself when you are sitting in a six-by-nine-foot jail cell every single day for a year. I dealt with a lot of the feelings I had pushed away from my time as a child in the woods. I realized how that had affected my relationship with MaryAnn. I had taken a broken woman and brought her with me on a whirlwind journey for a few years. What I had been blind to was that MaryAnn was not ready, or even interested in, being with only one man. She wanted love and she was willing to get it wherever it was coming from. That's what that hotel room and the bag of pills was about. That was what this baby, who really didn't look like me, was also about.

During my five years in prison, MaryAnn came to visit me one time. She brought Brian with her. When they walked in, it was clear that he looked a lot more like our dealer, Joe, than he did me.

Instead of broaching that subject, all she said was, "I just came to tell you that we are leaving. I cannot wait five years for you to get out."

I tried to talk her into waiting for me, but I knew that she was already gone, and that she might not ever have been with me in the first place. It was because of her that I went to jail the first time, and it was for her that I went to jail the second time. What I still have a hard time grasping is that she never really seemed to take any ownership of my jail time. It was as if I had wronged her somehow by getting busted buying her a fix. MaryAnn moved away from Long Branch and never came to visit me again.

Back in my cell, I truly felt as if everything had gone wrong. It was as if I was cursed. I came from the wrong family, made all the wrong choices, and was in the worst place in the world. I was in the one place where I could do nothing but think about all of the ways that I had failed. I thought back to that moment in the holding cell when I tried to drown myself in a combination of my own vomit and toilet water. I knew that something had to change, but that suicide was not the answer.

I put my books away and embarked on a mission to change my status in Trenton State. My time of solitude and reflection was over, and I needed some human contact, even if those humans were not humane. I started close to home and tried to talk to the man in the cell next to me. It turned out he was as quiet as I was. I asked his name and he held up a small mirror in order to see me around the wall.

"Well, that depends on who is asking," he said.

"Nobody, really. John is my name," was the best I could come up with after barely speaking for an entire year.

"Well, John, my name is Rubin, but I keep to myself and I do not need any more trouble." He put his mirror away.

"Me neither. I just wanted someone to talk to. What are you in for?" I asked in an attempt to keep the conversation going a little bit longer. This was the most I had said in a long time. When you get quiet, it is sometimes hard to get your words back once you try to rejoin humanity.

"I was accused of murdering two people in a bar," was all the information I got before he stopped answering me.

Now, I am no dummy, so I started thinking about what he said, running the details over and over in my head. Rubin, murder, Trenton State. Ring any bells? Well, it did for me. I was a big fan of boxing and I began to wonder, had I been living next to Rubin "the Hurricane" Carter?

I tried to leave Rubin alone, but my curiosity and excitement grew with each day. After a week of greeting him every time we entered or left our cells, he finally cracked and began to answer me back. It wasn't much, but we exchanged pleasantries several times a day.

Begrudgingly, I finally got him to admit to who he was and asked him the question that I had been dying to ask since we began talking.

"Did you do it?"

Rubin picked up his mirror again and studied my face. "You really want to know what happened? You can read this, and you decide for yourself. In case you haven't noticed, everyone in here is innocent, so it doesn't matter what I say. It only matters what the jury believes."

At that moment Rubin Carter gave me a handwritten copy of his manuscript that would later inspire not only Sam Chaiton and Terry Swinton, but also Bob Dylan to advocate for his innocence. Although I was not there that night in Paterson, New Jersey, in 1967, I can tell you what I believe. He did not do it. He is the only person I ever met in prison who did not tell me if he was guilty or innocent. He wanted everyone to decide for themselves. Instead of crying about his innocence, he let the legal system abuse him and steal twenty years of his life, in addition to the middleweight championship title, right out from under his nose.

One thing I learned from Rubin was that I still had a life to live, no matter where I was. I may have been locked up, but I could still do something while in prison. I decided to start working in the kitchen. It afforded some human interaction and put me in a place of power within the prison. Everyone has to eat and no one wants to piss off the guy serving you your meals. From here, I finally began to understand how the prison system worked. Cigarettes were the main currency, and if you had money, you could get anything you wanted.

I took my whole paycheck and some money that my mother sent me and started bargaining with one of the guards on my cellblock. I explained to him that with cigarettes came power and that I needed cartons of them. He was a bit of a tough sell, since he knew that they sold cigarettes in the canteen, so how much of a market could there really be? I told him that I would split my profits with him, and finally he relented. He snuck me in a few cartons and my stock shot straight up. I was suddenly everyone's friend. I had what everyone wanted, and I could give it to them cheaper than anyone else.

I started asking around and tried to find out what else people were looking for in the cellblock. It didn't take long before it became clear that people in jail are exactly the same as people outside of jail—at least in the 70s they were, anyway. They wanted food, smokes, and good pot. So here I was again, with a good connection and a whole crop of people who wanted to get high.

I took this information back to the guard who was helping me smuggle in cheap cigarettes. After explaining that we could double or even triple our proceeds if we started providing people with more options, he was interested. Of course, illegal drugs are a bit of a harder sell to a career corrections officer than cigarettes, but he still went for it. Another thing I'd learned is that if you make anything worth someone's while monetarily, they will most likely do it. Money makes the world go round, and it also keeps the prison up and running.

Basically, the guard, Steve, would take some cash from me and meet one of my connections on the outside. Marijuana could be gotten cheap and good in almost any area, and Trenton was no exception. Steve would get the product and then slip it into the prison through his work duffel bag. Once in the locker room, he would make the switch with a mailbag from the prison mailroom and have it delivered to my cell by one of our partners. Here I would divide it up into manageable portions during the times when Steve was supposed to be guarding my cellblock.

I would sell packs of cigarettes that were full of pre-rolled joints. That was the most expensive product, of course, ready to smoke and easily concealable. The other packages I sold were nickels for five dollars and dimes for ten. You would have thought I was giving it all away by the way people bought it up. People came from all over the prison to help me move my product. What I had been selling in a week was soon gone in a day. Another lesson learned in prison: make sure you can supply your demand.

The only problem I faced with my pot-selling operation was how to keep from getting ripped off. If people found out that I was running low and they did not have money to buy enough to last them a few days, they might get some crazy ideas about stealing my supply. In order to combat this potential pitfall, I had to turn to my friend Steve again. This time, I needed him to help us protect our investment. If we got robbed neither one of us would be getting our money back. If only it worked like this on the streets, the police protecting the drug dealers for a kickback. Oh wait, that is how it works. Anyway, that is what we did. If anyone messed with me, I would tell Steve and he would create a scene and throw the guy into solitary.

It was in this way that I was able to cope with prison. Selling drugs had once again proven to be a good way for me to make friends and gain protection from someone more powerful than myself. So I guess I know one way that the prison system failed me: I definitely had not learned that participating in illegal activities was wrong. The whole purpose of criminal justice passed me by while I was busy getting rich on selling pot in jail.

SYMPATHY FOR THE DEVIL

THE SOCIAL CLIMATE was friendly to felons, with many people focused on "rehabilitating" criminals. You have to love social activism and justice proponents. They are more willing to spend money on people living in prison than on those who have never committed a crime. Because of this, many prisons were operating college prep programs or doing some sort of job skills training for inmates who showed potential. The penitentiary had partnered with several local colleges, including Mercer County Community College, Trenton State College, and Princeton University. I made good impressions on some of the people involved in this college prep program, and they decided I should be invited to participate.

The counselor called me into his office and asked me if there was a program that interested me. I had my choice between college prep courses that would lead to an associate's degree, or I could choose one of the more traditional vocational trades. I could take culinary classes, work on cars, or learn to do construction. The only one of the three vocations that seemed like it would be worth my while was cooking, but I already knew how to do that. I decided to enroll in the academic track, and like many other college students in the early 70s, my focus was on the field of psychology. My counselor was thrilled, as he himself had been a psychology major during his undergraduate years. Of course, I did not say so at the time, but I don't think he should have been excited to have so much in common with a convicted felon.

I took a few classes and proved myself to be no dummy and perhaps maybe even worthy of a real college education. After my fourth semester of coursework in prison, my release date was finally close enough to seem real, and I decided to take the counselor up on his offer to allow me to take the college entrance exams.

I spent a good amount of time in the library studying as the fifth year grew to a close. I attribute my lack of test-taking abilities to my upbringing. If no one ever believes in you, then how can you believe in yourself? On the day of the test, I nervously sharpened and resharpened my pencils and paced the hall outside the library. Who did I think I was? I was a waste of time and money, and everyone knew it, or at least they would soon. I gathered my things to leave; this was nothing more than an exercise in futility. As I turned, the door to the library opened and my counselor walked out.

"They're ready for you, John. I know you'll do well. Just do exactly as you practiced and everything will be fine."

I walked in to take the test, and for the first time in my life there was no freak accident or bad luck that prevented me from reaching my potential. I flew through the pages of the test and surprised myself by knowing most of the answers. Sitting alone in that room, I asked myself questions and my brain answered them. After finishing the last page of questions, I slowly stacked up my papers and made sure they looked neat before allowing myself to smile. I had done it. Now all that was left was to wait for my results.

The exams were scored over a few weeks, and I had tested into the programs at both Princeton and Trenton State

College. While speaking with my advisor, we decided that it would probably be a very large culture shock for me to attend Princeton right out of jail. I would be on parole, and that is not something that many students at Princeton would even know how to respond, let alone relate to. So rather than take on a challenge that I might not have been able to handle, I decided to take the scholarship to Trenton State College starting the following fall semester.

Since my behavior had been good enough and I had done so well, both in school and on the exams, someone at the parole hearing decided that I was a perfect candidate for early release. If only the judge who had handed me three consecutive sentences could see me now. Just over five years after I entered the prison, I was granted permission to leave. Upon checkout, I was given back my few belongings and let into a side room to change out of the prison uniform. It was here that I transferred my small fortune and newfound luck into my civilian clothes and was allowed to exit the prison.

As that first breeze hit my face, I remembered what it was like to be on your own. Obviously, I was still on parole, but I was free. I knew that no one was going to be watching me take a shit or sleep for a good long time. I was willing to do anything to make sure I never landed back here.

When I had been processed into the penitentiary, I was a skinny, broke heroin addict with a losing attitude. Now I was able to hold my head high, ready for my new life to begin. I didn't know where MaryAnn and Brian had gone, but I was unattached for the first time in a long time and happy about it. I had a wallet full of cash and a ticket into Trenton State College. Basically, I had been given a new lease on life, a chance to function normally in society. Would I take advantage of this opportunity, or would it disappear from my fingers like dust in the wind?

FREE BIRD

AS I UNLEASHED myself into the community surrounding Trenton State, I had a few things that I needed to accomplish. First, I needed to find like-minded individuals who were also looking for a good time. Second, I needed a place to live. Third, I needed a source of income.

I found all three, under one roof, when I arrived on campus. I went with my first instinct and asked around about where to find good pot and possibly some sunshine LSD. I still remembered how much I liked that stuff while I was hanging out with Corey's crew in Miami. It didn't make you ugly like heroin—it was just a good time.

Everyone I asked seemed to say the same thing. "Check out that big blue house at the top of the hill. They get their shit straight from the farmers in Pennsylvania."

Well, if everyone was jumping off a bridge, I would've done that, too. I followed their instructions and headed up to the big blue house on the top of the hill. Here I met three kindred spirits in Nancy, Tim, and George. Tim and George were the sellers and Nancy was the beauty, and I was a sucker for a pretty face. I don't think she knew it at the time, but everyone who stepped into that house had a thing for her. She also was blissfully unaware of how much pot was moving through that house, but her innocence only increased her charm.

It turned out that the three of them were looking for a roommate who would be able to help them cover the rent. If there was one thing that I had at that time, it was a full wallet, thereby making me a great candidate for the role of fourth roommate. And it would afford me the opportunity to get to know Nancy better; maybe I would have a chance with her if she saw my face every single day. I wasted no time moving in, and things began much as they had with Corey. Our house and its inhabitants were the life of the party, and there was never a lack of money or drugs to go around. Of course, we were nothing on the scale of Corey and his circle, but this was Jersey, not Miami Beach.

While I had been locked up, a new drug emerged on the scene. It was called methamphetamine, or speed, and you could even make it yourself at home. The best part was that a little bit would allow you to stay up for days on end without even thinking about sleep. A little bump would let me take in the scene tirelessly. Somehow, speed made me feel better about having missed the last five years. I had always hated to miss out on anything, and it seemed that I had found the right drug for me. Heroin had never been my cup of tea, anyway. That addiction was just collateral damage to the primary addiction in my life, MaryAnn. The way I felt people looked at me when I was with her was the same feeling that I got when I did a little bit of speed. I had found a way to replace her.

With my secret adrenaline rush available whenever I needed it, I began to enjoy myself again. There was something dirty about doing heroin; maybe it was the needles or the feeling of being plastered to the couch that I didn't like, but I was finally flying high again. I made the rounds at every party, said all the right things, and made everyone laugh. I was back in business.

I guess it begs the question—yes, I did enroll in classes. Not with any plan in mind; that would have made too much sense. Instead, I went to the classes that interested me, and sometimes I was able to follow through and fill out the paperwork and write an essay or two. Overall, I think I attended at least seven courses my first semester, even though I was enrolled in just three. Again, this penchant for not sleeping was working to my advantage.

Sitting in the back of classrooms, mostly psychology classes, I took in as much information as I could. Like a lot of people who study psychology, I was eager to know more about myself. I was hoping to be able to find out how the events in the woods had shaped me. As I listened, the professors discussed the latest trends in psychology, including the emerging area called behaviorism. Here, I learned that even doctors abused their children, like Skinner locking his daughter inside one of his experiments. The difference was they called it science. Other professors talked about how Sigmund Freud was a genius for figuring out that all little girls were truly victims of penis envy. I heard still more about Oedipus and Electra complexes and how all children secretly want to have sex with their parents. I can tell you one thing about that: my mother did not want to have sex with her father, or her brother. The point here is that while I did learn some interesting things about self-esteem and its effect on confidence and self-image, most of what these professors said simply did not align with my life experiences.

I am not saying that I am the only person who has known suffering or the evils of abuse. I am simply saying that many of these professors lived their lives through their textbooks and controlled experiments. When you take away the control and the experiment is actually someone's reality, you may learn that you do not know what you think you know. Just because Freud wanted to do his mother does not mean that concept applies to the rest of the population. In life, there are always more variables than you can possibly control for.

Where I did find a home in class was in the new area of psychological study: the brain. Not much was known about the brain and its chemistry, with many of the imaging techniques available today still in the very early stages of development. Neuroscience was something that was a bit of a mystery to everyone, which made for very interesting class discussions. To be honest, though, the main reason I attended most of these classes was because Nancy was enrolled in them. I loved being around her. She didn't know anything about my history, and therefore I had a clean slate when it came to her. I wasn't a convicted felon in her eyes; I was just John. Wild and crazy, but still just John. Can you imagine what it feels like to have walked around for most of your life marked? As a child, I was known for being poor and living in the woods. Then I was known as a backwoods boy trying to survive in the big city. After that, it was for being short. Then it was for selling heroin to a cop. Nancy was the first person with whom I could truly reinvent myself. And that is exactly what I did.

With a natural gift for storytelling, I began to tell Nancy about my past, embellishing many of my experiences. Instead of just walking to school in the woods, I told her I'd walked barefoot and it took me hours. My tales from the Air Force painted me as a rapidly rising star whose time was cut short. The beauty of self-reinvention is that you can become whomever you want. I was more than an abused kid who had gotten away; I was a rebel without a cause. I was an asshole.

What I failed to realize was that by touting myself as a fascinating man with a storied past I was making other people jealous. To them, I was a golden child who'd gotten everything easily. They learned that I had been in jail, but I made sure to glorify myself, saying that I sold tons of pot. I told them stories about Corey and my time in Florida, but they thought I was the kingpin and Corey was my sidekick.

Not only was I golden, but it seemed like I was also lucky in love for a change. While Nancy always brushed aside my advances, I met a girl named Johnnie at one of our house parties. Our relationship was casual and fun. Johnnie liked to party, but she kept things pretty light; she dabbled in drugs here and there without showing a real affinity for any one thing. She came and went, breezing in and out of the social scene effortlessly. She was a lot of fun to be around, but I still had my eye on Nancy, hoping that she would finally come around to me.

After class one night, I decided to head across the river and visit my friend Harry in New Hope, Pennsylvania, a short trip from campus. I often went there when it seemed like we were in for a quiet night back home. After we smoked a bone, I started to think about Nancy and couldn't help but wonder if she was back from class for the night. I decided to call and check in. George answered the phone.

"Hey, John boy, where ya at?" he asked

"Oh, you know, just catching up with Harry. Nancy home yet?"

"Nah, just me and Tim, but she should be here soon. You should come back. We're getting ready to have a bit of a party," George said.

"Yeah, all right. I'll be right there."

What George didn't say was that the local police had just busted in the front door. He also failed to mention that Nancy was outside being questioned by the cops when I called. Pure chance had me make that call and it brought me home, right into the wolves' den.

I approached the house and saw the cop cars from the bottom of the hill. Already? *The party could not possibly have been that crazy yet,* I thought to myself. I headed up the hill to see what was going on. The first thing I remember seeing was Nancy. She was sitting in the backseat of a cruiser with the door open. She was crying.

"I have no idea what you're talking about!" she shouted at the cop.

"You mean to tell me that you had no idea there were fifty pounds of marijuana in your living room under the couch?" the cop demanded.

That was all I needed to hear. I turned to leave. I wanted no part of this shit. It was Timmy's pot anyway. Let him sort it out.

"There he is! There's the guy I was telling you about!" Timmy yelled.

Within seconds the cops had me on the ground again.

INSTANT KARMA

APPARENTLY, I SHOULD have kept my mouth shout. Maybe I shouldn't have gone looking for the biggest dealers on campus to make my home with. Maybe I shouldn't have pissed everyone off with my stories of grandeur. Maybe it was chance that made me make the phone call, or maybe it was karma. I'll never know for sure, but I was back behind bars again.

When I had called the house, I had provided the perfect cover story for George and Timmy. They claimed that I'd approached them eighteen months before, looking for a place to set up a drug-dealing operation right out of prison. They told the police that all the pot in the house was mine, and my connection was a guy named Harry who lived in New Hope. The next line was that they could prove it was mine because there was some in my bathroom. You see, the bulk of the pot was in the living room, a common area, thereby making it any-one's. The ounce in the pocket of the bathrobe hanging on the door of my bathroom, however, made it mine. Busted. I was busted again.

What judge would believe that it was not mine, again? Who would think that maybe the college kids with no prior arrests, charges, or convictions were the ones selling pot all over campus? Certainly not the head of the Trenton State court system. I was guilty as far as they were concerned. I was in violation of my parole, and I was probably going to end up going back to jail for the remainder of the original sentence and then whatever they charged me with for this offence.

While I was sitting in the holding cell, I thought of everyone I knew who might possibly be able to help me get the hell out of there. I needed to post bail and fast. I called my brother, mother, and Johnnie. All three of them got back to me, and together they would be able to post bail and I would be out in just a few days. I gave my brother Johnnie's information and he sent her the checks from Florida. Johnnie posted all of the bail money under her name and I was released in under two days.

Lucky for me, Nancy wanted to make a deal. As I said, she was about as innocent as they come and the court system offered her a one-time free pass in exchange for a signed statement. Nancy told the truth: we all smoked some of the pot in the house, but Timmy and George were the principal dealers. She signed her pretrial intervention paperwork and with that helped to set me free. Since she had not corroborated Timmy and George's story, I was off the hook, somewhat.

The courts decided to let me finish school and seemingly left the case open. There was no warrant issued for my arrest and every time my court date approached, I would receive a notice that a continuance had been filed on my behalf. I cannot know for sure, but it seemed that the justice system in New Jersey was allowing the charges to quietly die. They already had two people they could charge and hold responsible in Timmy and George, and Nancy's signed statement cleared my name. The whole case wasn't dismissed, probably because of my record, but at least I was not going back to jail. Not yet, anyway.

When I was released on bail, I thought I had two women who were seriously interested in me. Johnnie had always been more of friend with benefits than a true love interest, so I told her about what Nancy had done to get me out and what I thought the implications were for my future with her. Johnnie seemed to understand that I had to see the situation with Nancy through, that my heart was all wrapped up in another woman, and she told me I could take my time, that there was no need for us to get serious just because she helped me out.

With Johnnie's blessing, I turned my attention to Nancy. It quickly became apparent that Nancy only signed that statement because it was the truth; it had nothing to do with her feelings for me. When I tried to call her, I found out from some mutual friends that her parents had taken her home. She would have to finish college as a commuter rather than have her own place on campus. I did get the number for her parents' place and tried to get in touch.

"Nancy wants nothing to do with you. Don't call here again!" her father shouted into the phone. I called a few more times, but I never got through. I was alone and on my own again.

I returned to finish taking classes on campus, but upon meeting with my school advisor, I discovered that I had managed to accumulate 170 credits. The minimum requirement for graduation was 124 and the college wanted me to graduate now. There was only one problem. Back in prison I had expressed an interest in psychology and had earned an associate's degree from Mercer County Community College, but upon entering Trenton State College I had never officially declared a major. I was going to have to figure out if I was anywhere close to a degree. That's the problem with showing up for only the classes you feel like taking.

When we reviewed my transcript, I was surprised to see I had managed to take many of the classes required for a Bachelor of Science with a concentration in psychology. I was only one class short, so all I had to do was register and complete the course. For once, this was actually as easy as it seemed to be on paper. Without the distractions of Nancy, Johnnie, or the party house, I was able to take the course and graduate the following semester.

ALONE AGAIN (NATURALLY)

THE HARDEST TIMES of my life were usually transition times. After the Air Force, while in prison, after I lost MaryAnn—these were all times when I had no direction, no structure, no one to hold myself accountable to. Lack of a plan was a dangerous thing for me, and after college, transitioning was no easier.

You would think that after earning my degree in psychology, I would pursue a job in that field. What job? In the late seventies, there was an overabundance of qualified mental health professionals and only so many jobs in the healthcare and social service industries to be filled. As I hadn't planned for graduation, I was left without a place to go.

I had already lived in Virginia, North Carolina, Maryland, Florida, California, and New Jersey, and that is just what I remember for sure. I was a vagabond, a man without a place to call home. Where should I go? Who would want me around? I wasn't sure yet. I decided to go back to the place where I had lived most recently: Long Branch. Hoping for a few friendly faces in the area, I moved into the Fountains Motel while I tried to get my bearings. Just a few days after I arrived, there came a knock on the door, and there stood Johnnie, holding her bags.

"I heard you were in town," she said. She placed her bags on the dresser and began to unpack. And just like that, Johnnie was in my life.

The next few days we spent wandering around town, looking for help-wanted signs and asking everyone we saw if they knew of any opportunities. One afternoon, walking by Seven Presidents beach, we saw a restaurant with a grand opening sign hanging above the front door. It was called Yesterday's.

We walked in and filled out job applications while talking to the owner. He was looking to hire a whole staff, front of the house and back. I told him I could cook, and he brought me into the kitchen. I did a demo for him and made him some red sauce with penne pasta. After tasting my food, he offered me a job on the spot. Then he turned to Johnnie. He took one look at her and decided she would make an excellent hostess. Who wouldn't want to eat at a place that had her standing at the door? Now we had both a place to stay and a place to work.

I still had my drug connections from when I lived in the area with MaryAnn, but Johnnie was a good influence on me; we only really smoked pot and drank a lot. We were having too much fun to need to dull our pain.

Johnnie and I had never established whether or not we were an official couple. We just took things as they came and usually ended up home together at the end of the night. Neither one of us brought other people back to our place at the Fountains, but we both stepped outside the relationship occasionally. Working at Yesterday's, we met so many new and interesting people that we did not bother tying ourselves down to only each other. I had learned the hard way from MaryAnn that people will do whatever they want, no matter what labels you try to assign to yourselves. By not defining our relationship, we had no expectations from each other. We could just be together and see where things went on their own.

I was living altogether footloose and fancy free when I finally got a letter from MaryAnn. I don't know if someone contacted her to let her know I was out of prison and working again at the shore, or if she could sense I was happy and felt the need to destroy it for me. In addition to divorce papers, she sent me a letter demanding money for Brian, and a lot of it. She claimed that she was entitled to wages I earned in prison and anything I now made from Yesterday's. There was no mention of visitation or a relationship with him in return, but since I wanted to avoid having to hire my own lawyer and any possibility of going to court, I signed her divorce papers and agreed to send money for Brian. I didn't send a set dollar amount; I chose to send her as much as I could spare. Some weeks I sent more than others, but I did the best I could. I wasn't exactly sure that Brian was mine, but I still felt a level of responsibility for bringing him into this world.

Getting back in touch with MaryAnn was like getting visits from a ghost. I had not thought that much about her while I was in college and had done well for myself as a result. It was as if someone out there had decided that I was too happy and that I needed to be brought back down. Aside from sending her money, I also spent a lot of time talking about her and Brian to Johnnie. Although she never said anything about it, I could feel Johnnie begin to pull back slightly. When the person you are with is sending most of his money to, and talking incessantly about, an ex-lover, how can you maintain the same level of attachment that you had before?

Looking back, I can't be sure how long I lived with Johnnie. It could have been a couple of months or even a couple of years. All I know is that one night I came home and Johnnie was standing near our dresser like she had on the day she came to me.

"I'm going to be leaving for a while," she said as she picked up her bag and put her sunglasses on. "I'm going to Florida with Billy. I don't know when we'll be back."

Billy . . . Billy . . . who was Billy? Billy was that quiet new waiter we had hired over at Yesterday's. I had been so consumed with myself that I hadn't noticed she had stopped coming home most nights. Just by being unaware, I had lost her. She left later that day and didn't leave a number or address where I could reach her.

I couldn't afford to pay weekly rent at the Fountains without Johnnie's help while still sending MaryAnn money for Brian. A buddy from work was leaving his place on Westwood Avenue, and he said he paid a lot less than I did. I took him up on his offer and moved across town. I still had a place to work, but without Johnnie I had a lot more free time on my hands. My natural reaction was to do what I did best when things were not going my way: get high.

I started going down to the pool hall—Mike's Tavern—and blowing all my money, including the money I was supposed to be sending to MaryAnn, on booze and games of pool. I would drink scotch, Johnny Walker to be exact, as quickly as possible from the minute I got there until the time I left. The bartenders all knew what was expected of them when I walked through their door. They would line up four shots and I would take them down, one after another. Then I would walk to the nearest table and challenge the guy playing. We played for money and we played for keeps, but mostly we just played ourselves and the demons that lived inside us.

WALK ON THE WILD SIDE

IT BECAME A ritual. Get off work, head over to Mike's, get wasted, and then go home. Nothing really changed from night to night. Over and over, the same scenes played themselves out. I would play pool, get all the way to the end of a match, and then forget to call my pocket. The other guy would always win and I would go home a loser.

That is until one night when everything changed. I walked into Mike's, and the usual crowd settled in. I was totally caught up in my routine, and it took me a while to notice the two new girls sitting at the bar. They were getting hammered, and it seemed that one of them was trying to distract, or was it console, the other one.

The skinny girl with the long brown hair caught my attention. She was absolutely beautiful, but there was a seriousness about her. Or was it a sadness? I took my fourth shot and, instead of going to the tables, I walked to the other end of the bar.

"Hey, you, uh, wanna go smoke a bone?" was the best I could come up with.

The brunette turned her stool to face me and responded, "I don't do that." She quickly went back to her friend.

"Well, do you want to come with me while I do?" I tried again.

"No, not really," was all she said back.

"Will you be here when I get back?" I asked again. There was just something about her, something that screamed, *I'm out of your league, pal.*

She looked back at me this time and gave me her undivided attention. I could feel her sizing me up. I did not know what she was looking for but, man, I was hoping I had whatever it was. "Yes, I guess I will," she answered.

It turned out her name was Nancy, too. I could not help but think, "Here we go again." Of course, this Nancy was nothing like the other one. All they really shared was that I was attracted to both of them and they both were far more innocent than I deserved.

Nancy's house was around the corner from me and she was currently living alone. Apparently, she had been married, just like I had, but it had not worked out for a whole host of reasons. The only difference was that she was still living in the house she had shared with her husband, whereas I had lived in a prison, a pothouse, an apartment, a motel, and now a rooming house since leaving my spouse.

I was lucky enough to have met Nancy because her best friend, Peggy, had been trying to get her out of a rut. Since Nancy split with her husband, she had been keeping to herself most of the time and most likely assigning the blame for the relationship's failure to herself. Peggy had decided that perhaps a night out would be just the pick-me-up Nancy needed. She had certainly gotten picked up, but only time would tell if it would improve her situation.

Nancy and I saw each other often over the next few weeks. We went dancing, ate out, and went to the movies, and I think we really enjoyed each other's company. Nancy was unlike anyone

I had ever been with. She always had a plan, an idea of what she was looking for and where she was going. She had expectations for herself and anyone else in her life. If I said I was going to be somewhere or do something, I had better do it.

One Friday night, I was supposed to meet her after I got out of work. Instead I went to Mike's, got drunk, and didn't even bother to call to let her know I wasn't going to make it over to take her out. When I called the following morning, she was not pleased. I had never had someone take me for my word so easily. Anything I told her, she believed, and that included when I told her I would be somewhere. Nancy told me that our relationship was not going to work if I was not going to be able to hold up my end of the deal. Trust was a major issue for her and she had already lost some with me. I decided I was going to make it up to her. Nancy made me want to be a better man.

I wrote her a note and asked for another chance. I told her I would pick her up and take her anywhere she wanted, even if it was only to walk on the beach. The romantic in me was born.

Falling for Nancy was the most natural thing that had ever happened to me. We saw each other almost every day. Living around the corner made it very convenient, and the only glitch was that I was now working several jobs. I left Yesterday's slowly, mostly because I had moved and it was not right next door anymore. I cooked most nights at Mike's Tavern and then would hang out at the bar. Nancy would come in just as I was switching from working to drinking, and she would stay to watch me play pool.

I won most of my matches, though I still continuously forgot to call the pocket for the eight ball, which would result in me losing on a technicality. Nancy was much better at remembering to call it than I was, so there were many nights right before I shot where she would shout out, "Call the pocket, John!" I loved that she was looking out for me.

Since a lot of our time was spent in a bar, I was doing a lot of drinking. A day didn't go by that I wasn't passed out or unable to recall details from the night before. I guess that's why a lot of the time we spent together in those early days is lost to me. That is one of the hardest things about looking back on my life. I have extremely vivid memories from my childhood, complete with pictures, ingrained images, and even smells that can bring me right back to the woods and our time in Florida. I am not sure if it was the brain damage I sustained from the car accident or if it is from all the drinking and drugs, but so many of my memories of my adult life are foggy. The times I remember the best are the stories that have been told to me by my friends and family. I believe that most of what I "remember" is actually just remembering being told about a particular event after it occurred. Attempting to piece together my past is like working with a jigsaw puzzle that is completely devoid of color. All of the pieces are there; I just have no way to differentiate any of them.

Hanging out at Mike's must have been interesting for Nancy because, aside from that first night when I met her, she really never drank. As I got to know her better, I found out that her life had been very unlike mine. She grew up in a middle-class family that moved around a lot; her dad had been in the Service. There may have been some problems, like with any family, but for the most part they were normal through and through. There weren't any beatings, no one murdered anyone, and she didn't flee her home as soon as she was able to.

Nancy emanated stability. She graduated at the top of her class from a local high school in New Jersey and went to the University of Maryland, where she studied psychology. I often wonder if that is part of what drew her to me. Nancy seemed to have an attraction for the abnormal and attracted a lot of weirdos. She was a good listener and showed genuine concern for the people around her. After she got her bachelor's degree, she went on to Rider University, where she got a degree in counseling. She married her high school sweetheart, and the rest of her life was supposed to be happily ever after. Unfortunately, her husband had other plans.

Nancy didn't make mistakes, and getting a divorce was probably one of the hardest things she had ever endured. The night I met her in Mike's Tavern was one of the only times that Nancy got drunk. It seems fitting that she met me under the influence.

Our relationship progressed rather quickly, and I moved in after about six months. We spent most of our free time together, but I am not sure exactly what we did. You know the song lyrics, "Don't smoke, don't drink, what do you do?" Well, that summed up a lot of our relationship. I got drunk and high every day, and Nancy had a nine-to-five job that she went to every day. She also went to church every Sunday with her parents and was involved in the local community. I don't know if I was some sort of project for Nancy at first or if she really loved me for me, but we were getting serious quickly.

I bought an engagement ring at a local jewelry store. I placed the small box inside a larger box, wrapped it up, and placed it under the tree, nestled among the other presents. On Christmas morning of 1982, Nancy agreed to marry me. We decided that since we had been lied to so many times in our previous relationships, we would get married on Honest Abe's birthday: February 12. This would symbolize our commitment to being truthful and honest in our relationship.

We flew to Florida to prepare for the wedding. The actual ceremony would be performed at my mother's house, and then we would have a small reception at a local restaurant. We also planned to have a larger reception when we got back to New Jersey, at a restaurant called Christie's, where I had recently

Nancy and John Wagner—1983

started working part-time. From what I recall, which is not that much, Nancy looked beautiful and the ceremony went off without a hitch.

Of course, things couldn't remain that positive for long. As soon as the festivities were over, my mother handed me a letter. The return address was from MaryAnn's parents' home, close to where we lived in New Jersey. She was back. MaryAnn had no way of contacting me once I'd moved out of the Fountains, so she'd reached out to my mother. I opened the letter to find MaryAnn's telltale scrawl staring back at me. Even after all these years, I still knew her handwriting. She wanted to arrange a meeting. Brian was getting older now, and he had starting asking a lot of questions about his father. While I may have had my doubts about who Brian's father really was, it seemed like I was the only shot he had at having a father figure.

I tried to avoid dragging Nancy into it; we had just been married, after all, but she was extremely perceptive. She wouldn't let me alone until I showed her the letter. Of course, I had told her about Brian and MaryAnn, but hearing about it and seeing evidence of a past marriage and child are two different stories. To her credit, she took it quite well. She thought I should be as involved as possible with Brian. She believed children needed to know both of their parents, and I guess I agreed with her. She told me to think about my own childhood without my father and what that had done to me. I felt awful that I had not reached out to Brian sooner.

COCAINE

NANCY KNEW THAT I drank and smoked some pot, but I really don't think it ever occurred to her that I also did hard drugs regularly. With our opposite work schedules, so much of what I did occurred while she slept. I had reduced my consumption of LSD and heroin over the years, but cocaine use was now becoming much more widespread. It used to be that only hippies and Wall Street types used coke; now it was fashionable for everyone to have a rolled-up bill, small silver spoon, long pinkie nail, or other cocaine-using utensil on them at all times in the early 80s. Eventually, it became a pretty consuming force in my life.

I was working full-time at Christie's and had made friends with a few other guys who liked to party. Brandon Harris, Big Al, and Daryl were my partners in crime and we were having fun. We had a good contact in Hollywood Ray, a friend in addition to a dealer. We would spend nights at work waiting to get off so the fun could begin. We sneaked drinks while we were working and had a fairly decent buzz going by the time our shifts ended. That was when the games would really begin.

We would head over to Hollywood's and score a big bag. We didn't mess around like a lot of people did with little lines or small bumps; those were just teasers to me. One Friday night, we all got paid and headed straight to Hollywood's. Picking up an ounce, we brought the bag back to my house. Nancy was in bed, and she slept like the dead, so there was no chance we would wake her up. I took down one of the mirrors from our bedroom, a large square mirror with a little wooden border. I dumped most, if not all, of the bag right into the center of it. Then I took out my driver's license and shaped the coke into a huge happy face: two eyes, a nose, lips, and eyebrows. I started on the left side and, in one fell swoop, took down half the face. I felt the drip almost instantly and then my heart started to pound. The numbing tingle spread quickly as the boys finished off the rest of the face. We sat around and smoked a few bones, drank some booze, and waited for the sun to come up.

I often went to bed right before Nancy got up. Sometimes I would pass out on the couch and she would wake me up on her way out the door. Our relationship was still good, but I knew I needed to give her something or she was going to lose interest with my antics. When Nancy said she wanted to have a baby, I figured this was my chance. I could give Nancy something no one else—including her ex-husband—had ever given her. She was a natural mother, and I knew everything would be all right if there was someone for us both to care for; the baby would bring us closer.

We were married in early February of 1983 and Nancy got pregnant as soon as we started trying a few months later. The baby was due in March of 1984. Life seemed to be racing by me and I was standing still.

I guess all the talk of our own baby was making Nancy nervous about my other child, so we made arrangements to have a visit with Brian. I called the number MaryAnn had written in the letter and waited for her to answer. When you haven't spoken to someone in so long and you were once as close as

MaryAnn and I, it's almost eerie when you do hear their voice. It was like I had traveled back in time to the last moment I had seen her, sitting across the table from her in prison. Our conversation was stiff and guarded—what do you say to someone you were once so close with? She wanted me to take Brian, who was now twelve, for a few days to a week so that we could really get to know each other. Nancy agreed and the plans were set in motion for him to come visit for a week at the end of the summer.

I was starting to get nervous about the new pressures being placed on me, and my drug use began to pick up pace. How was I going to be able to afford my habits, a new baby, and Brian? A normal person might back off from the drugs, but my behavior only got worse. I was isolating myself from my friends and getting high by myself.

For Christmas the year we got engaged, Nancy had bought me a nice telescope. I had always had an interest in the stars and it was a great gift. The telescope started out in one of the back rooms of our house. There were a set of French doors that led out onto a small flat roof area that overlooked our backyard and some of the neighbors' property, and from there I could get a nice clear shot of the sky overhead. One night after getting high, I got the idea to go play around with the telescope. While I was looking through the lens, I got the feeling that I was being watched.

I pointed the telescope toward our neighbor's house on the left. I studied the house for a while—nothing. Then I turned to the right—again, nothing. As I looked at each house, the feeling of being watched was growing stronger and stronger. I was sure now that someone was watching me; it was just a question of who. Finally, I turned to the house that was opposite our property. Our backyards fed into each other, separated by a thin forest. There it was, a flash, a reflection, something in the window. I dropped to my knees and crawled to my bedroom. I had found the perpetrator.

The next day I went over to our neighbor on the left, an old Italian man named Peter who seemed friendly enough. I asked him if he knew the people behind us.

"Of course," he said. "That's Officer Spinnoza's house."

My worst fears had been confirmed. The cops were watching me. That night after work, I came home with another big bag and again went to the room with French doors. I looked at Spinnoza's house and realized he was watching me again. I panicked at first and then came up with a plan. I would communicate with him and see what he wanted. First, I got out some paper and wrote a note that read, "What do you want?" and hung it next to the telescope. Nothing happened. Then I realized that maybe the lighting was bad. I would have to work out how to make the sign more visible. I got out a flashlight and began turning it on and off, waiting for a response. Still nothing. Finally, I had the courage to walk over to the house and check some things out. I realized that both of his cars, his family car and his squad car, had license plates that started with the letter Z. I became convinced that all cars I saw that had plates that began with Z were from the same law enforcement agency as Spinnoza. The whole town was watching me.

This went on for a few weeks. I would attempt to communicate with the officer and get nothing back. I couldn't figure out what they wanted me for. Maybe they knew about the scandal from Trenton State College, maybe it was from the MaryAnn problem, or maybe they had been following me since Florida. I couldn't be sure, but I knew they wanted something. One night I was off work early and Nancy had come home from the grocery store. All the lights were out and I was sitting in the middle of the floor in the back bedroom. The telescope was gone.

"John, what are you doing in here?" Nancy questioned. I couldn't tell if it was fear in her voice, or maybe she already knew. Maybe she was working with Spinnoza, too. I didn't respond.

"John, I asked you what you were doing. Where is your telescope?" she demanded, getting more agitated by the second.

My response came in a whisper. "They took it apart."

"Who took it apart? John, what are you talking about?" Her voice was shrill now.

"Spinnoza's men. They took it to keep me from watching them watch me. I was onto them, and they couldn't stand it."

Nancy looked at me hard. I was sitting in the middle of the floor in a dark room with pieces of the telescope scattered around me. There were pieces hidden all over the room. "John, Officer Spinnoza has lived behind this house for years. He's lived here longer than me. Why would you think he is watching the house?"

"Why wouldn't he, Nancy? Don't you understand? They have been following me for years. That's why I always get caught—they're always watching!" I yelled as I leapt off the floor. I continued to get more and more irate as the conversation continued. Eventually, Nancy left the room.

Even twenty-five years later—which is how long it's been since that night—I still don't know how the telescope came apart. I would say that someone else did it, and that would be partly true. If you consider me a different person on drugs, that is. I know deep down somewhere that I must have done it myself; I just can't remember doing it because I was too high. Again.

Soon enough it was time for Brian's big visit. Nancy took a week off from work and I did the same. We planned trips to the beach and baseball games. It was nerve-wracking to think we were going to meet my child, and he was old enough to have a personality, thoughts, feelings, and expectations. What was he looking for from me? A constant presence? Guidance? Only time would tell.

The day Brian came to us, we were both nervous with excitement. The doorbell rang. I opened the front door and saw a lanky African American boy of about ten.

"Is there anything I can do for you?" Nancy asked.

"Ummmm, yeah. I am here to meet my father, John Wagner. Is he here?" Brian answered.

He looked nothing like what I remembered, and MaryAnn had never sent me pictures, but we wasted no time inviting him inside. I couldn't just make him wait on the porch while we adjusted to his appearance. Nancy quickly got Brian something to drink while I showed him around the house. He was a very polite and fun-loving kid. He asked questions and showed a genuine excitement and interest in my life. He just didn't look like he was mine.

After that first day, Nancy and I lay down in bed and talked about what had happened. She was supportive and accepting of Brian and told me not to focus on how he looked. We agreed to enjoy our time with him and deal with the issue of paternity later. It was exactly what I needed to hear. We went through the rest of the week and just enjoyed ourselves. Brian was a lot of fun, and it was nice having him around. For the first time, I got a taste of what it was like to be a father. I told him he was welcome to come back anytime.

It took a few weeks, but eventually I got another letter from MaryAnn. She wanted money—and lots of it. She claimed that except for my time in prison, I had never sent her and Brian any money. While I had done my best to send cash whenever possible, it was probably only for a few years out of what had quickly become more than a decade of Brian's life.

When Nancy got home from work that night, I showed her the letter. I told Nancy that we needed to send some of my savings for the new baby and give it to MaryAnn to get her off my back.

"I'm not exactly sure how to handle this, John," Nancy began, "but Brian isn't your son."

I wasn't the only one who thought so. It felt so good to have confirmation from her.

"I know you've told me before that MaryAnn explained Brian's looks by telling you it was probably from the drugs you were doing. I have never heard of such a thing before, and after seeing him I truly believe he is part African American. If MaryAnn is white and you are white, how could he possibly be yours?"

I signed Brian's birth certificate at the hospital and had agreed to send him money to avoid court all those years ago. How was I going to work my way out of this mess? I needed some answers, especially because I had another baby on the way. I could not send money to Brian if he wasn't mine, not while Nancy was pregnant with a child who would bear not only my name but my genetic ties as well.

I have never been one to go to court willingly, and I certainly never thought that I would be the one to request a day before a judge. My previous experiences with judges had not been all that pleasant, so I shocked myself when I filed a motion to determine Brian's paternity. It was in response to another letter that I got from MaryAnn, actually from her lawyer, that she was suing me for child support.

While I was sure that Nancy was right and Brian was not my real son, I still had a small nagging doubt. Part of me was still kind of nervous that he would be mine and I would have turned out to be as big a deadbeat as my own father. I had only spent time with him once that I remembered, and when he passed away, he hadn't left anything for my mom or me. He clearly didn't care about me, and I was afraid I may have been making the same mistakes with Brian. As court approached, I started to get more and more anxious, which led to more and more drugs. Nancy was also getting huge and starting to get more aggressive with me around the house.

When I would come home wasted, she would be waiting up for me. Ready for an argument. She would follow me from room to room, demanding, "Where have you been?" and "Who were you with?" As my life spun further and further out of control, the lies I was telling also grew much larger. I began making up stories that I thought she would find more acceptable than "Oh, you know, honey. I was just doing the usual, a few eight balls with the boys."

By the time our court date arrived, there was a lot to be anxious about in my life. As per usual, I had brought it upon myself, but that didn't make me feel any better about it. As we entered the courtroom, my heart began to pound. Standing in front of me was MaryAnn, looking well for the first time since I had met her. She had gained some weight, had gotten rid of her bleached-blonde locks, and had a healthy glow about her. I realized she might win this case after all. I looked nowhere near as good as her. I was thin, my once thick, long hair looked stringy, and my face had a sallow, scary look. Basically, I looked like MaryAnn had looked before Brian was born. Clearly, having a child had given her some sense of responsibility and she had responded well to it.

The court proceedings began smoothly with the judge reading the complaint filed against me. I was accused of reneging on ten years of child support. MaryAnn produced the birth certificate that I had signed twelve years before, right before I went into jail. There it was, my signature clear as day.

"Why haven't you paid to support the welfare of your child, sir?" the judge asked sternly.

"I am not sure he is mine," I answered, my voice shaking.

"Well, your name is on the birth certificate. Why would you sign for a child that you were not sure to be yours?"

Good question. "Well, Your Honor, the child looks nothing like me. At first it was hard to tell, but now that he is older it's really kind of obvious he's not mine."

The judge shook his head, "John Wagner, you have been in and out of jail for drug-related charges, you have not paid child support in ten years, and your defense is that he doesn't look like you? Many children resemble one parent much more than the other. Is that your only defense?"

"Well, sir, as you can see, his mother and I are both Caucasian," I stuttered.

Nancy handed me a picture taken from our recent beach vacation with Brian and told me to give it to the judge. "Also, Your Honor, I have a picture here I'd like to show you, and I think I would like to ask for a paternity test."

The judge took the picture. Then he looked at MaryAnn. Then he looked at me. Then back. And forth. Finally, he spoke. "Ma'am"—he was looking at MaryAnn now—"did you engage in sexual relations with any other man during or around the time this child was conceived? Specifically, were you seeing anyone of African American descent?"

She hesitated, and then turned her big blue eyes right on me. "Yes, sir, I did. I did have an affair with a man named Joe."

And just like that, MaryAnn and Brian were out of my life. Joe was Brian's real father, not me. Now you might be wondering why she hadn't contacted Joe for child support. I am sorry to say that Joe was one of the first victims of the AIDS epidemic and had already passed away. Brian would never get to meet his real father. Because of my own childhood, I felt guilty just turning my back on Brian, so I continued to send small amounts of money and Christmas and birthday presents for a few years. He would send thank-you cards back, but eventually the cards stopped coming and so did the gifts. I was ready to have my own family, and it's a good thing, because my child was about to be born.

Brian Wagner—taken during his visit in 1983

SWEET CHILD O' MINE

NANCY'S WATER BROKE on a cold spring morning during a rare late March blizzard. She spent the next twenty-four hours bringing our first child into the world. Lauren Danielle Wagner was born at 5:49 am on March 26, 1984. There was something about holding her for the first time that was very different from what it had been with Brian. Maybe it was because I wasn't worried about getting dragged off to prison the next day. It also could have been because she was mine and I knew it. She would turn those little eyes up to me, squeeze them shut, and let out a wail like I had never heard before. But that wail was for me. I was a father.

Once she was home, things returned to normal fairly quickly. She was a low-maintenance baby and slept through the night after only two weeks. She ate well for Nancy. My god, she had this smile. It was hypnotizing. I thought that Big Al and Darryl would stop coming around because I had a kid now, but, if anything, her arrival had the opposite effect. They loved her, too.

Our routine was regular and easy and didn't change much day to day. I was still drinking and using drugs but not quite as much as right before she was born. Nancy was happier. I continued to work at Christie's, moving up in the ranks until I was one of several main cooks. Nancy worked as a day care provider and took Lauren with her. The program, Mother's Day Out, was held at the church that Nancy went to with her parents. This way, Nancy could get paid, have a sitter and see her parents all in the same day.

With my growing family and drug habit to support, I needed a higher salary than what they could offer me at Christie's. Local places weren't paying that well, and the only place I could find that could afford me was all the way in Newark, about forty minutes away. Ordinarily, I wouldn't have considered commuting to a cooking job, but it did occur to me that I would be able to score better in Newark, and no one knew me as a father and husband there. There was something about people knowing you had a family that made it more difficult for them to sell you drugs. I guess everyone has some level of a conscience, something that seemed to be missing from my brain chemistry.

The Marriott at the Newark Airport was my first large-volume cooking job. In addition to being a line cook, I was also in a chef preparatory program there. They trained us in classical cooking techniques such as French cuisine and even let us dabble a bit in some of the newer fields, like Neo-American and Asian fusion styles. The only problem with the job was that it was so far from home that I had to spend a lot more time away from the family and more time on my own. Taking care of myself was never something I did well, and this time was no different. Instead of getting out of work and coming home, I would circle around Newark, looking for someone selling coke. After I got what I was looking for, I drove back to Long Branch, using my supply. Right around the corner from home, I would stop off at Falvo's Liquors and pick up a quart of Johnnie Walker Black Label scotch. I would finish it before I walked in the door.

This may seem no different from my behavior when I worked at Christie's, but now there was this child waiting for me when I got home and I would have to attempt to pull it together. Of course, Nancy would have put her to bed long before I got home, but Lauren would wake up as soon as she heard the door open. Like many little girls, she loved her daddy and wanted nothing more than to hear a story and spend some time with me.

At a loss for what to say to this curious, bright-eyed three-year-old, I began to make up stories for her entertainment. I would do anything to hear her sweet giggle and get a hug. There was almost a mini-series, if you will, that I made up about a blue tiger that lived in our garage. I told Lauren that Mr. Sinuto, a name I stole from the people who had owned our home before us, had been an adventurer and often went on safaris to Africa in search of rare and beautiful things. One year, while Mr. Sinuto was traveling through the jungle, he spotted something out of the corner of his eye, something blue and large and fast. *Oh, what could it be?* Mr. Sinuto had wondered, and he set out to find whatever it was that he had seen in the jungle. It took him years of searching. He looked until he was quite the old man, and then, finally, entering a clearing in the jungle, he was face-to-face with the blue creature: it was a tiger. A tiger that could speak.

Mr. Sinuto captured the tiger and brought him back to America. He let the tiger live in his garage, the very garage that was located behind our house. Lauren ate these stories up night after night, asking to hear them again or to hear new stories about the tiger. Since the tiger didn't have a name of his own, he took on the name of his captor, Mr. Sinuto, when the real Mr. Sinuto died of old age. The tiger started moving around the town in search of food. He wore roller skates and would attach the garage to himself and pull it behind him on his way to 7-Eleven. There, he would buy Cheetos, Fritos, or Doritos to eat for dinner. One night, Mr. Sinuto came out of 7-Eleven and heard crying coming from the garage. Inside, he found a newborn baby. There was no note, nothing to tell him where the child had come from—that is, until he caught a whiff of her. She smelled like Ralph Lauren perfume! He wanted to call her Ralph but decided that was no name for a little girl; hence, he gave her the name Lauren.

This is just a silly series of stories, not worth recalling, except that to me it was one of the most important pieces of who I am. When I think of the story of the blue tiger, I remember the way Lauren would laugh and I could remind myself that I was a decent father. I may not have always been in all the right places at the right times, I may not have been sober often enough, but I told her stories that she would never forget. Nighttime after work was our time, and she didn't know or care that I was high.

Nancy had a doctor's appointment one afternoon, and Big Al and Darryl and I were supposed to be watching Lauren. Instead, we got high. We sent Lauren upstairs so that she wouldn't see what we were up to, but the second we were done she came bounding down the stairs with every single stuffed animal she owned wrapped up in a sheet. If there was one thing that she had a lot of, it was toys. Stuffed animals, Barbies, baby dolls, tons of them, everywhere, all the time. She dragged her toys down the stairs while we tried to regain some composure and un-numb our facial expressions. She arranged them all on the sheet in a row on the couch and directed us to each take a corner. The four of us—a three-year-old and three drug addicts—picked up the blanket full of toys and swung it back and forth, back and forth, until she screamed, "Let go!" and everything fell on the floor. That is kind of how my life was going at the time, up and down, just waiting for everything to go flying.

Having Lauren was a blessing and a curse. She was fun to have around and the love she gave was immeasurable, but she came with a lot of responsibility. Nancy wanted me to be "more of a father," take her places, be there when I said I was going to be there, and make sure she came home in one piece. This may sound simple, but to me it was a whole lot of expectations that hadn't been placed on me before. I didn't know how to be accountable to myself, let alone to someone else.

Working at the Marriott was a great gig for me. Nancy expected a paycheck, which motivated me to go to work every day—and that was an advantage in holding down the job. This may be a bit of a stereotype, but most people who work in the food service industry do so partly because they have some trouble with authority and have a hard time showing up at regular hours. The result is that what the higher-ups expect from chefs, cooks, and waitstaff is a bit less than a traditional nine-to-five job. As I continued to excel at work, I was quickly climbing the corporate ladder.

John and Lauren Danielle—1986

JUST GIMME SOME TRUTH

ONE NIGHT AS I was leaving the restaurant, my boss approached me.

"John, I need a favor," he said.

"What's up?" I replied. I was anxious to get out of there, but it was pretty rare that anyone asked me for a favor.

"I forgot the keys to the office, so I can't lock up the register. Usually, I just take it with me, but I'm not going straight home tonight. Do you think you could take it?"

I didn't hesitate. "Sure, I can do that. Should I just bring it back with me tomorrow?"

Pulling out of the parking lot, I slid the cash drawer under the front seat. I went and met my dealer and he came to the car window to make his drop. I stopped at the liquor store around the corner from my house about an hour after that. I picked up a bottle of scotch and turned the corner to go toward my house. I walked into the house just as I emptied the bottle of Johnnie Walker. Then I walked over to my favorite spot on the couch and passed out.

When I woke up the next morning, I went out to warm the car up. Then I remembered the cash register. As I opened the passenger side door and slid my hand up under the seat,

I realized with a sinking feeling that it was gone. Damn, who was going to believe this? I hadn't stolen the money, but no one would buy that story.

I pleaded my case to my boss, but I was right to be worried; they fired me on the spot. Losing my job at the Marriot marked the beginning of the end for me. Nancy was pregnant again, and she was constantly pissed off with me. I can't say that I blame her. Who wants her husband to be unemployed while she's busy building a family? I tried to hide behind my bottle of booze, but it always seemed like she could see right through it, straight through me, even.

As money got tighter, we started fighting more and more. I tried to find a new job and even managed to pick up a few shifts here and there at places around town that knew my reputation as a talented cook. The problem was that I wasn't sober enough to show up all the time. There were weeks where all I did was sleep. Depression began to creep in.

I always knew that my brain was different from others. Most people see left and right, up and down, right and wrong. In my universe, the most mundane situations and choices lie along a grey continuum that would baffle the paint department at Home Depot. The credit cards I had reserved only for emergencies or family necessities became increasingly enticing. I finally figured out how to buy Nancy the things we needed, get me the drugs that kept me happy, and be able to check out whenever I wanted. Charge it. Not only did cards work at stores, but they also worked with dealers. I could buy them anything they wanted, which was almost as good as cash. TVs, cigarettes, jewelry. Things were flowing freely again and I could feel like myself. I had no idea that the rug was about to be ripped out from under my feet.

Jonathan Peter Wagner was born on August 14, 1988. My first true son. I should have been overjoyed with his arrival, but

I was already too far gone to connect. Compounding the issue, Jon-boy was born with asthma, and he suffered almost incessantly. Suddenly, there were machines in my house to help him breathe. Late nights were spent in the emergency room. And Nancy was just not herself. Things were much more serious to her now. She had definitely changed some over the years, but caring for Jonathan brought out a whole new side to her. The part of her that longed for freedom and carefree days became buried so deeply inside her that I almost couldn't see it anymore. I had almost no connection to this family that I had created, and the divide between us continued to grow.

Nancy's father was an extremely successful international businessman. His successes only magnified my failures, but sometimes you take a handout no matter where it comes from. Each year, he would take twelve of us—his wife, their children, and their grandchildren—on vacation somewhere exotic. We had been to Hawaii, and Mexico a few times as well. I enjoyed myself on these vacations, but, of course, there was part of me that resented not being able to do this for my wife and children myself. The vacations we could afford were usually trips to visit my mother in Florida or somewhere else domestic and inexpensive.

For our first big trip after Jonathan was born, we would all be heading to a big resort in Acapulco. I was absolutely dreading the trip. How was I going to be able to get away with using when there would be twelve pairs of eyes on me all the time? I did the only thing I knew how to do: hide. I kept different hours than the rest of the family. I stayed up all night using the drugs I bought off the Mexican street kids and then slept all day. I was never at the family dinner, never around during the swimming pool hours, and I certainly had no involvement with anything having to do with my in-laws. The questions about my whereabouts did not faze me one bit; how could they, since they were never directed to me? Nancy fielded all the questions from her family. The woman who never lied was turning into a pretty good storyteller. I forced this good woman to lie for me, to hide my behavior from everyone close to her. By isolating myself from the world, I was also forcing Nancy to join me in my pseudo-reality.

I managed to evade everyone for almost the whole trip because Nancy told them I was sick. Truthfully, I *was* sick. But one night, Nancy demanded I make an appearance.

"I can't do this anymore," she exclaimed, coming in from yet another day at the pool without me. "I will not lie again for you. You have to at least pretend to socialize. You have to get out of that bed, now. Dinner is in an hour. Try and clean yourself up before then." The door slammed before I even got a chance to open my mouth.

Here we go, I thought. I pulled my bag out from the night before and looked at the dust stuck to the side of the plastic. Empty. Well, almost. There was a little bit left. Maybe if I scraped all of the baggies from the whole week, I would be able to come up with enough to get my ass out of bed. I started the process and was able to get at least a thin line going. Up it went and I felt the familiar burn. Showered and dressed, I thought I looked pretty damn good; that was the depth of my delusion.

I strolled into the lobby and was immediately blindsided by a flash of pink and sunburn.

"Daddy!" Lauren screamed. She tackled me and instantly began talking. "I'm so glad you feel better. Today we went out into town and . . ." The rest of her story was lost on my ears. My heightened senses made me acutely aware that my every facial expression and movement was being scrutinized. I looked up to find the whole clan glaring at me. I guess they hadn't necessarily believed Nancy's story about my "sickness."

"Come on, kid. Let's go for a ride," I said, dragging Lauren toward the exit. I had to escape. I whistled and a horse-drawn carriage covered in balloons pulled up in front of us.

"Ooooh, Dad, can we really ride in the carriage?" Lauren asked, her face lit up.

"Of course, we can," I replied.

There was no way she could know that this was about getting away. But really, what difference did it make? I looked like the caring father, Lauren was happy, and I had the chance to get the hell out of there. Good enough for me. The horse drove us around the city, Nancy—tight-lipped and pissed off—on one side of the carriage holding the baby and Lauren beaming and pointing out all of the places they had been that week. Me, I was just hanging on to life by the skin of my teeth.

That was how I spent the family vacation, hiding and retreating to the confines of our room when I could have been out enjoying life. Using was becoming less and less fun and more about escape. I couldn't look my family in the eye, and Nancy was finally on to me. It was only going to be a matter of time before it all came crumbling down. "Rock bottom," the place that you end up when things can't get any worse. You lose everything—your money, your job, your family, and sometimes even your life.

The grand total of my drug abuse came to $300,000 in cash advances on the family credit cards. I had been stealing the bills and hiding them from Nancy for years with no repercussions. I used one card to pay another and so on until I didn't have any cards left to use. I even maxed out the gas card, buying cigarettes and trading them for coke. That's when the phone calls started.

"Hi, I'm calling on behalf of MasterCard. I'm looking for John Wagner."

I'd hang up and disconnect the phone when I was home. I knew I was slipping; I just didn't know how to stop the fall. That's when I went to bed. For three months, I didn't leave the bedroom. Dealers would come to the house when Nancy was out and give me drugs on credit. They made bedside deliveries.

It was obvious that I was out of control, and Nancy started taking the kids to stay at her parents' house. She was afraid to leave them alone with me. Truthfully, I deserved it. The straw that broke the camel's back was when she asked me to watch Jonathan while she ran out to the grocery store. She left him on the floor, sitting on his blanket, and went shopping. She came home about a half hour later and found him playing with his toy fort. I was asleep on the couch next to him. After a minute Nancy realized that he wasn't shooting the regular missiles and boulders that had come with his toy set. He was catapulting coke vials at his enemy assailants.

I woke up to Nancy closing the car door in the backyard. I thought she was just getting home. I rolled over to look at Jonathan on the floor and realized he was missing. Just then Nancy came back in.

"You're going to get out of this house tonight. You will not come back, and you will not be with these children again. I knew you had problems, but this? You just jeopardized the life of our son who I have been fighting to keep alive for three years. Did you know he's three years old, John?"

At that moment, my seven-year-old daughter walked in through the back door.

"What's going on, Mommy? Why are you so mad at Daddy?" Lauren asked.

I could always count on her to be on my side.

"Your mother thinks I'm using drugs," I began. I bit my lip. When had she gotten so big? "You don't think Daddy's on drugs, do you, sweetheart?"

Nancy turned a shade of purple I didn't know a human could be.

Lauren came and sat on my lap in the dining room. "I don't know. Are you, Dad?"

There it was again. Black and white. Right and wrong. So simple, so clear.

"Of course not, sweetie," I said, pulling her close.

Lauren may have believed me, but Nancy surely did not. She packed up her stuff and went to stay at her mother's while I was supposed to pack my things and get out. The only problem with that was that I had nowhere to go. My mother was in Florida, I hadn't spoken to my brother in years, and I owed money to all of the people I knew in Long Branch.

A few weeks went by like this, with the creditors calling and the dealers trying to beat the door down. I knew something had to give. My family was gone. My job was gone. My money was gone. The only thing left for me to do was die.

John and Lauren on vacation in Acapulco——1998

THE SMILE HAS LEFT YOUR EYES

I CHOSE TO abuse, but I tried to inflict the abuse only upon myself. I abused drugs and alcohol in an attempt to dull the pain I still felt from the early years I spent in the woods. Somehow, I thought that I would be able to break the cycle of abuse and violence by not hitting my kids. What I failed to realize was that I abused them by coming home drunk all the time; they didn't get the love or attention they deserved. By literally blowing all of our money, I stole a childhood from my children that I wasn't even conscious of.

Realizing this, I couldn't imagine how I could go on living. Quickly and painlessly, I longed to escape into the next life. Nancy had other ideas. Rehab was among them. Once Jonathan was born, Nancy had started working as a social worker. She spent her days trying to help other losers like myself get it together for their families. With her contacts, she easily found a place that would take me in and that her insurance was willing to pay for. She also found herself a good divorce attorney and some of our maxed-out credit card bills.

I knew then that the only chance I had for survival and to get to see Nancy and the kids again was by doing what she said. I also knew that if I didn't get out of Long Branch soon, someone was going to come for me. I owed a lot of bad people a lot of money.

I checked into Hampton Hospital, about an hour's drive from Long Branch, in the winter of 1992. The program wasn't a thirty-day program to sobriety; it was a program you stayed in until they deemed you healthy enough to leave. The first few weeks I spent my time trying to figure out how I was going to get out of the enormous mess I had made of my life. I also tried to trick the counselors into believing my stories and lies about wanting to get sober for myself. Unfortunately for me, all of the other patients at Hampton Hospital were as good at lying as I was. The counselors were better than a polygraph at detecting falsehood.

They preached the program, twelve steps to salvation. When we woke in the morning, we had a group session, which was more like a devotional meeting than therapy. We thanked our higher power for giving us one more day to live and also for keeping us sober. A lot of the people in the program had a real problem with this concept, that something larger than ourselves could take control over our lives. Personally, I never had a problem giving up responsibility for my actions. If anything, it was easier to put the onus on someone or something else.

After group, we would eat breakfast, followed by art therapy sessions. We were given time to make things with our hands that we could be proud of and that could be given as gifts to our families. I began to see how good it felt to give rather than to take from others. Growing up, I never had anything that anyone else would want, except for the things I stole from the store, so the sensation of giving a gift was new to me. It was also an isolating feeling, to work on toy cars or suncatchers for a family that I wasn't with, that I wasn't allowed to be with. I would spend hours in the art room, putting together toys for the kids or a picture for Nancy, and I would think about how far away from them I really was.

The kids knew I was sick and that I had checked into the hospital. I was definitely ill—at least, mentally. Who takes every blessing he is given, including a wife, two beautiful children, and a safe home, and throws it away for something as elusive as a high? A sick, selfish loser, that's who. For the first month, that's how I saw myself, a man so narcissistic that I had been willing to trade the love of my children and my family for drugs. I wondered how I could ever ask them to forgive me for the pain I caused them, for the memories that the children wouldn't be able to erase. As the first weekend for family visits approached, I found myself afraid of seeing them.

We spent a lot of time in therapy trying to prepare for this moment. Seeing my family would be difficult, but maybe it would also allow me to begin the healing process, something that had been eluding me despite all my sessions with the counselors. Maybe if Nancy, or at least the kids, could forgive me, I could begin to forgive myself.

As the other patients began to leave the waiting area with their families, my anxiety only increased. What if they didn't come? What if Nancy decided that the kids shouldn't see me in here? What would I do if I really were all alone in this?

Just as the downward spiral reached the point where I thought I was going to be physically ill, the doors slid open and in walked Nancy and the kids. She scanned the room, and when she saw me, I watched her stiffen. No forgiveness there. I looked over at Lauren and Jonathan. Lauren's whole face lit up when she saw me. That's when I remembered the love, the immeasurable, unconditional love that seemed to emanate from her being. She sprinted across the room and flung herself at me.

"Daddy! Are you okay? I missed you," she exclaimed all in one breath.

I stroked her hair and smelled her smell and then burst into tears. I was never good at hiding my emotions, and the relief that coursed through my body washed over me with such intensity I couldn't breathe.

"I'm fine, sweetheart. I just missed you so much," was all I could get out. While all of this was going on, Nancy walked toward me with Jonathan. He was too young to really know where he was or what was happening. I reached behind me and grabbed the bag full of the toys I had made for them. Suddenly, they seemed meaningless, not good enough to present to them. How had I thought a wooden car or purple suncatcher was going to make this be all right?

Lauren grabbed the bag out of my hand. "What's this?" she asked.

"Oh it's, uh, nothing. Well, I guess it's something. I made these for you guys in the art room. I wanted you to have something to play with while you were here visiting me," I mumbled.

I still hadn't met Nancy's eyes.

As I handed the toys to the kids, I forced myself to look up. "Hi, Nancy," I said.

I looked at her beautiful face. It was tight, her expression stretched to the breaking point. So that is what it looks like when you've forced someone to change their nature. The trusting and loving woman I had swept off her feet had been replaced by a hardened, determined mother who wanted nothing but to protect her children from me. Her expression softened some when she returned my greeting, but I saw how far away from me she was. How long had she seen me this way and I was too high or too stupid to really see her? That thought rocked me to my core. I had missed years of our life together. When Jonathan first got sick, I should have been there. When Lauren graduated kindergarten, I should have been there. Why had I thrown it all away?

The rest of the day was more of the same. I was happy to have them there with me, if only for a few hours, but I was exhausted by the time they left. I had a lot of soul-searching to do if I was going to find a way to fix everything I had broken.

"God grant me the serenity to accept the things I cannot change, the courage to change the things I can, and the wisdom to know the difference." The serenity prayer. I repeated it daily, like my mantra in prison from years before: "Do nothing." The time for doing nothing was over, and I had to show what I could do. If I couldn't change the past and I couldn't change Nancy's feelings about me, I would have to prove to her that I could at least change myself.

I threw myself into the work of recovery with a zeal that only a first-timer in rehab can possess. The counselors said things like, "Out of the hundred people in your graduating class, only one of you will stay sober without having to come back." I believed I was that one. I thought I could beat the odds. And that's exactly what I was planning to do.

During one of my sessions, the psychiatrist on staff took off her glasses and looked me in the eyes.

"John, have you ever heard of manic depression?" she asked.

Courtesy of Jimi Hendrix, most of the world had heard of this mental illness.

"Yes, of course," I answered her.

"Are you aware that most people who abuse drugs tend to gravitate toward one end of the spectrum? That it's very rare for someone to abuse alcohol, heroin, methamphetamine, and cocaine?"

"I've never really thought about it, I guess. I just did whatever I was in the mood for."

"After listening to your therapy sessions, paired with the information of your drug use, I believe you were self-medicating. I think the main reason you abuse drugs is a chemical imbalance in your brain, and your drug use was a way to try to balance yourself out. I am going to write you a prescription for lithium. This drug, paired with the skills you have learned here about sober living, will give you the best chance to stay clean on the outside."

A diagnosis of manic depression was certainly not what I expected to get from that day's therapy session. But it did sound like a good explanation for all my ups and downs. Armed with my new prescription, I was ready to be discharged, almost two months after my arrival.

The day I left Hampton Hospital was bittersweet for me. I had been deemed well enough to leave by the hospital staff, but I was no longer welcome in my home. This was a problem, since all of the friends I had in New Jersey were either drug buddies or had gotten screwed over by me while I was using. Nancy was adamant that I could not come back to our house. I was too untrustworthy to live under her roof, and by this point our divorce was final.

Divorcing me had been important for a few reasons. Nancy needed to distance herself from me, not only emotionally but also financially. Since the house was in her name alone and the bills I had racked up were either only mine or on some of our joint accounts, by divorcing me Nancy ensured that she would be able to keep her house and also not be held responsible for my bills. I knew that this was the safest choice for her to make and of course the responsible thing to do to protect herself and the kids, but that didn't make it sting any less.

That first day out was the first time I truly opened my eyes to my situation. I was forty-five, divorced again, and had two kids to support, no job, and nowhere to go. For the old John, this would have been the perfect kind of situation to send me off on a bender for a few months. I was close to the edge and

I knew it. I had a few options, but only one of them involved staying sober: I needed to go to a meeting.

I had been to AA before. I knew all the clichés: the miserable, washed-up addicts sitting around in a circle, feeling sorry for themselves, hashing and rehashing things they did, things they shouldn't have done, and what they would give to just go back and do it all again. The reason I went is the same reason I kept going back. This was part of the "cure," the prescription for maintaining sobriety. It included getting a job, maintaining a home on my own, getting a sponsor, and, above all else, going to meetings. One day at a time, they say, but so much of the first day involves planning for many days. Jobs don't materialize out of thin air and neither do homes. I tried very hard to focus on the first day as a day unto itself, but the big questions persisted.

Nancy helped find me a place to stay, a few towns away from her in a rooming house. It would be easier if I was out of her sight, unable to see her and the kids on a daily basis, kept at arm's length. I wasn't crazy about the idea, but it was better than my other option, which was homelessness. The room was tiny and bare, but it was also warm and dry.

There was another good reason to stay out of town for a little while—debt collectors. While I was away, many of my dealers had come looking for me. Thankfully, none of them were truly malicious and they left my family alone. They did make one thing clear: if I came back to town and I was using again, I would owe every penny in debt that I racked up before I left. Apparently, news of my release had made it to most of my dealers and they came knocking. The day I was released, Nancy had four visitors, all of them looking to help me "celebrate" getting out. Of course, everything would be on the house the first time; they just had to get me back. I may have owed them money, but no one likes to lose a customer. I don't know if

I would have had the resolve or inner strength to turn them away. For that, I am thankful she didn't let me come home.

While the question of housing had been answered for the moment, I still needed a job. I didn't have many contacts left. News of the lost money from the Marriott had gotten around and most would-be employers were wary of me. I could have sat around and done nothing, collected unemployment, but I knew that if Nancy was going to let me see the kids, I needed to get a job no matter where it was.

Walking into McDonald's was one of the most shameful experiences I have ever had. After ten years in the business, extensive training from world-renowned top chefs and working for one of the most successful hotel chains in the country, working at McDonald's was going to be a lot to swallow. When I first walked in, I was just planning to get a burger. Actually, I guess I really don't know what I was planning. Maybe some small part of me knew that it was more than that, but I certainly couldn't admit that to myself.

I ordered my food and went to sit at one of the booths near the front door. I watched people come and go, and I watched children coming in with huge smiles on their faces when they got their Happy Meals. I would have given anything to have Lauren there, and that's when I remembered bringing her in before school. On days when Lauren missed the bus, I would drive her to school because Nancy had to leave for work right away; I loved those stolen moments, no matter how short they were. On the way to school, I would stop at McDonald's and let her order anything she wanted, usually a breakfast burrito with hash browns. She would have been late, regardless, so I figured it couldn't hurt. I was wrong. It did hurt to imagine never being able to do that again. Before I knew what I was doing, I was at the counter asking for a job application.

"Excuse me," I said. "I need one of those employment applications."

I didn't meet the clerk's eyes as he handed it over to me. I also didn't stay to fill it out. I turned it in the next morning, and the manager on duty took one look at my experience and handed me my uniform. Pairing this job with my new apartment met most of Nancy's requirements for seeing the kids.

She didn't want the kids at the rooming house, at least not right away, so I got to go to the house to visit with Lauren and Jonathan. Nancy was there, too; she didn't trust me as far as she could throw me, and that wasn't too far. I loved getting to see the kids, but it truly made me miss what I lost to drugs. I longed to go upstairs and lie in my bed. I wished desperately to be able to tuck the kids in, but Nancy wouldn't have it. There was no way I was coming back. She said it over and over.

"But I'm sorry," I said, and I actually meant it. "I won't do it again. It won't be like before."

"You can't do this to us. You can't just get out of rehab and come back into our lives like that. The kids have had a hard enough time adjusting to you being gone. Letting you back in would set them back. And for what? You think you're going to make it?"

She didn't yell. That was what scared me the most. Before I left she would have been yelling at me, done anything to get through to me. Not now, though. She was done.

"I miss you, Nancy. I love you, damn it! What will it take for you to give me another chance?" I pleaded.

"If you can live for one year on your own, with your own income, and keep a nice place to stay and pay off your debts, we can talk about you coming back. But until you have proven that we can trust you again, I just can't let you come home. I can't do it. It's not fair to us."

She looked at me, her brown eyes serious and full of pain. It was then that I knew she was genuine. I had to earn back everything that had been mine. I wasn't going to be given the easy way out. Nancy meant business, and I would have to deliver if I wanted the slightest chance of getting them back. She let me visit with the kids a few times a week, but never by myself. I couldn't pick them up from school or do anything with them alone. I had been a lot of things before I went to rehab, but a danger to my children? I had a hard time with that, but I knew this wasn't a fight I would be able to win easily. I had to try, though.

One night after I got off work I brought burgers by for dinner and Lauren was fuming as she opened the door. Her tiny features were all screwed up and her eyes were puffy from her tears. She had always been a dramatic kid, but this time she genuinely looked like something was wrong.

"What's up, pumpkin head?" I asked as I put the burgers on the dining room table.

She glared at her mother. "Mommy went out with someone else. And I don't like that! I want you to come back! How can you come back home if he's here?" she exclaimed.

Now I glared at her mother. "Nancy?" was all I asked.

"This is not a conversation to have in front of the children, John." She spun on her heel and headed out the back door.

I followed quickly behind her. "I went out a few times," she spat, "but God only knows what you were doing all those nights. I have a right to a life, too!"

I hadn't counted on that one. "Nancy, I have done a lot of things. I have lied, I have stolen, but I have never cheated. Isn't that one of the things we promised each other? Never to cheat?"

"No, John. We promised to be honest, and that's something you have never been capable of doing. I haven't done anything with him, not that it's any of your business—we are divorced after all. It's just nice to go out with a normal adult and have dinner and go to a movie. Living with your addiction all day and all night is exhausting. When do I have time for me?"

Again, unexpected. One of the problems addicts have is seeing only themselves. Of course, we think about other people, but most of the time we are worried about things that directly affect us: Where am *I* going to get my next fix? How am *I* going to get myself out of this one? What can *I* do to get ahead? I knew my using had cost Nancy part of her life, but I was so incredibly wrapped up in how *I* was going to get *my* family back that *I* never thought about what all of this was doing to *them*.

HOW CAN YOU MEND A BROKEN HEART?

THE PROGRAM HAD also helped me take ownership of my actions, instead of excusing myself for my transgressions because of some previous hardship. The only way to move forward was to go back and try to right some of my wrongs. I had already started on the journey. What I needed then was something to be passionate about. Something that would motivate me to get out of bed and fight the good fight no matter what. I needed my children.

The pure, unadulterated love of a parent for a child is nothing compared to the love that Lauren gave me every time she saw me. Even after all I had put the family through, she still believed in me. If I said I was going to move mountains, she would have been right behind me, pushing away. The issue I faced was how to get more time with her, especially with Nancy seeing someone new. I wanted to live closer. Nancy said I couldn't live at the house. There was only one obvious answer: move into the garage.

I figured that, this way, I would be able to see the kids every day and maybe fend off the swarm of single men trying to take Nancy away from me forever. The garage was an unattached building designed around the turn of the century, termed a "carriage house," and it was about one hundred yards from the back door to Nancy's house. There was some electricity back there, but only enough to operate a single overhead light. I ran a line from the back of the house via an extension cord so that I'd be able to have a table lamp and heat. It was fall, but the season was changing fast and I knew it would be freezing in the uninsulated cement building within a few weeks.

"What the hell are you doing?" Nancy was home.

"Moving in some things," I replied. I tried to play it cool; I knew that this would not be well-received. "I just realized that it would make more sense for me to pay you rent instead of some landlord. That way, the money can go right to the kids. I'll stay out of the way back here. You'll barely even know I'm here."

"John, I am only going to say this one time. You cannot, under any circumstances, live in this garage. You're going to freeze. Where will you go the bathroom? How about showering?"

"Well, if those are your only issues, this could definitely work for both of us. I have a space heater, and I already have an extension cord ready to plug in. Bathroom stuff I can do during the day while you and the kids are out, and I work at night so you'll hardly ever see me." I paused. "And Nancy, I need to see the kids. I need to see them and touch them and be with them every single day. I cannot live without them."

She opened her mouth. She shut it. She opened it again. Then she turned and stalked back to the house, shaking her head. She hadn't said yes, but she hadn't said no either.

"Good morning!" Lauren called as she shoved open the carriage door. Light came streaming into the darkened garage.

She bounced up onto the bed I had placed in the far corner. The cup of tea she brought me every morning sat on the coffee table a few feet away. The steam rose quickly from the hot mug; even with the space heater, the garage was freezing.

"Hi, puddin' head," I mumbled, reaching for the jar I kept my teeth in. I popped in my dentures and sat up. As I ran my hands through my hair, I thought, *One more night I hadn't caught on fire from the space heater; only two more months of this miserable New Jersey winter to go.*

Since I had moved in, I had set up a decent living space and sometimes I could even forget that I was living in the garage. Almost forget, that is, until a squirrel would run up on the coffee table and steal some of my food. In some ways, the move helped me remember where I came from. The place was a lot like the log cabin in North Carolina, minus all the cousins and, of course, Jim. When you looked at it from that perspective, the garage was not a bad place to live.

Tugging on my arm, Lauren pulled me back to reality. "I only have a few minutes before I leave for school, and there's something I wanted to tell you," she said.

"What is it, honey?" I asked.

"I wanted to tell you that I love you!" she screamed as she jumped up and down on the bed. Laughing, she ran out of the door, slamming it shut behind her.

That was how almost every day started. Talk about waking up happy and content. If nothing else, I felt loved again. That void that was ripped open in rehab was slowly starting to fill itself in. Nothing like the love of a child to heal a broken soul.

I could feel the strength returning to me on a daily basis. The feeling that I had options, opportunities, and places to turn to was humming through my veins. I was on the verge of something, something that might just be good for me. There was a change in the air—the karmic wheel was spinning.

Riding around in my car, with the music loud and the windows down, I was driving without a destination and just enjoying the sun on my face, the wind in my hair. I turned off Route 36 onto a small side street and realized I was starving. The Capri Lounge, a restaurant I had never heard of, was the only place on the street that looked worth going into. I parked the car and went inside.

The restaurant was vacant. Not a soul was sitting down to eat, even though it was just about time for the lunch rush. A young guy pushed open the double doors from the kitchen.

"You want a table or do you want to eat at the bar?" the man said.

"Neither. I want to cook you lunch," I said, surprising myself. I had no idea that was what I had come in to do, and maybe it wasn't actually me talking. Maybe it was the higher power I had been working so hard to turn my life over to.

No matter whose idea it was, the man extended his hand. "Sammy's the name. You're one ballsy guy, aren't you?"

"Just need to get back in the game, is all," I replied. "I haven't cooked in a real kitchen in eighteen months, but I definitely want to get my hands dirty."

By the end of the afternoon, I had made Sammy lamb chops, macadamia-encrusted sea bass, and a happy restaurateur. The details of our agreement were hazy, but it went something like, I would help redesign the menu, put bodies in his seats, and help turn his empty bar into a bustling restaurant in a few months' time. A tall order for a guy working at McDonald's, but I really thought I could do it.

While I had the charisma and personality of a top chef, I still had a lot to learn. At Marriott they taught classical cuisine, slowly, with implicit instruction from certified instructors. While at Sammy's I learned to cook serious Italian food. The head cook, Vinnie, made amazing sauces. Under his lead,

I learned how to make pasta all'Amatriaciana, vodka sauce, and creamy alfredo, and most importantly I learned that I was still extremely teachable. I worked with Vinnie every day and through trial and error learned the very best ways to make sauces for my dishes. I began to realize that with a little guidance and a clear head, I could go a long way in this field.

Not only was I learning to be a better cook but also how to be a better partner and father. Nancy was letting me see the children on more normal terms, and she invited me into the house most evenings after work and before bed. Working at the Capri Lounge had shown her a side of me that excited us both. I was passionate, engaged, and above all else, I was sober.

Celebrating my first year of sobriety sneaked up on me. I had been spending most of my time at the Capri Lounge, conversing with customers and learning all I could about running a successful restaurant. Without much free time for meetings, Nancy had to remind me that it had been a full year since I got out of rehab. To celebrate, I invited her and the kids to Sammy's for dinner.

We had a good crowd that night and a band playing on a small stage at the end of the bar. Of course, the family had been here before, but this time was different. I spoke with the hostess and had a nice table reserved for them in the main dining room. As I walked them to their table, several customers called me by name and gave compliments to the chef for their dinners. I sat them down and went back in the kitchen to cook. They didn't need menus; I knew what they all liked. As dinner came out, I went to sit with them. Everyone was happy, even Jon-boy with his chicken fingers. It was shaping up to be a great night, and it wasn't over yet.

I walked through the dining room and into the bar area. I told the leader of the band what I wanted: a few songs Nancy and I could dance to. I was always a good dancer, but together we were quite the pair. The singer acquiesced and I walked back into the dining room. I bent down and offered Nancy my arm. She definitely had not anticipated this. I could feel her hesitation, but also her desire to be back on the dance floor.

The next few songs passed by in a blur. The third song ended and the bar patrons clapped politely. Nancy grabbed my hand as we left the dance floor. With a glow of contentment, I knew I was back.

It was a gradual transition, but slowly I moved back into the house. My nights with the squirrels were over.

I left Sammy's much the way I started, on a whim with an appetite. I was driving around in Shrewsbury when I ended up at the Grove Mall. There was something nostalgic for me in the outdoor shopping area, something that reminded me of my teenage days in the shooting galleries in Coconut Grove, Florida. I was going to buy a present for Nancy, and this place had everything. There was a nice jeweler, a few high-end clothing stores, and a couple cafés. I walked into Caroline's Restaurant around three-thirty in the afternoon and they were getting ready to close up for the day. I talked the lady behind the counter into letting me eat anyway, and soon I was seated in the empty dining room. I don't remember what I ordered, but I do remember that it was terrible. Awful. I mean disgusting—food I wouldn't have fed to my dog. No wonder they were done for the day. When my server, a tall blonde named Tara, asked what I thought of my meal, I told her exactly that.

"I have never heard anyone be so honest," she said, laughing. "But you're right, the food here is terrible."

I asked Tara if the cook was still around. She came back to table and said that he was. I followed her through the double doors and into the kitchen. There I met three guys in jeans and T-shirts. No one was in a uniform and there didn't seem to be any indication as to who was in charge. I asked who the head chef was. One of the kitchen guys pointed to himself and stuck out his hand. "Tomas," was all he said.

Looking around the kitchen, I realized with a shock that this was why the food was terrible—no one who worked here had been trained to cook. These people were sitting on a gold mine, a high-end shopping district with a disgrace for a café as one of only two options for all of the hungry shoppers. I thanked Tomas for my lunch and asked Tara if the owner was in. She said the owner's husband, Mark, was there.

I introduced myself to Mark and told him that I'd like to turn his business around. Namely, I wanted to transform his café into a place that could cater to the upscale clientele he had available at his fingertips, if he only served the right kind of food. I still had a lot to learn, but for some reason I knew that I could do this. I spoke with the confidence of a man who knows his place in the world, a man I had never been up until now. Something about me must have appealed to Mark because he hired me on the spot. I was to start the following week.

GLORY DAYS

WHEN I TOLD Sammy I was leaving, he just shook his head.

"I knew we weren't going to be able to keep you long. Go on. You just keep moving straight on up, you hear me?"

With Sammy's blessing, I started at Caroline's the following Monday. The first thing I did was pull everything out of the kitchen. The layout was all wrong. They had the dishwasher next to the chopping block and the stoves spread out all over the place. Luckily, the space was small so I could pretty much move anything I wanted without the risk of needing to run new gas, water, or electric lines. The next step was to tackle the walk-in freezer.

I realized what was wrong with the food in a hurry: everything was frozen. All the vegetables, fish, meat, and dairy—literally everything. There was not a single fresh ingredient. The reason they did that was because they couldn't move their products and were afraid to throw out their entire inventory each week. You buy fresh foods, don't sell them, and then are forced to toss them out when it goes bad, and all of that waste goes into the loss column. What Caroline and Mark didn't seem to realize was that it was equally dangerous to pair poor food quality with a bad reputation. There are always new people who come into a place for the first time unsuspectingly, but if what they eat is horrible, they will never make that mistake again.

I explained these concepts to the owners, who seemed willing to listen. They wanted a profitable business as much as anyone else, but it was still a tough sell. In the end I had to explain my strategy in vivid detail. The reason they had to throw out "perfectly good" ingredients was because their menu was too scattered. They needed to pick main ingredients that went into most of their dishes. This way, even if they sold only fifteen lunches in a day, at least they could use most of the same items in these meals, thereby cutting down on waste. If you buy specialty ingredients for every plate and then don't sell those plates, your waste is much higher than a restaurant that can use their produce in every dish. This was a trick that I picked up working at the Capri Lounge, and that Italian restaurants all over the country have used with success. I called up some of the contacts I made working with Sammy and arranged to get new food purveyors. We would have fresh ingredients and new recipes. Now all we needed were customers.

I began walking from store to store, passing out the new menu and inviting the workers at the Grove Mall for lunch. I figured if I could get them to like it, they would spread the word to their customers. The first few days, no one came in. With no one to feed, I spent the days training the boys in the back. Tomas in particular seemed to be very receptive to my lessons. He soaked up everything I showed him, and the best part was he could replicate my recipes without oversight.

If there was one thing I knew how to do well, it was to move a product. I went around to all the shops again and again, and slowly but surely people started to drop in. I served crab cakes with a honey Dijon and balsamic reduction. I made them lamb chops in a brown demi glaze. Within weeks we were getting takeout orders from every shop in the mall. And I had been right: they started to tell their customers about us, too. In a few short months we ended up with a wait for a table every day of the week. We now had a new problem. Closing at three-thirty was simply not enough time to feed the number of people coming through the doors.

"Mark, I think we need to stay open for dinner," I began. "We are losing out on so much revenue turning the evening shoppers away."

"I don't see how we can stay open. We'd need a new night menu, a whole new waitstaff, and either myself or Caroline would have to stay all night. That's just not something we're comfortable with, John."

Mark and Caroline needed to be able to trust me in order for this to work. How could these two people, who had worked their entire lives to open this restaurant and finally begun to turn a profit, put their faith in a junkie.

"Leave it to me. I will do everything that needs to be done, and as soon as everything is in place, we will talk again."

I was a man on a mission.

Every morning before the rush, I would come in and help the guys prep everything we would need for the day. As they became more self-sufficient, I began to spend my time experimenting with new recipes. Instead of chicken two ways for lunch, I needed to make it five ways and three of them needed to be dinner portions. With a little time and a lot of tasting, I began to craft a menu that would appeal to the masses. My goal was to make Caroline's restaurant a destination not just for shoppers but for people who lived in the area, too.

One afternoon, just as we were wrapping up, a group of guys wandered in. They weren't your typical clientele of the Grove Mall. Each guy's hair was longer than the next, and they wore ripped up T-shirts, and leather pants—can you say acid wash? I heard Mark telling them that we were closing for the day, so I came running out of the back with my new menus. I shot Mark a look that screamed for an opportunity. I handed the menus to Tara and she led them to a table in the back half of the dining room. Explaining that we were testing out a dinner menu, I asked them for their feedback. And feedback is exactly what I got. These guys ate for what seemed like hours. Every time Tara would tell me she had cleared the table, I'd come out and they would order something new. Finally, when they had ordered every item on the new menu, they asked for the bill.

I watched them walk out and I headed over to the table. Inside the bill fold was the money to pay for their meal and a handwritten note. "John, keep doing what you're doing and people will come. Thank you for your hospitality and the best meal we've eaten on the shore—Snake." I handed the note to Tara.

"Snake?" was all I asked.

I watched Tara's green eyes light up as recognition spread across her face. "John! That was Skid Row! I can't believe I didn't recognize them. They are one of the hottest bands to come out of Jersey right now!"

As we cleaned up the table, I felt Mark walk up behind me.

"If that is any indication of how dinner service will go, I'm all for it. I'll speak with Caroline tonight, and we'll figure out who will be here which days. Great job."

With dinner service a go, I had finally gotten to the place where I needed to be. The restaurant was blossoming and I was making a great paycheck—the only thing missing was time with the kids. Since dinner started at five and lunch was basically over around three, I would go home in between, shower, and change into a fresh uniform. Nancy and I had reestablished a basic level of trust, so I felt comfortable asking her to mix things up. Jonathan went to an all-day day care close to where Nancy worked, so he was off-limits. But we agreed, one day a week, I would pick Lauren up from school and take her with me to the restaurant while Nancy finished up at work.

At first, most of the time was spent with Lauren sitting at the counter doing her homework while I prepped the back half of the house for dinner.

One day she finished early. "I'm done with my homework, Dad. What can I make?" Lauren asked as she pushed through the double doors to the kitchen.

"Um, well, I'm making crab cakes right now. You can help me mix the ingredients."

I handed her the bowl and she immediately started squishing the jumbo lump crabmeat between her fingers, pulverizing it.

"Whoa, whoa, whoa." I held up my hands. "The meat is delicate. We pay extra to have it come in those lumps so the customers need to be able to see the lumps when we serve it."

Coming around to where she was standing, I began to show her how to gently toss the ingredients together. Almost instantly she mimicked my motions, so I decided to teach her the rest of the steps. One hour and a hundred perfectly formed crab cakes later, Nancy came to pick up Lauren and brought Jonathan with her.

"Mom, look what I made!" Lauren grinned as she held up one of her prized cakes.

"Wow, honey, that looks great! Did you do your homework, though?" Nancy asked.

"Yep, all done. It's right here," Lauren said, gesturing to the counter.

Nancy was impressed. We had done good. Nancy and the kids stayed for dinner that night, which grew into our routine. Lauren would come with me to work, I'd teach her a new recipe, and then they'd all have dinner while I worked. I had never felt this proud before.

"John, one of the tables wants to see you," Tara said one night as she dropped dishes into the bus bucket.

I wiped my hands on my apron, threw a towel over my shoulder, and headed out into the dining room. I scanned the room and saw a couple of ladies sitting in the corner, gesturing for me to come over.

"Hello, John. My name is Dorothea, and this is my mother. We really enjoyed lunch today. I wanted to talk to you about catering a party at my house next month," the younger woman said.

Catering. This was new. I thought for a minute and replied, "I'm sure we could work something out. What did you have in mind?"

That was how I ended up standing in front of Jon Bon Jovi's mansion in Rumson on a bright and sunny summer morning a month later. Shaking like a leaf, I rang the doorbell. The maid answered the door and showed me into the kitchen. I had been a lot of places in my life, but never had I seen a home like this. The large kitchen had soaring ceilings, and floor-to-ceiling windows, and it opened to a grand living room. I had worked in professional kitchens for most of my life, but never had I been in a chef's kitchen before. I took a few deep breaths and began to unload the car. As each item came inside, I began to get more and more comfortable. With all of the tools of my trade around me, I remembered that I could do this.

It was Bon Jovi's daughter's fourth birthday and a party rental group had already been out to set up the rows of tables and chairs in the sprawling backyard. I began to dress the buffet table. I had brought cases of kale, fresh fruits, and flowers to make the table holding the chafing dishes look presentable. Lauren and Tara were also with me: Lauren to help me set up—she was mature beyond her twelve years of age—and Tara to wait on the tables. The three of us were scurrying around prepping when we started to hear loud banging noises and cursing coming from what appeared to be the garage. Too busy to pay much attention to the clanging, we proceeded with our setup. We were right in the groove when the garage door went up and the man himself came out.

Bon Jovi exited the garage and strode across the lawn. He seemed to be looking for someone when his eyes rested on our little gang.

"You guys, could you watch my kids for a while? I have to run out," he said.

Lauren and I exchanged glances. "Sure," she said.

Bon Jovi turned on his heel, slammed the door to his truck, and peeled out of the driveway.

"What was that about?" Tara asked.

Without much more thought, we went back to work, the kids playing in the grass on their own. Thirty minutes later, the pickup truck zoomed back into the backyard. In the back was a fully assembled little girl's bicycle replete with streamers. So that's what he had been up to; he was trying to put the bike together himself. That moment was when I realized I could relax. I may have been out of my league, but I had discovered our common ground: our love for our daughters. With my composure fully restored, I delivered the best four-year old's birthday party luncheon that Rumson had seen in quite some time.

Catering that party changed the way that I did business. In addition to my job at Caroline's, more and more calls came in, asking for catered parties on the weekends. The size of the party and how many resources I needed to pull from the restaurant determined whether the job would get funneled through

Caroline's or if I did it myself for cash. Obviously, the latter was more lucrative, but it is infinitely easier to cook for fifty or a hundred guests in a professional kitchen than it was out of our home.

As my clientele base grew and expanded, so did the budgets I had to work with. I went from simple pasta dishes and lemon chicken to filet mignon and crab salad. I had a creative outlet for expression and I was flourishing. I needed waitstaff to work the weekend parties, so in addition to Tara and Lauren, Nancy also started working with me. She already knew I was doing well—she was in and out of the restaurant frequently enough to see what was happening—but some of my favorite memories are from the large parties that we would all work together. To have my family be a part of the success only made it more real. It was easy to think that I was simply blowing things out of proportion, but when we'd get home and talk about what Heather Locklear was wearing at our latest party there was no denying our achievements.

Watching my catering business grow was amazing, but with it came increased tensions with Caroline and Mark. While they loved what I had done for their restaurant, they also wanted more and more of the catering business. I began to resent their incessant nagging about using their kitchen for the parties. My tolerance for them was growing thin.

While I needed the freedom that the restaurant business afforded me, Nancy thrived in a much more structured environment. She worked at the local hospital, Monmouth Medical Center, as a social worker. As good as I was at my job, Nancy was better at hers. She moved through hospital populations with ease. She began in pediatrics, but as our children grew up, she needed to separate herself from the world of sick kids, so she moved to geriatrics. It was here that she met Samaira, a case manager, with whom she shared an office. As they grew to know one another, Nancy began telling her stories of our catering escapades and how successful Caroline's was becoming. Samaira and her husband, Mani, came to eat at the restaurant and became huge fans of my cooking. They started coming in more and more often and were becoming some of my best regular customers.

Mani was a businessman. Since moving to New Jersey from India, he and his wife had purchased a series of Buy-Rite liquor stores in and around Long Branch. Some of their locations did better than others, but overall they were quite successful. A large piece of property in the West End of Long Branch had recently come onto the market and Mani was considering buying it to put in a new liquor store. The only issue was that the retail space was easily over ten thousand square feet. That would be one of the biggest liquor stores ever and was overkill for that kind of business. He was telling me all about the property details one night when Mark came rushing into the dining room.

"You have another party this weekend?" he huffed. "That's two this month and neither one have you paid us out for!"

"Look, Mark, it's a small party. I'm going to do most of the prep at my house," I replied. I hated that he was doing this here, in front of Samaira and Mani in the middle of the dining room.

"That's what you said last time, yet you were here until almost three in the morning using the kitchen. Caroline and I talked about it. You aren't allowed to use the kitchen here at all unless you give us our cut upfront."

Furious, I threw down the towel on my shoulder and yelled, "If I can't use the kitchen, then I guess I should go home. It's pretty hard to cook your dinner service if I can't be in the kitchen."

"Oh no, you don't! You can't just leave in the middle of the dinner rush." An exasperated Mark ran after me as I strode through the doors into the kitchen and out the back door into the parking lot.

"Mark, I don't think you understand. No one tells me what I can and can't do, especially not you. Don't you see what I've done for you? How ungrateful can one man be?" I slammed the car door in his face.

I threw the car into reverse and hit the gas. Mark scrambled to get out of the way. As I peeled out of the parking lot, I knew it was time to move on. I needed a new gig, and one with more liberty. What Mark and Caroline were asking for wasn't unreasonable—I just didn't want to share. With my adrenaline pumping I didn't care whether or not I was being fair to them.

Being out of work was different than it ever had been before for me. Whereas I was used to scraping my way along, trying to figure out how to make ends meet, I was now one of the most desirable chefs in the area, and everyone wanted a piece of me. Job offers couldn't be made fast enough. There was only one catch for me, and it was that I wanted clearance to be able to run my catering jobs out of the professional kitchen. I knew how to separate the jobs and was confident I would be able to find a place where we could make the arrangement work.

I was standing in the kitchen at home, making a cup of coffee when Mani called.

"John, could you meet me at the property on Ocean Avenue that I was telling you about?" he asked.

"Sure, I can be there in ten minutes. It's right down the street."

I parked in the back lot and looked at the large building. It was pinkish stucco and looked almost like a house, but larger. I saw Mani pull into the parking lot and got out to meet him. I followed him to the back door and watched as he entered the code into the lock box. As the door slowly creaked open, we were hit with a musty smell. The room was dark, cold, and old.

"This is going to be my new store," Mani said proudly, gesturing to the decrepit room we were standing in.

"Uh, well, its very large," I managed.

"John, I want this room to be a dining room. And over here, a bar. And that back area? That's where the liquor store will be." He pointed and spun around as he spoke; his excitement was overwhelming.

I looked around this poorly lit, musty old building and thought about what it could be with a little guidance and expertise.

"You've got your work cut out for you here." I kept my face neutral as I asked, "What am I doing here, Mani?"

"I want you to design it—all of it. You create the kitchen, the dining rooms, the bar—the only thing I will do is design the liquor store."

I tried to keep the emotion from my voice. "You know I can do this. We can make a successful restaurant here. I have one condition: that I can use the kitchen after hours, whenever I need to, to cater parties. And those parties will belong to me."

Mani looked at me and smiled his electrifying smile. "Of course, John. I don't want any part of that messy off-site nonsense."

With that response, all of the anxiety and fear melted away. I looked around the room again, and this time I could hear the bustle of a busy waitstaff, the soft music playing in the background, the smell of my food wafting through the kitchen doors. This place was going to be something special.

WINNING

I WAS BUSIER than I had ever been. Designing the layout of the restaurant turned into a full-time job. I met with architects, contractors, and tradesmen daily to make sure our vision was being executed. Mani and I couldn't agree on whether this restaurant should be fine dining or a more casual bar atmosphere, so we compromised and had both. In the front of the building, there was a rounded bay window and a room screaming for elegance. I dubbed it the Peacock Room and used that as our theme. We brought in large, high-backed, over-stuffed upholstered chairs and plush carpeting. The walls were done in a vibrant wallpaper and thick drapes wrapped around the edges of the windows. On the other side of the kitchen was a smaller room with a view of the large oval mahogany bar. For this room we kept the lines clean and went with contemporary table and chair sets that could be wiped down without the use of table linens. The bar area was massive, with seating for fifty and a TV in every direction you looked. There was also a back room, with the large walk-in refrigerator section for the liquor store. We kept the area right outside of the beer coolers clear, tiled the floor, and put in a small stage. The space was versatile. You could have dancing and a band going in the back half of the house with a quiet dining room at the other end of the building serving high-end cuisine in a relaxing environment.

It took a few months, but we were ready to open in what felt like no time. We had been so wrapped up in the design of the building that I almost forgot to create the menus. With so many different spaces, it was quite the challenge to make a cohesive menu that followed my basic principle of using as much of the same inventory as possible. For the casual dining room, we used the same menu as the bar. The Peacock Room was a different story entirely. Poring through my cookbooks, I took my time developing a menu that was guaranteed to be a winner. I integrated a lot of my Asian fusion cooking into traditional dishes and created a menu that I was excited and proud to begin cooking. Based on the size of Mani's, I couldn't handle all the cooking myself. I needed someone who knew my recipes and could be trusted to pull them off without much oversight or direction. I called Tomas and the boys from Caroline's. It was easy to get them to jump ship. Mani was paying well, and the excitement of the new restaurant was contagious.

Opening night came, and I invited Nancy and the kids to come out. You could see the sense of awe washing over them as they walked from room to room. By the time they made it to the Peacock Room, their smiles were ear to ear.

"I guess this is where we should sit, just like at home," Nancy said, gesturing to a nice table near the window.

"Sure, you can sit anywhere you want," I replied, not catching her meaning.

"John, I was joking. The furniture in this room is disturbingly familiar." She laughed.

When I was picking the furniture for the restaurant, I bought an extra set of chairs and a table for our house. Nancy, Lauren, and Jonathan had been eating dinner in an identical setting for the past three months.

Laughing, I pulled out the chairs for them. "Have a seat and prepare to enjoy."

Our success was unprecedented in the area. My reputation alone filled both dining rooms the first week. Reservations were being booked up to a month in advance, and money was pouring in. Mani couldn't have been happier with his investment and we began to coast through those first six months that most new restaurants struggle with, without any real effort. I was cooking some but, with the strong team we had in the kitchen, my role had changed. My job was more the executive chef. I handled all of the ordering, food cost calculations, and quality control. On our busiest nights, I helped expedite the food and keep the guys on track.

As we steamrolled through our first year, I had some extra time on my hands for the first time in a long while. I wanted to get into something with the kids, so I rifled through the closet under the back staircase in the kitchen until I found what I was searching for—a wooden Slazenger tennis racket. I had gotten the racket in college and played around with it some. I was never great, but it was fun to hit balls around.

That Sunday, I took Lauren and Jonathan out to the high school tennis courts for a lesson. Jon-boy was more into swinging for the fences rather than keeping it in the lines, but at least he had fun out there. Lauren seemed to really enjoy herself. She got into a rhythm almost instantly. Spending time on the courts was a great way to spend some waking hours with the kids and get some much-needed fresh air. We started to make it a habit, and each Sunday after the kids got home from church with Nancy, I would take them out to practice.

As winter approached, Mani and I were looking for ways to keep the place busy without the help of the summer beach crowd. We decided that we should utilize our dance floor more and promote the bar aspect. We booked Line Drive, a hot local band, for a New Year's Eve party. Flyers were handed out, and we used the big marquis sign out front to let people know that Mani's was the place to be on NYE. We did a special menu, had multiple courses for the Peacock Room, passed hors d'oeuvres, and offered a buffet for the bar room. Filling the place was my obsession, and it didn't take long for us to be booked solid.

With a large steady paycheck and things going so well between me and Nancy, I wanted to make a grand gesture for her. I went to the jewelry store near Caroline's to speak with Yule, the store owner, with whom I had grown quite close. With his help, I picked out a marquis-cut diamond flanked on either side by rows of smaller stones. The ring was a knockout, and I planned to give it to Nancy on Christmas morning.

With the whole family gathered around the tree, I waited as they opened all their gifts. Aside from the ring, I had really outdone myself. There were tons of new clothes for both kids, a small leather purse for Lauren, and outfit after outfit that I had picked out for Nancy. Jon-boy, I had gotten a new skateboard deck. I had no idea about that stuff, but I picked the most expensive one they had, figuring it had to be the best. When Nancy grabbed her stocking and reached inside, I held my breath. I hadn't realized I was nervous until just that moment. As she pulled out the small box wrapped in gold foil paper, I remembered proposing to her on Christmas morning all those years ago. She excitedly looked up at me and began to open the box. As it popped open, I dropped to my knee.

"Nancy, will you marry me?" I asked.

Lauren squealed and Jonathan's smile spread from ear to ear. Nancy paused, took a breath, and said, "Yes. Yes, I will."

I had gotten my family back.

On New Year's Eve, I pressed my best uniform and took a look at myself in the mirror. Looking back at me was a well-polished, healthy, lively guy with a sparkle in his eye and pep in his step. *If only the little boy with the old overalls and hand-me-down shoes could see me now,* I thought. I had arrived.

Nancy was going to join me around nine. That way, the kids would be in bed, the main portion of dinner service would be completed, and we could dance and enjoy the band. One of my catering clients owned an upscale women's clothing store in Deal. Occasionally, they would trade me clothes for Nancy in exchange for a small party or brunch. For New Year's Eve, they sent me this gorgeous champagne-colored mini dress. I knew Nancy would look amazing in it so I laid it out for her on the bed to wear that night.

Mani's was buzzing as I pushed through the doors and walked inside. The waitstaff was busily setting up, dressing the tables, and laying out silverware and stemware. Tomas and the boys had the kitchen in full swing, with every burner being used to cook something. I threw on an apron and started tasting all of the sauces, each one better than the last. The boys were on fire, and this party was going to blow everyone away.

Prep continued at a breakneck pace, and before we knew what had happened, guests had arrived. Mani and Samaira were both dressed to the nines and greeting and seating people themselves. It was go time.

Party service went off without a hitch. Food came and went on trays served by capable hands. The drinks flowed perfectly from the bar to the guests, and the band, my God, the band brought the party to life. They played a lot of Earth, Wind & Fire type dance music. They were just hitting their groove as I saw the back door swing open. Guests were coming in the main entrance, so I knew it could only be one person.

Nancy was glowing as she came through the door. The champagne dress clung tightly in all the right places and the dance floor lights seemed to illuminate only her. I was frozen in place watching her come in; when she finally spotted me in the crowd, it was as if I awakened from a trance. I strode toward her across the crowded dance floor and we did what we did best—danced. The area in front of the stage was packed from the start of the first song and stayed that way as midnight approached. Nancy and I swirled among the guests for what seemed like hours. With five minutes left to go before the New Year, the band quieted down and the servers began circulating with trays of champagne flutes. I grabbed two and handed one to Nancy. This night was too perfect not to indulge a little. To her credit, Nancy didn't comment on the drink in my hand. I don't think she wanted to spoil the moment. As the clock struck midnight and the band started playing "Auld Lang Syne," the crowd clinked glasses and cheered.

As the champagne hit my lips, and the bubbles filled my mouth, I was on top of the world. My restaurant was a success, Nancy was proud of me, and the night itself couldn't have gone any better. I handed the glass to the waiter and turned to look at Nancy.

"I am so glad you were here with me tonight. Sharing this moment is so important to me," I told her.

She smiled up at me. "John, you really outdid yourself. Tonight was amazing."

We kissed and began slowly walking off the dance floor. I said good night to Mani and Samaira and pushed open the door to the parking lot. The crisp air hit me in the face and I realized I had a slight buzz from the champagne. It felt good. Too good. I fought the urge to turn and go back inside to the bar and order a scotch, but instead I opened the car door for Nancy. As we drove home, my mind was racing.

How could I get another drink? Did we have anything in the house? Were any stores still open that would sell liquor? I parked in the driveway and went inside with Nancy. My skin was absolutely crawling. I couldn't sit still. I needed a drink. While Nancy went upstairs to change, I weighed my options. There was really only one—go back to the bar.

Racing like a madman, I made my way back to Mani's. As I walked in, Mani looked at me.

"I thought you went home. I'm glad you're still here—let's celebrate!" he exclaimed.

I don't think I answered him well. I mumbled about forgetting something behind the bar and made a beeline for the liquor. I pulled out the scotch and the shot glasses used for measuring liquor to add to cocktails and lined them up. I filled the whole row and slammed back each shot. It only took me a few minutes to forget everything. I forgot about my recovery, Nancy and the kids, and all of the work I put into the restaurant. I was immediately transported back in time, when I hadn't a care in the world other than where my next drink was coming from.

LIFE'S BEEN GOOD

MY EYES BLURRED as I tried in vain to open them. Oh God, my head was killing me. I sat up too quickly and grabbed my head to keep it steady. Spinning. As the room came into focus, I realized I was on the couch in my living room. No one else was there. I tried to stand, but my body was so sore. I sat back down and tried to take stock of what was happening. I had a hangover; that much was clear. I looked down and to see why I was so sore. I had a couple of bruises on my knees, and a large scrape across my elbow. As I turned my hands over to check out my palms, I realized that my pinky ring was missing. The ring was a gift from my mother. She gave it to me when I got out of prison, and I believed it to be my lucky charm. Damn.

I heard some chatter in the kitchen and realized Nancy and the kids were in there. I looked at the clock; it was noon. They had all been tiptoeing around me for hours. I walked toward the back of the house with trepidation. This was going to be a tough one. And for once, I didn't have a good story waiting to cover my ass. I couldn't remember a thing.

As I walked into the kitchen, the kids stared at me. Jonathan and Lauren looked at me with wide eyes; they were scared.

What had I done? I could barely meet Nancy's eyes. She looked calmer than I would have expected, but clearly we needed to talk.

"Lauren, Jonathan, I need to talk to your mother. I know I need to talk to you both, too, but right now go to the living room." I spoke slowly.

As the kids left the kitchen, Nancy continued to brew her cup of tea.

"What happened last night?" I asked.

"I don't know," she started. "We came home from a lovely night at the restaurant and I went upstairs to change. When I came back down, you and your car were gone."

I vaguely remembered that. "I went back to the restaurant."

"You could have told me where you were going. I had no idea where you were and then at three-thirty in the morning, I heard you screaming from the front lawn. Moaning and yelling, 'I'm sorry, Mom.' I went out to get you and you looked like this. You were blacked-out drunk, bleeding, and your car wasn't in the driveway," Nancy retorted.

I opened my mouth, but Nancy cut me off.

"Your friend Kevin called this morning. I had to go and get your car keys from him, and on the keychain was your pinkie ring. He had your car at his gas station. But all of this is beside the point. What are you going to do, John? Do you need to go back to rehab? You can't do this again! We were finally in a good place."

She was right. I needed to say the right thing. I had to talk to Lauren and Jonathan and make them feel okay, too.

"I'm going to a meeting as soon as I shower." This was going to be a very long day.

Ultimately, I was able to reel it back in after that night. I had gotten overly confident and thought myself invincible. That single glass of champagne was enough to throw many years of hard work off-kilter. What a fragile thing, recovery. Such a tiny decision, but its effects spanned my whole universe. After speaking with the kids, Mani, and Nancy—and after attending meetings every day over the course of the next week, I felt steady enough to put myself back out there.

In February, we were planning a trip to Mexico with Nancy's family, and it happened to fall on our original wedding anniversary. I knew that Nancy was nervous about going through with our decision to remarry, but I really needed this commitment from her. I needed something to work for again, and it was this family. I pushed her to continue to plan the wedding—just a small ceremony, more of a renewal of vows—for our trip to Mexico. I bought both of our outfits: a white linen suit for me and a seafoam green dress for Nancy. Nancy arranged for a justice of the peace and found a location for the ceremony. As our trip approached, the whole family grew more excited.

Arriving in Mexico, the first thing Nancy did was call to confirm with the justice of the peace. Nancy had planned for the ceremony during the last week of December, which meant that all of the information she got was accurate for 1997. On January 1, 1998, some of the rules and regulations had changed. We were short a few pieces of paper in order to be legally married in Mexico.

I don't know who was more upset. Nancy, because she was such a thorough planner, or me, because I really wanted to cement this commitment to the family. But it was probably Lauren. The kid was hanging on to the idea that we were getting remarried. She was planning to use the new video camera to record the ceremony and was absolutely crushed that it wasn't going to happen.

On February 12, the day we were supposed to get remarried, Lauren woke us up early.

"So, since this wedding was more for you guys than anyone else, I don't see why you still can't do it," she said.

"We've been through this, honey," Nancy replied groggily. "We can't get married here. We are missing some paperwork, so we will have to wait until we get back home."

"Right, but that's not your anniversary. I think you should both get up, get dressed like you were going to, and say your vows anyway. I will record it and officiate." She walked across the room and opened the wooden slatted blinds. "I'll see you downstairs when you're ready," Lauren directed.

I chuckled and looked at Nancy. She was smiling, too.

We walked down the white marble staircase, arm in arm. In front of the pool, at our private villa, in front of Nancy's family, we renewed our vows. As promised, Lauren videotaped the whole affair. And at the end, she said, "By the power vested in me, as your daughter, I now pronounce you Mommy and Daddy. You may kiss the bride." What could have been a complete washout turned out to be the best wedding Nancy and I could have imagined.

SHE'S NOT THERE

I TRIED TO stay focused at Mani's but the place pretty much ran itself. I had designed the perfect restaurant, a restaurant that didn't need me running it in order to be successful. As boredom crept in, I fought daily with my sobriety. It didn't take me long to realize that I needed a new project. I let Mani know that I was looking for something new, and he really didn't seem to care. He had already gotten the restaurant of his dreams out of me. The truth is, I was sick of making other people money, getting paid only a fraction of what I brought in. I needed my own restaurant. Money, my lifelong nemesis, was the only thing keeping me from it. The only way this was going to work was if I found the impossible: a free restaurant.

One of my catering clients, Christopher Ciafletti, was a member at one of the local beach clubs. He invited me to meet him at the club, though the official season hadn't started yet. As we walked around, he explained to me that the beach club had a huge attached restaurant and with it guaranteed business from the members. The previous two summers, the club had auctioned off the right to run the concession to a local restaurant owner who had run the place into the ground. Stories of rotten food, undercooked meat, and rude waitstaff had resulted in an empty restaurant by the end of the second year. The members were angry. They paid high prices each year to belong to the club and one of the major amenities—the food—was terrible. They were in the market for a new proprietor. All I had to do was submit a bid for the place, and provided I was the highest bidder, I could run this restaurant as my own.

I submitted a bid the following week: one dollar. According to my friend Christopher, there weren't going to be any other bids that year. As is the case with many small towns, word had gotten around that things turned sour between the previous concession owner and the club. No one wanted to get in the middle of that. Except me, that is. I had absolutely no problem getting in the middle, and with a bid of one dollar, I really had nothing to lose. If we didn't get a single customer, all I stood to lose was the cost to purchase the food. The tip from Christopher turned out to be exactly right. The club owner called me the next week to let me know that I had won the concession for the upcoming summer.

The planning was more than I could tackle alone. Nancy jumped on board and decided to manage the books. She had always had a knack with numbers and, Lord knows, I shouldn't be in charge of the money. Together, we ordered the makings of a restaurant; from serving trays to dish soap, we stocked the house. As we busily prepared, Nancy interviewed waitstaff and hired lots of local kids looking for summer work. Many of them were untrained, but it was going to be nice to have a fresh slate and young energy.

With both me and Nancy at the restaurant, Lauren and Jonathan really had nowhere else to be. Lauren was about to enter high school and had been helping me cater parties for years. We gave her a job as a waitress so she could earn a little spending money. Jon-boy was on the younger side, but he still wanted to help and be involved. He washed dishes and did some basic side work like rolling silverware into napkins and refilling ketchup bottles.

That summer, the four of us took the Allenhurst Beach Club restaurant, newly named Windows on the Water, by storm. Used to crappy hamburgers and undercooked chicken sandwiches, the customers were blown away by our fresh cuisine and peppy staff. The restaurant was big, with room for forty tables, and we managed to keep it full most of the time. Running a restaurant as a family was an exhausting, all-consuming job. We worked hard, we worked late, but mostly we just worked together.

After a long weekend at the restaurant, Nancy, Jonathan, and I were unwinding at home. Lauren was out with some friends. Jon was tossing a baseball in the air and catching it in his new glove. Nancy was upstairs, putting away laundry, while I was watching a Yankees game. The ringing of the phone pierced through the quiet calm of the evening. I reached for the receiver.

"John, is that you?" It was my brother, Tony.

"Yeah, Tony. It's me. What's up?" I turned the volume down on the game and gestured for Jon to find somewhere else to play.

"It's Mom, John. She's gone."

It felt like someone had let all the air out of the room. My mind spun, looking for a place to grab onto, something to gain a sense of traction. Words. I had to say words.

"What?" was all I could muster; my tongue was lead in my mouth.

Leroy, my stepfather, called Tony that morning. He had given my mother her heart pill the night before like he always did, then he went to bed. When he woke in the morning, she wasn't in bed next to him; she was still sitting in the same chair in the living room that she had been in the night before. He put his hand on her arm and she was ice-cold. When Tony got there, he shook her, and the pill fell out of her mouth. She had never swallowed it. They called for an ambulance, but it was too late. Cecile Belle had suffered a massive heart attack; there was nothing anyone could do for her.

The realization that my mother was actually gone took a while to sink in. Frozen and numb, I struggled to figure out my next move. I had moved away from her a lifetime ago, but I carried her with me everywhere I went. I bore the scars of our tortured relationship, yet at the same time I knew that she had loved me deeply and had truly always done her best.

Thank God for Nancy. She did what she always did when I fell apart. She picked up the pieces and started to put me back together. She made arrangements for us to fly out the next morning. Leroy, Tony, and his daughter, Melissa, met us at the airport. It was surreal for us all to be sitting in my mother's living room without her there. Everywhere I looked, I saw her. Glancing into the living room, I saw her overstuffed armchair that she sat in each night to watch television. The kitchen still smelled like her cooking. And when I looked into my brother's blue eyes, it was like gazing into hers. That week was harder than I ever could have imagined it to be. There were pictures, reminiscing sessions, and funeral services, but mostly I just remember becoming acutely aware of the raw spot where I kept her close to my heart.

When we came home, we got right back to work. It was the end of the summer and we had just a few weeks left for the season at the beach club. My heart wasn't in it anymore, but I knew we had to finish strong and cement our place for the following year. We threw a Labor Day party for the members of the club. It was a beautiful party, but I just didn't feel like celebrating. I had started the year with huge successes at Mani's, and now I felt like I had lost my place in the world.

LIKE A ROLLING STONE

WITHOUT THE PROSPECT of work for the winter, I was unnerved. To try and keep some form of routine going, I woke up each morning, got dressed, went to 7-Eleven to grab my morning cup of coffee, and then rode around town until I got bored. Then I'd drive back home. Wake, dress, coffee, drive, home, repeat. The weekends were a bit better. Jonathan had begun playing baseball that summer and the Little League was still going in the fall. During the busy months at the restaurant, I had made it to a few games, but now I went to every single one.

He was a pitcher, in addition to playing the field. The rules stated that each child could only pitch a few innings in a row, to make sure none of the kids got hurt or wore out their arms. That made partial sense to me, but I loved to see the boy throw.

"Fire that rock, Jon-boy!" I called.

He looked at me from the mound, then toward home plate. He focused and threw home. Strike!

"Yeah, that's what I'm talking about. That's my boy!" I exclaimed as I paced behind the dugout. Games were always exciting to me. It had never mattered who was playing, but with my son out there, I became a fixture at the field, stalking each ball thrown and cheering for the team. Of course, in Little League there are also a fair amount of mistakes made on the field. When the games would get too bad, I'd take a break, resuming my regular routine of visiting 7-Eleven and driving aimlessly.

One afternoon I strolled in for my cup of coffee and in front of me was my friend from Mani's, Kevin Nassur. He was in the middle of a conversation with Baba, the owner of the store, as I came up behind them.

"Yeah, I was surprised it was available, too," Kevin was saying.

"What's up, buddy? It's been a while," I said, patting him on the back.

Kevin turned toward me and his eyes lit up. "You aren't going to believe this, John, I have something amazing to show you! You got some time to take a ride with me over to Asbury Park?"

Did I ever. I drove the familiar route down Ocean Avenue, through Elberon, Deal, Allenhurst, and then into Asbury Park. Asbury was the only town in the area in worse shape than Long Branch. After driving through Deal with its large summer homes, we entered the desolation of this once-bustling city. Big, beautiful Victorian mansions dotted the streets in dire need of restoration. Half-finished buildings littered the beachfront. Even the carousel and boardwalk had been closed down. I followed Kevin through town, wondering where we were heading, when his car stopped in front of a decrepit old building with a for-sale sign stuck on the door.

Kevin had driven to the Stone Pony, a notorious bar that had once been a great spot to catch local talent. The Pony had a cult following and over time it attracted a crowd. A series of lawsuits over drunk driving accidents bankrupted the owners. Developers in the area, the same ones who attempted to build buildings they couldn't finish, had bought and sold the Pony countless times in the mid nineties, without getting anywhere. I had been a patron here before I went to rehab, always had a good time, but I couldn't see what I was doing here now.

"I can't stand to see it like this." Kevin shook his head. "It's a piece of history!"

"Kevin, there's nobody in this town." I gestured at the vacant lots around us.

"People need somewhere to hear music, John! This place was a beacon. If Asbury has any chance of returning to its former glory, the Pony is its lifeline. I already have a promoter lined up to help with getting the musical acts. I need you to help me with the layout and putting in a kitchen. People won't get pulled over for drunk driving as often if they have some food in their bellies."

I thought about it. Logically, I couldn't see it working, but that really wasn't my problem. I didn't have a gig, and I was bored out of my mind. I needed something to take my mind off my mother and to pay some bills.

I agreed to work with Kevin. We mapped out the building, changed the layout, and began to talk through the details. The more I heard him and his promoter, Anthony, talk, the more I realized how serious these two were. They weren't looking to recreate the scene from the 80s; they were going to reinvent the Pony and turn it into an intimate venue for major names.

While work was steady, it still wasn't as fast-paced as I was accustomed to. The kitchen was a side note in a large-scale production, so I was still left with free time. Jonathan's team had made the playoffs and I had ball games to go to most weekends. It was becoming harder for me to watch the games. I found myself wanting to tell the kids what to do, but every time I opened my mouth, the coach would throw a hard look in my direction. Jonathan looked embarrassed when I'd call out from the stands, so I tried my best to keep it under wraps.

At the last game of the season, I watched as the umpire called ball after ball on Jonathan. The kid he was pitching to couldn't have been much above three feet tall. He would scrunch down in his stance, making the strike zone almost nonexistent. I paced, drank coffee, and shook my head. I made it through the kid's first at bat with my mouth firmly clamped shut.

"Ball one," called the umpire.

Jon-boy had thrown a perfect pitch, straight down the middle.

"Come on, ump. You gotta call that like it is," I said.

Jonathan wound up, threw across home—ball two.

"Are you kidding me?" I exclaimed, as I walked toward home. "How low are you gonna let this pipsqueak get in the box? If he goes any lower, he'd be sitting next to the plate!"

The ump turned toward our bench. "If you don't get this guy under control, I'm going to have him removed," the ump said, warning Jonathan's coach.

As I made my way back toward the bleachers, a short little bald man stepped in front of me. "You called my kid a pipsqueak." He poked his finger at my chest accusingly.

"Ball three," called the ump, taunting me.

I dropped my coffee cup into the dirt. "Listen, you little jerk. Your kid is purposefully trying to weasel a walk every time he's at bat. How about you teach him to stand up like a man," I retorted.

"This is Little League, remember. They're just kids," the guy said, backing away.

"I don't have to remember anything," I said, pushing him backward.

Suddenly, I felt people behind me. I spun and a couple of parents, both coaches, and the umpire had gathered in back of me.

The ump spoke for the group. "You're out of line, pal. You leave now, or I'm calling the cops."

No cops, no thank you. I gave them a piece of mind as I stormed back to the car. I saw Jonathan standing on the mound, looking nervous or embarrassed, or both.

"You fire that rock, Jon-boy! I'll see you at home."

But I couldn't go home; I was too wound up. I drove toward the Pony, needing something to take my mind off that idiotic scene at the ball game.

When I pulled up, the construction crew was hard at work. The massive dumpster took up most of the parking lot. Kevin and Anthony wouldn't be there; this was a demo day. I leaned on the hood of my car, lit a cigarette, and watched as parts of music history were thrown into the garbage, piece by piece.

By Monday, I had recovered from the spectacle of the weekend, but I was bored again. I made it to midafternoon with my usual routine, but I had lost interest in riding around town by three. The fall had marked the beginning of a transition for Lauren, who was now a high school freshman. With the start of the school year, she had decided to go out for the girl's tennis team. As my car slid into the lot behind the tennis courts, I saw twenty or so girls gathered around the coach.

The girls broke up and started pairing off with hitting partners, and I spotted Lauren. She was short for her age and didn't know how good she was yet, but I could see the competitive gleam in her eye a mile away. She started off strong, nailing her groundstrokes cleanly. She was playing well, until the older player's confidence level took control. When we played Sunday tennis together, Lauren would hit an entire bucket of forehands and then walk up to the net to count how many she missed.

Jonathan playing baseball——1996——age 8

If the number was too high, she would start beating herself up about it and mope around the court. As I watched from the parking lot, it looked like she was starting to slip into that routine. With every forehand or backhand that didn't paint the lines, her head dropped a little farther forward and her shoulders slumped.

I stayed in the car as long as I could, but I knew she needed encouragement.

"It's easy, kid. Racket back. Move your feet," I said as I approached the fence.

She spun around at the sound of my voice.

"Dad," she exclaimed, her excitement giving way to nerves almost instantly. "None of the other parents are here. I don't know if you should be here." She glanced around to see if the other girls were looking our way, but none were.

"It's okay. I'm not going to stay long. I have to get to the restaurant," I lied. "I just came by to remind you to keep your racket back when you're running for a ball and not to swing until your feet are set up."

"I know, I know," she muttered. "I can do it, Dad." She turned away from me and walked back up to the baseline. Her opponent hit a nice shot to her backhand. Lauren turned, brought her racket back, squared up, and fired a bullet up the line.

She glanced back at me. "See?"

I smiled and turned back toward the car.

SATISFACTION

WE WORKED STRAIGHT through that winter, installing new floors, putting in the makings of a kitchen, and most importantly getting the stage ready for opening night. Anthony was on the phone nonstop calling agents and at times, even musicians themselves. He, more than any of us, wanted the opening night to have the big names we needed to show people that not only was the Stone Pony back, it was better than ever. Eventually, he nailed down the acts for the first night. The headliner was Jimmy Paige, playing with his own band.

Radio promotions in conjunction with flyers and advertisements at other concert venues had apparently been very effective, and the line stretched around the block. Watching Jimmy take the stage, hearing the roar of the eager crowd as the drummer hit the first downbeat—it was an incredible moment for rock and roll. As the party swelled around me, I realized I was completely disconnected from it. This wasn't my project and my heart wasn't in it. I managed to feel completely alone while standing in the middle of a crowded room. On my way out, I thanked Kevin for the opportunity to help him reopen this musical icon, and I knew that it was time to move on.

Staying in one place was not something that I was good at. When I was a kid we had moved around in order to survive, and I think that stuck with me. I was constantly in motion, dodging and weaving, attempting to find a place for myself. It was still cold outside, despite the fact that spring had arrived. Living in New Jersey for twenty years, you'd think that I would have adjusted to the seasons, but winter just wasn't for me. It was so easy to feel depressed, bleak, and desolate. I needed the sun on my face in order to feel alive. I decided to focus on the summer, as if thinking about it hard enough would will it into existence.

I reached out to the beach club. It was about time for them to hold their auction for the concession for that year. Based on the previous year, it had been promised to me, but I knew that we still had to go through the formality of allowing others to submit their bids. Nancy, the kids, and I had turned that restaurant into a profitable business, and there was likely going to be more competition.

I called the office of the beach club daily, never getting anyone on the line. I left voicemails asking about when they were going to start accepting bids, but no one was returning my calls. Keeping calm was difficult for me, despite my regular lithium intake. When I got focused on something, it could very quickly grow into an obsession. I began driving to the club on a daily basis, but being winter, the office was closed most days. Finally, on the seventh day of sitting in the parking lot, I saw Jerry, the office manager, slowly turn into the lot.

As she started to get out of the car, I approached. "Hey, Jerry. I am glad to see you. I left a couple messages about the bids for this season, but I never heard anything back."

"Oh yeah, I did hear those." She fumbled in her purse for her keys. "You know, John, we have already received a couple of offers. If you'd like to submit a bid as well, you can draw it up and drop it in the mail."

Drop it in the mail? Was she serious? This wasn't what we had planned at the end of the season.

"Uh, Jerry. I think you know we had an arrangement. I turned this place around and was guaranteed the club for the second year if I did that. I already got the liquor license approved for this year. No one else will be able to secure one in time, not to mention the $5,000 price tag on that."

She finally looked right at me. "John, things have changed. Last year was last year. This season we will be having a proper auction. The offers we've received will benefit the club. We cannot just give this place away for free anymore. If you'd like to submit a bid, all I can do is give you a tip. Don't submit anything under ten grand. You'll never get it."

Jerry walked into the office and shut the door behind her. As I heard her lock the door, it began to sink in that I was out. It had been a rocky year, and it looked like I was off to a bad start for the upcoming season.

Looking for work is never fun, and I wanted something different. I wanted something with staying power, but for me to last longer than a few months—or even a year—I knew that the restaurant would have to be adaptable and able to change with me. Caroline's had been such a good fit for exactly that reason; it had grown with me and was easily molded to meet customer demand.

I drove around town, chatting with old friends and business acquaintances to see if anyone had any suggestions for me. No one did. With no one left to turn to, I called Tomas at Mani's to see if any of his cousins knew of a place looking for a chef. Tomas lived in a two-bedroom apartment, shared with at least eight other men, mostly relatives. The guys all worked in the restaurant business, from dishwashers to line cooks; they spanned all aspects of kitchen life. Some had worked for me over the years, and they all knew what I had done for Tomas's career. He promised to get back to me if he heard anything.

After a week of spinning my wheels, not really getting any leads, Tomas called me back and asked to meet at a local pool hall on Monday night, his day off. I hadn't played pool in years, but knew that it might be fun to get out, and at the least this would be interesting. The pool hall was close to the parkway entrance, not close to any residential neighborhoods except for Fort Monmouth and all of its housing. I don't know what I expected it to be like when I got there, but it wasn't this. The parking lot was slammed with cars, and there was a wait, on a Monday, in a room that housed at least twenty tables.

As I scanned the room for Tomas, I began to see the allure. There was a small bar with two bartenders keeping the drinks flowing and waiters carrying in trays of bar food. I didn't see the kitchen, and as far as I could tell the waiters and waitresses didn't look like they worked in the pool hall.

"Juanito," Tomas called, using his nickname for me.

I turned and saw him coming in behind me. He had another man with him.

"This is Nervine. He is the head cook across the hall."

I shook his hand and Nervine broke into a huge grin. "Very nice to meet you, Juanito. I've heard a lot about you. Tomas's brother Antonio works with me. I hear you are looking for work?"

"I am, but I don't know if you could use me. It looks like you've got the food under control in here," I replied, gesturing toward the packed tables.

"Oh, you haven't seen anything yet." Nervine laughed as he led me back outside.

I followed him across the hall and through another entrance into a large, mostly empty dining room. "This is Redhead's, the restaurant. We supply the food for the pool hall, but we also serve lunch and dinner. We have a sushi bar up front and on Friday nights, we are a *discoteca*."

Pool hall, restaurant, sushi bar, and club all in one? This was a first—an interesting, adaptable, ever-changing first. I glanced over at Tomas, who was positively beaming.

"Juanito, I got this for you." He clapped his hand on my back.

Once we got the management on board, Nervine and I made quick work of overhauling the menu. Based on sales and how busy the pool hall was, we decided not to touch that part of the business. They were mostly selling buffalo wings and quesadillas anyway, so it wasn't a stretch to leave those items in place. The restaurant menu really wasn't too bad either; it was the technique that needed tweaking. We went through the menu, recipe by recipe, teaching each line cook the necessary steps to properly execute each item. With the basic menu starting to get under control, I began to design daily specials, with a few appetizers and several of my upscale favorites from Mani's and the beach club.

The only other restaurant in the area was an Applebee's. As long as we kept our prices somewhat competitive and served a slightly better product, we had an easy victory. The hit-or-miss dining room slowly began to fill up. I took on a similar role to the one I had at Mani's. In the mornings, I would come in and supervise setup, meet with vendors, check inventory, and make sure everything was prepped for dinner service. Around one I'd head home to rest, shower, and change into my uniform before heading back by five o'clock for the rush. Redhead's was an ideal job; there was constantly something going on, and if one area was slower than the others, that would be my focus until it caught up. With so many balls to juggle, it was impossible to get bored.

Since we weren't located right on the oceanfront, our busy season started in the fall. Once the seasons fully changed over, we were slammed each night. Sonnie, the manager, was looking to hire some new waitstaff and also beef up the support staff. Lauren wanted a part-time job so she could save money for a car. I know, unbelievable, right? The kid was old enough to think about driving. I created a position for her at the restaurant as the dessert and cappuccino server on the weekends. People are much more likely to order dessert when they see it rather than looking at a paper menu, and it's a very easy way to increase each check by ten percent or more. With Lauren there, it was a win-win; the average check increased across the board, Lauren made money, and I got to steal a few extra hours with her each week. Since she'd started high school, I had seen less and less of her. Not to mention keeping her busy on Friday and Saturday nights was a perfect way to keep her out of harm's way.

Being a teenager was hard for her. She struggled with her identity in a way that was unfamiliar to me. She had always been smart; she was enrolled in all honors classes and didn't have to try very hard to get straight As. That set her apart from her classmates. The other aspect that caused her angst was her firecracker personality. The kids she related to the most were not in her classes. They were a rough and edgy group with sharp tongues and serious wit. Dripping with sarcasm, they would banter endlessly with one another, stopping only when one person had enough and walked out. Lastly, was her boyfriend, Frank. He was older by a couple years and completely different from her. He never did well in school, but he was an over-the-top athletic. Captain of everything from golf to the state champion football team, the guy was a total jock. And with him came yet another group of kids who drank keg beer and partied late into the night. To say that Lauren was a kid in conflict with herself would be a huge understatement. She fit in everywhere but never felt at home with any one group of friends. She needed all of these groups to satisfy different parts of her. I didn't know where she would land; I just knew it wouldn't be in this town. The quicker she could get out, the better it would be for her.

I pushed her to pick up more shifts at the restaurant as I saw the changes in her becoming more and more pronounced. She stayed out until the last minute of her curfew and came home looking wrecked. She grew distant from Nancy and me, and it was all we could do to keep from grounding her for years at a time. Nancy was a huge proponent of keeping her within our sight at all times, but I knew from my own past that when someone was going to go off, it didn't matter how close a watch you kept on them. We needed to find an escape for her, and the only one I could think of was still a whole year away: college.

As if the new job and dealing with Lauren weren't enough, there was also Jon-boy to consider. He was skateboarding pretty regularly and was also running with a tougher crowd than in previous years. Baseball, I had been able to relate to—but skating? I just didn't get it. As had been the case for years, Nancy had a much better handle on him. I listened when he talked to me, using words I had never heard of: nollie, kickflip, tailslide—what? Really, I tried, but he might as well have been speaking Martian.

I focused on Redhead's. My regular clientele, who had been growing since Caroline's, came religiously. I tried to keep the menu specials fresh and new, but inevitably they repeated. One night when I went out into the dining room to check the front of the house, I saw Kimberly and Christopher, my old friends who had helped me secure the beach club. As I approached the table, I took a deep breath. I liked working at Redhead's, but it definitely was not an upscale enough destination for customers like them.

"John!" Kimberly squealed as I made my way over to their booth. "So nice to see you."

I kissed her on the cheek and shook Christopher's hand. "It's been a long time. So glad you two could make it out."

"Of course, of course. We wouldn't miss a chance to eat your food," she replied, smiling.

As we settled in to talk, I could feel my mind drifting away from the conversation. I just wasn't proud of this place the way I had been at Caroline's, Mani's, and even the beach club. I felt a lull in the conversation and realized that both Kim and Christopher were looking at me, expectantly.

"I'm sorry. What did you say?" I asked.

"Brunch? I asked you about whether or not you were going to do a Sunday brunch here?" Kimberly questioned.

"That's not a bad idea. I don't know exactly how that would work, but it's worth looking into," I replied. "Guys, it's been great catching up with you—order the sea bass. I've gotta run, though."

I needed a way to take some ownership of the restaurant. Basically, I was making minor modifications to an already well-run establishment. If I wanted to be proud of this place, I needed a way to make it my own. At Caroline's, adding the dinner service and catering had given me the sense of contributing to the bigger picture, and at Mani's the design process had made me feel included. Redhead's already had such an established culture that it felt like there was little I could do to make my mark. Perhaps instituting a Sunday brunch would build business at an otherwise dead time. Ordinarily, we had ten, maybe fifteen tables over the course of the eleven to three time span on Sundays.

I ran the idea by Sonnie, and he was game. Truthfully, the man didn't care much what I did so long as I didn't mess with his Friday nightclub. I found his obsession with the club odd, especially considering the work that went into clearing the restaurant, breaking down the tables, and moving them out of the way. Next was shutting down the sushi bar, setting up a moveable dance floor, bringing in bouncers, and then convincing waitstaff that they wanted to stay on for cocktail service that would bring them little in the way of tips. It seemed like an awful lot of work for such a small reward until I noticed the second cash register. Like clockwork, every Friday night, Sonnie would come in with a small gray cash register and set it up by the entrance. As people showed up for the DJ, they were charged a five- or ten-dollar cover charge, depending on how early or late they got there. This money would go straight into the gray register, bypassing the Point of Sale system and main cash drawer. Sonnie explained he did this because it was "easier" to keep the cash separate so it didn't interfere with the numbers from the restaurant. As a schemer, I knew there must be more to this cash register, but I just couldn't put my finger on it yet.

During the first few weeks of brunch service, we worked the kinks out. We decided to do buffet-style instead of à la carte. The food could all be prepped in advance, and then only a handful of the hot items would need to be made in the morning. This would allow the kitchen to get set up for dinner without much interference. We started slow, as it took some time for the customers to hear that we were offering brunch, and then that the brunch was worth coming in for. Because there were buffet tables preset in the dining room, I was able to dress the tables, something I hadn't done much of since my catering days. There was a raised platform, similar to a small stage, set back into a bay window. I placed most of the food on display in that window, surrounded by heads of purple cabbage, fresh fruit, and small flower accents. If nothing else, the table was beautiful.

Most Sundays I would head home after setting up brunch to shower and relax before coming back in for dinner. After the first month, though, I began to notice that something was off with the numbers for brunch. We were charging a flat fee, so our food cost-to-profit ratio should have remained steady; in fact, our profits should have grown as we adjusted to demand and cut down on waste. Curiously, our profit margin was shrinking with each week, so I had to look deeper. It didn't take long to see where we were losing our money; it was the shrimp cocktail and crab claws. With each brunch, we were serving more seafood than we had the week before. At this point we had doubled our initial seafood purchase order and then some. I spoke with the guys in the back and instructed them to change the display. We needed to place the seafood in a less conspicuous location and instead put something much less expensive, like the bagels and cream cheese, front and center.

I stuck around to make sure that my changes were executed and also to see if there was something missing. Pouring myself a cup of coffee, I grabbed a seat in the bar area. Dressed in my regular street clothes, I blended right in. I watched as people filtered in and took their seats. Every fifteen to thirty minutes, I walked up to the buffet to check supplies. Everything seemed to be in order and the seafood was being eaten at the same rate as the other food. It seemed as though the change in presentation had solved the problem. I went in the back to grab my coat and tell the guys I would be back in the afternoon. On my way back to the front of the house to leave, I noticed a bottleneck at the buffet. I slowly walked up and saw an enormous woman and her two kids, also giant, standing near the seafood; the platters were suddenly empty.

"Can I help you?" I asked the woman.

"Yes, where is the shrimp cocktail?" she asked, haughtily. "I paid for a full buffet, but half of the items are missing."

"Half of the items aren't missing; they are being restocked. If you wait a few minutes, more will be out. Please have a seat, and we'll make sure we refill this area," I replied, trying my best not to show my disgust.

The woman shook her head and reluctantly made her way back to her table. I watched her join her husband, one of the largest men I had ever seen, who sat with a heaping plate of shrimp and crab claws in front of him. The man easily had three pounds of expensive seafood in front of him, and he was paying $14.95 for everything. Frustrated, I took off my coat, grabbed the seafood tray, and made my way back into kitchen.

"Fat asses," I mumbled as I refilled the platters.

When I walked back into the dining room, the woman and her family spotted me and got up to walk over to the buffet. Unbelievable. Before the tray was even settled onto the table she pushed past me and began loading up a plate. And then another. And then another. As I watched, the woman loaded up plates for herself and her children. There had to be at least seven pounds of seafood there.

I tried to restrain myself, I really did, as she sat back down at her table. She began to gobble up the crab and shrimp, pausing only to swirl each bite into her massive bowl of cocktail sauce. It was just too much. I approached the table swiftly and began to take the silverware off the table.

"What are you doing?" the woman shrieked, her mouth full and dripping cocktail sauce.

"You've had enough," I snapped. "Do you realize you and your disgusting family have eaten ten pounds of seafood this morning?! If you want an all-you-can-eat seafood buffet, head to Red Lobster. We don't want people like you here."

As I headed back to the kitchen, I knew I was in trouble. I just didn't care. A lot of things can disgust you working in a restaurant, but wasting food like this was absolutely sickening.

The double doors didn't have time to stop swinging before Sonnie scurried through the doors.

"John, have you lost your mind?" he demanded, wringing his hands.

"Yeah, maybe I have," I sneered. "That elephant and her family are single-handedly ruining the profitability of brunch. What do you want me to do? Just sit back and watch it happen?"

"They are paying customers, you lunatic! You absolutely cannot talk to our patrons like that! You will go back out there and apologize, and their bill will be on the house—wait, it'll come out of your pay!"

"What the hell do you expect me to say to that beast?" I shouted.

"I don't know what you're going to say, but I suggest you figure it out fast, or it's your job!" he roared as he turned and spun out of the kitchen.

That day marked a drastic change in my relationship with Sonnie. Of course, I knew that I shouldn't have talked to those people like that, but the truth was the man had been there to witness the behavior of those people for the past month and he had done nothing to stop them. We could have structured several ways to avoid this sort of problem, such as adding in a separate charge for raw bar items or adding shrimp cocktail as an à la carte add-on. Sonnie hadn't even noticed the amount of waste from brunch. The kitchen and food cost was primarily my domain, but he was the general manager, making every-thing his ultimate responsibility. The more I thought about it, the more I couldn't shake the feeling that something was off with the place. The owner, Mr. Donafrio, had many restau-rants in the area, and Sonnie managed quite a few of them, though he spent all of his time at Redhead's. I couldn't imagine why a seemingly intelligent businessman would have someone run a significant portion of his holdings when he clearly did not care about where the money was going. I didn't know what I was going to find, but I decided to make it my mission to figure out what Sonnie was up to.

Chef John, Lauren, Nervine, and Jesus At Redhead's—2002

MONEY

IT WASN'T GOING to be easy to unravel whatever web Sonnie was spinning, so I focused on the aspects of the restaurant that I enjoyed while I waited for the opportunity to present itself. My initial assessment had been correct; this was a place with enough different facets to hold my interest.

The sushi bar in particular intrigued me. I had eaten a little sushi but not enough to really know anything about it. Charlie, the owner of the sushi bar concession, walked me through the basic differences between the types of rolls and ultimately through each menu item. Once I was done with my taste test, I felt I was in a good position to help him make the bar more profitable. Up until that point, our regular waitstaff covered the sushi bar as one of the less desirable sections of the restaurant. While that was fine from a coverage standpoint, none of them had ever received any special training on the items served at the bar.

Charlie and I designed a sampling and a basic overview for some of the servers and invited them to come in before lunch one morning to try it out. From that point on, only trained waitstaff would be scheduled to work the bar. This would help increase revenue, as they would now have a better understanding of what to recommend to customers and how to try and upsell them.

Charlie was happy that people were taking an interest in what his crew did, and he began to take ownership of the relationship between the sushi bar and the rest of the restaurant. It was time to turn my attention to other areas of need. As I moved methodically through the business, I would ultimately be left with only one area: the club. I worked through jazzing up our lunch offerings, featuring quick and fresh sandwiches and wraps that would appeal to people on a short break. Then I was on to the pool hall. There, I just focused on small things, like adding a sweet teriyaki glaze to our traditional wings already on the menu. The pool hall was the busiest part of the restaurant and I didn't want to waste too much time there.

Sonnie was so secretive about the club that I had no idea whether or not we were even making or losing money on it. I wanted to tread lightly so that I could weasel my way in without him noticing. At that point, the club only served alcohol. We shut down the kitchen right before the DJ would start spinning. To me, that seemed to be a good place to start. I could design a small late-night menu with easy items that people could eat standing up at the high-top cocktail tables. It wouldn't cut down on the flow of the night and would actually encourage people to order more drinks, since they would no longer have to drink on an empty stomach.

I brought my suggested menu in to Sonnie and honestly was completely surprised by his positive reaction. He was almost enthusiastic about the possibility of gaining some revenue from food at the club. I was still suspicious, but his response made me question whether I was wrong to think there was something dirty about the club.

We advertised the change for a couple of weeks and decided that we would only need one kitchen guy to stay on

board to run the finger food items, at least initially. I picked
my most trustworthy guy, Nervine, and told him that I wanted
him to keep an eye on things while he was there late. Sonnie
had worked with all of these guys long before me, but I knew
that the kitchen staff had no respect for him whatsoever. He
had ignored their suggestions for years and treated them like
second-class citizens. While I didn't come right out and tell
Nervine what I was looking for, he was smart enough to know
that "keep an eye on things" really meant keeping an eye on
Sonnie.

My phone rang at twelve-thirty in the morning.

"Juanito, I'm going home now," Nervine reported, sound-
ing tired. "I saw something."

I cleared my throat. "Go on. What did you see?"

"They stopped letting people in at midnight. About five
minutes ago, I was cleaning the kitchen and I saw Sonnie take
all of the money out of his gray register, put it in a brown takeout bag with his dinner, and get in his car."

Bingo.

"That's very good, Nervine. You did a great job. Thank you
for staying to work tonight. You can come in at noon instead of
ten tomorrow morning."

The restaurant was equipped with a safe, so there was very
little reason for Sonnie to take the cash home with him. There
was only one way that this was going to be legitimate, and
that would be if I saw the total amount of cash and deposit
slip the following morning in the books. I usually didn't check
the books, as making the bank deposits and pickups for cash
was Sonnie's territory. But since we had just started the new
late-night menu, I had an excuse to get my hands on the
book—to check on sales.

Turns out, I didn't even need an excuse. When I went into
the office, the book was right on the desk. I hung up my jacket

and flipped it open to the previous night's entries. The dinner service numbers were there, and even late-night sales were recorded, but the cover charge did not appear as a line item. No record of that cash whatsoever. I flipped to the previous week, no cover charge entered. The week before that? Nada. Sonnie had been pocketing the money every Friday since I started working there, and probably even before that. By my rough calculations, Sonnie had stolen between $500 and $1,000 every week for at least a year. Nice extra paycheck. I didn't waste any time. On the bulletin board in the office were the phone numbers of the management, as well as the owner. I dialed Mr. Donafrio's number and held my breath.

"Hello," came the gravely voice on the other end.

"Mr. Donafrio?" I inquired.

"Yes, this is he. Who is this?" he asked.

"It's me, John, from Redhead's," I began. This was going to be fun.

Mr. Donafrio thanked me for the information but did not sound as shocked as I had expected. I had nailed Sonnie stealing thousands of dollars a year from him, but Donafrio never even raised his voice. As I sat in the office, mulling over what had happened, it dawned on me that Mr. Donafrio must have already known or somehow approved of Sonnie taking the cash. I began to feel sick as I thought of the implications of what I had done.

I didn't stick around to wait for the ball to drop. I put my jacket on and walked out to the car. As I opened the car door, I saw Sonnie's white Jaguar come screaming into the parking lot. Good news always traveled fast. I shut the door and waited to take my licks.

"You arrogant prick," Sonnie said. "Who do you think you are, you rat? If you think you still have a job here, you're out of your mind."

"I realize that, Sonnie. Congratulations. You won."

My reply must have caught him off guard. He looked at me, confused, and then I saw him crack a smile.

"You designed that whole late-night menu just to mess with me, didn't you?"

I nodded. "Yeah, I knew you were up to something and I had to know what it was."

"Well, now you know. Get the hell out of my restaurant. I can't have a snitch working for me."

I was so pissed at myself for not thinking it through before calling the boss. How could I have known that Donafrio was in on it? Who just knowingly lets someone take home cash from their restaurant? I paced around the house, not really knowing what to do with myself. Taxes? Could it be about unreported earnings? If it never came in and it never went out, both of them could save a few bucks. Was that how they paid the guys who were off the books? Spinning through possibilities, I was becoming more resigned to the fact that my ego had just cost me my job, again.

When the phone rang, I almost didn't answer it.

"Yeah?" I said, snatching the ringing annoyance out of its cradle.

"Hey, John. It's Davey, up at the Farm House."

"Oh hey. Listen Davey, I don't think you've heard yet, but I got let go this morning, so I don't think you can count on me to split orders this month."

Dave worked at one of Donafrio's other restaurants. We had worked together years before at one of my first jobs in Long Branch, so we had a good rapport and enjoyed getting to rub elbows again.

"Oh, I heard, you idiot." Dave laughed. "That's why I'm calling. Donafrio called to let me know that Sonnie fired you for snitching on him but that I am supposed to offer you a job up here. He said that Sonnie may not like a rat, but he liked that you reported what you thought was theft. Take the day off and then take a ride up here tomorrow, and we'll see what we can work out."

SHEER HEART ATTACK

THE FARM HOUSE was a bitch of a restaurant. The main prep kitchen was in the basement, with only a small firing kitchen on the first floor. The largest cooking area was down a flight of at least twenty stairs, and they were narrow. Big vats of sauce and trays of food would be prepped and precooked in the basement and then lugged up the stairs. Working with Davey was nice, but he was already the executive chef there, which made me a sous chef. I hadn't actually cooked this much in years, and while I enjoyed it, I did not enjoy the ridiculous gymnastic routine involved in getting the food up those stairs.

The pains came quickly. One minute I was hauling a bucket of sauce up the staircase, the next I was on my knees gasping for breath. As I sat on the floor, I felt my chest tighten, my arm growing numb, and my senses dulling. It's strange how your whole body reacts to a sensation in a seemingly isolated area. I had tunnel vision, and what little I could see was growing smaller. I reached inside myself and began to focus only on my breathing. I counted to eight for each inhale and exhale. As I counted, again and again, my body began to come back to me. When I looked up in the kitchen around me, there were the rest of guys, circled up, staring.

"John, I'm going to call 911," Davey said, his voice tight.

"No, no, I'm fine." I struggled to my feet. "Really, it's okay. I feel fine now."

Davey looked at me. "You're the whitest white boy I've ever seen. You're not all right—anyone can see that."

"I just gotta rest. I was dizzy, is all," I mumbled, making my way through the kitchen to where my coat hung on the hook.

Running his hand through his hair, Davey exhaled sharply. "Fine. Fine. Go home, then. But call me tonight and let me know how you're doing."

"Davey, really, I'm fine. But if it'll make you feel better, I'll call," I reassured him as I put on my coat.

I let the engine run for a good five minutes while I got a grip in the car. What the hell was that? There had been a lot of horrible feelings in my lifetime, but nothing like that. It was like the life was being squeezed out of me, pulsating and punishing as the grip on my chest radiated outward.

I drove straight home, anxious that the feeling would come back. As I drew closer, I began to calm down. Maybe it hadn't been that bad. Maybe I was just dizzy and I'd feel fine after dinner and a good night's sleep. It took the rest of the forty-minute drive to convince myself, but by the time I pulled into the driveway, the experience at Davey's felt like it had happened to someone else.

Nancy was in the kitchen, arms crossed. Damn it, Davey must've called her.

Smiling, I said, "Nance, I'm okay. You don't have to look at me like that."

"He told me you couldn't make it up the stairs. That you half-fell, half-walked back down the steps and collapsed on the ground holding your chest. That sounds like a heart attack to me," she said.

"Yeah, well, that's true. But if I had a heart attack, I wouldn't feel this way now. It completely went away," I said.

"You have to go get it checked out." Nancy was exasperated.

"No, I don't. I'm going to shower and lie down," I said.

I was most definitely not going to the hospital.

The next thing I knew she was shaking me awake while clicking on the bedside lamp. "Lauren is on the phone for you," Nancy said.

"Dad?" I heard the concern in her voice immediately. "How are you feeling?"

I cleared my throat and sat up. My head was throbbing. "I'm fine, sweetheart."

"Listen," she said, "I'm glad you feel okay, but you have to go to the hospital. It's probably nothing, but you'll never know if you don't go."

Not her, too. "Lauren. I do not need to go to the hospital. Really, I'm fine and I just needed to rest."

"That's not good enough!" she yelled. I could hear her voice rising a few octaves as she got more worked up. "Either you go now, or I'm coming home to pick you up. You cannot play around with chest pains and a potential heart attack."

She wasn't going to let this go. The same way she had nagged me into quitting smoking, she was going to nag me through the doors to the emergency room. When I glanced up at Nancy, I saw her smile; she knew she had won.

Having your wife work at the same hospital for fifteen years had a few perks. Whenever we had to take one of the kids, we'd always gotten great care and we'd gotten it fast. Now it was my turn to be the recipient of special treatment. I was assessed quickly and, much to my dismay, admitted almost instantly.

I had classic heart attack symptoms, down to the tingling sensation in my left arm. The only good news was that I had survived. As specialists came and went, it began to sink in that this was much more serious than I had thought. It took about twenty-four hours for the doctors and nurses to poke me a sufficient amount of times in order to satisfy whatever quota they needed to fill to convince themselves that they had been thorough.

"Good afternoon, Mr. Wagner. My name is Dr. Ferry," a short, stocky older man began as he peered at me over his clipboard. "I am your cardiologist."

I didn't trust myself to speak so I simply nodded in his direction.

"You are very lucky you came in. According to the EKG, your heart is not functioning well at all. We used that information to order a cardiac catheterization. The results of that were even worse than we first suspected. One of your arteries is fully occluded and an additional two have partial occlusions."

Staring, slack-jawed, I realized he was waiting for me to say something before he went on. "Uh, well, Doc, I have no idea what you're talking about to be honest," I responded.

"Mr. Wagner, you have three clogged arteries. It is a miracle that your heart is pumping blood at all at this point. You need a triple bypass in order for us to attempt to repair the proper functioning of your heart. Open-heart surgery."

Stunning. That was stunning information. Clearly, I didn't really know what he meant, but having my chest cracked open for heart surgery was not something I had been expecting him to suggest. Aside from the accident with the eighteen-wheeler, I had never needed a surgery in my life. The recovery from getting hit by the truck had taken months, and it was extremely painful. The main reason I avoided hospitals, and doctors in general for that matter, was because of how grueling it had been to come back from that accident. Surgery was not for me.

"Thanks, Doc. I appreciate you seeing me," I said as I pivoted to swing my legs out of the hospital bed. "I won't be having any surgery, so I guess I should get going."

Dr. Ferry's eyes bugged out his head. "Mr. Wagner, you are a very sick man! I really must impress upon you how important this operation is for you. You could die without it."

"Yeah, well, then I guess it's my time. My father died when he was fifty-five, so it must be in the genes," I replied, realizing that I was still attached to the IV. I pulled the needle out of my arm and grabbed a tissue from the side table to press over the blood spurting out of the wound.

"Mr. Wagner! If you leave, you will be leaving against medical advice. Please, just sit down so we can discuss this." Dr. Ferry had put down the clipboard and was gesticulating wildly.

At that moment, I heard a familiar click-clack in the corridor. Nancy. Damn it. Her eyes widened as she took in the scene in my room. There was the doctor, red in the face and yelling on one side of the small room. On the other side, I stood half-dressed with blood dripping down my forearm, fumbling to get my jeans on.

Her eyes never left mine as she spoke with icy calm. "Dr. Ferry, would you please excuse us for a moment? We have some decisions to make as a family."

They transferred me to Newark Beth Israel for the procedure. Apparently, they were the best in the area, and our little hometown hospital wasn't going to cut it. Despite my best objections, Nancy and the kids convinced me that there was no other option for me than to have the surgery. I used work as an excuse, reminding them that I would most likely lose my job as a result of being out of work for the two-month recovery. Nancy countered that I had been out of work before and had always managed to find something new. For some reason, I just couldn't shake the feeling that this was going to be different. I had always believed in letting nature take its course, and having my heart operated on scared the shit out of me. If I was meant to die, what was going to be there for me if I woke up from the surgery?

Lauren and Nancy were both there as they prepped me for surgery. Jonathan stayed with a friend, as waiting all day in the hospital would have been too much for him. I could tell they were worried, but Nancy kept the tone upbeat. It was hard to tell if it was for Lauren's benefit or to make sure I went through with it, but I guess the reason didn't really matter. Having them there helped keep me from running out the door and having Lauren melt down. They each took a turn telling me they loved me and kissing me on the forehead. It was go time.

After a six-hour operation, I awoke to a dull ache in the center of my chest and a horrible burning sensation in my throat. I tried to take a breath, but I couldn't get any air in; there was something blocking my airway. I struggled to pull it out of the way, but I felt hands pushing it in and then holding my arms down. The ache in my chest grew sharper as I fought to breathe. When the pain become so unbearable that I thought I was dying, I felt a sliding sensation in the back of my throat and the blockage was removed. Extubated, I could breathe again. The recovery room nurses wheeled me back to my room and sent for the family. I could see the fear melt off Lauren's face as she entered the room. She was clutching a turquoise pillow in the shape of a heart.

"Dad, this is for you," she said. "The nurses gave it to me, and it's for you to hold to your chest when you have to cough. We all signed it."

I tried to reach for the pillow, but searing pain slowed my arms and nailed them in place. Gasping, I fought the urge to cry out.

"Thank you, honey," was the best I could manage.

Luckily, the nurses didn't let them stay long, so I only had to hold it together a short time. The hooked me up to a morphine drip, and I slowly faded off to a fitful sleep.

The next few days passed quickly, or slowly, depending on how you looked at it. Each day felt like an eternity, an endless haze of prodding and poking with visits from family interspersed in between. Jonathan came to visit, Lauren came and went with her boyfriend, and Nancy checked on me daily. I tried as hard as humanly possible not to let on how much pain I was in. I wanted nothing more than to get the hell out of the hospital and home to the safety on my own bed. My logic was that if I didn't complain, they would discharge me faster. On day four, I got my wish. After a triple bypass, it would take months for my body to fully heal, but I was only under the supervision of trained medical professionals for half a week. The rest of my recovery would take place under the watchful eyes of my family.

Aside from the pain, there was the boredom to contend with. I really couldn't do anything. At all. Standing upright hurt my chest. Washing my hair hurt my chest. Driving a car hurt my chest. Opening the fridge hurt my chest. Not being able to have my independence turned me into an asshole. Asking for help and being watched all the time made my skin crawl. And puttering around the house like some sort of invalid was infuriating. Fifty-five is too young for a man to lose control of his health. It's unnatural to go from being a relatively healthy, independent, middle-aged man to a fully dependent loser incapable of making a sandwich.

I called Davey to check in and let him know how my recovery was going. The doctors told me that the absolute earliest I would be cleared to go back to work was six weeks, and likely it would be longer. Davey was completely reassuring and promised my job would be waiting for me when I got back.

Slowly, excruciatingly slowly, some strength came back as my rib cage healed. Once I was cleared to drive, I began to head over to the tennis courts daily to watch Lauren practice. Early September was always a great time to be outside at the Jersey Shore once the crowds from the summer had died down. The weather was still warm enough to be enjoyable, and you could move freely about the town without the traffic and congestion of July and August. Day after day, I waited for school to let out at three, so I could meet the team as they went onto the courts. After a couple weeks of that routine, waiting until three became too hard. I started going over at one, bringing my own gear. I would work on my serve or hit around with anyone else who happened to stop by the courts. My strength continued to improve and honestly, I was getting in pretty good shape. As my form improved, so did my mental state. I felt alive on the courts, with the sun on my face, the wind blowing my hair, and the satisfying pop of the ball when you struck it right in the sweet spot ringing in my ears.

Eventually, the six weeks passed and the doctor cleared me to go back to work. The same morning, I drove—okay, I raced—up the parkway to the restaurant. I didn't bother to call first to let Davey know I was coming; there was too much adrenaline driving me. I felt really good, maybe better than I ever had, and cooking was to be like a homecoming.

As I made my way through the restaurant and headed back into the kitchen, I felt a smile spread across my face and lightness in my step. When I came in, I caught Davey coming out of the walk-in box with his arms full of crates of potatoes. I grabbed the top box off the stack so he could see me and carried it over near the sinks.

"Hey, John! Holy shit, man, you look great!" he exclaimed.

"I feel great," I replied. "I'm cleared, Davey! I can start tomorrow, or today if you want. I'm back!"

The smile faded from his face. Davey shifted his gaze to the floor. "Oh, man. John, listen. The owners told me I had to cut a few guys from the staff. We're starting to slow down for the season, and we just don't need as many guys. I'd love to keep you on, but I've had to let go some of my top people. I just don't have anything for you right now."

"Are you kidding me? Christ, Davey, that's not right, and you know it. I need this job, Dave. What else am I going to do?"

But Davey didn't have any other answers for me. "It wasn't personal," he'd said. But it was personal to me. I had given the better part of my adult life to an industry that just didn't care about people. Busting my butt and doing my best just didn't seem to be good enough anymore. If the restaurant business was going to turn its back on me yet again, maybe I needed to find some other way to make a living.

Restaurants had been my business for so long, I really hadn't thought about any other kind of job in years. Everywhere I went, there seemed to be help-wanted signs. At the hardware store, they were hiring cashiers. At 7-Eleven, they were hiring a store manager. The more my eyes were opened to the possibilities, the more excited I became. Healthy and free for the first time in years, it slowly dawned on me that I could be anything. Not many people choose to start a new career at fifty-six, but for me, nothing had ever seemed so clear.

Whenever I saw a job posting, the urge to go in and inquire was too tempting to pass up. I spoke to half of the people in Long Branch about potential job offers and that was just in one city. The more we spoke, the easier my search became. I thought about the things that had been great for me at the restaurant and the things that hadn't worked for me. Setting my own hours, designing menus, and interacting with customers were my strongest points. The areas where I struggled were interacting with management and handling monotony. Most of the available jobs in Long Branch were not going to give me the freedom I needed to thrive and would definitely require brainless repetition. This was an opportunity for me to change my life and I couldn't squander it.

On a sunny October afternoon, I was at the courts, taking full advantage of my freedom. I heard the bell ring at the nearby middle school and checked my watch: three o'clock. I took the ball hopper around the court and picked up the balls I had scattered about. As I packed up the trunk, I saw Lauren and her team making their way over to the courts. When she spotted me I could see her expression cloud over in annoyance.

I kept my distance as they warmed up. They had a match against Asbury Park that day and actually had a good chance of winning. One of the hardest parts of watching the Long Branch tennis team play was that they almost always lost. We were among the least well-to-do towns in the area, so our team seemed to be born at a disadvantage. Schools like Red Bank Catholic, St. John Vianney, and Middletown South were in the same division as our girls and many of them had been taking private tennis lessons since they were little kids. The majority of our best players had held a racket for the first time in ninth-grade gym class.

Around three-thirty, a school bus pulled into the parking lot and the girls from Asbury unloaded. They were even less prepared, with too few players. Each meet was made up of five matches—three singles and then two doubles matches. Asbury would automatically forfeit their third singles match, as they didn't have a player for that spot. It was Lauren's senior year, so the first singles position was all hers, and she always faced the best player on the opposing team. Almost every town had at least one solid player, so victory never came easily.

Lauren won the first set 6-2 and was fired up to start the second. She went down 0-1; it was her turn to serve. She served and missed and then missed again, double fault. She shook her head and walked to the other side of the box where I watched her do the exact same thing. I ran from the hood of the car out to where she was standing.

"You gotta toss the ball out in front of you. Let it fall if it's not a good toss," I instructed.

She glared at me. She tossed the ball up again and missed, driving the ball into the bottom of the net.

"Damn it, kid. You have to keep your shoulder up," I said.

She spun around and approached the fence. "Listen, this is my match to win or lose, and you have no idea what you're talking about. Just because you play all the time by yourself doesn't make you a tennis coach!"

"Lauren, I do know what's wrong. You can't see yourself! It's clear as day what you need to do!"

"Dad! You're driving me nuts here every day. If you know so much about tennis, then why don't you become a professional coach! Right now you're just a professional asshole," she retorted.

Her words stung and struck a place deep inside me. She knew me well enough to say the exact thing to hurt me, but her anger was fleeting. Within minutes she would flash me her winning smile as she fired a backhand shot down the line. I took a few breaths as I headed back to the car, knowing that if I responded, I would just distract her more from the match, and that wasn't my intention. Sitting back down, I played the conversation over again and thought about what she had said.

Professional tennis coach; could that be the ticket? It was so far outside the realm of what I did that the thought had never occurred to me. I looked at the girls and thought about how affordable lessons would have dramatically improved the course of play that day. Maybe there was something there, if only I could figure out how to make it work.

HERE I GO AGAIN

"THAT'S IT, RACKET back now, and move your feet, Sarah! Yes, that's excellent! Who's up next?" I asked, looking at the line of kids behind the baseline.

The energy under the dome at the Atlantic Club was fast-paced and seemingly boundless. It had taken me a couple of months, but I studied for and took the Professional Tennis Registry licensing exams over the winter and passed with flying colors. While I knew I wanted to bring tennis to the kids of Long Branch, there weren't any indoor courts in town, so the last piece of the puzzle would have to wait until the summer.

Coaching was turning out to be the most enjoyable job I had ever had. I controlled the number of lessons I gave each week and I got paid well per hour. So with just a few lessons each day, I was making a decent living. The best part was that it didn't really feel like working. Buzzing around the courts felt more like playing around than anything else. It seemed like each lesson was over almost before it began. Time was flying, and so was I.

The only real issue at the Atlantic Club was my own jealousy. There are different levels of certifications from the PTR: Associate Instructor, Instructor, Professional, and Master of

Tennis. The club paid based on your ranking and also gave those with higher rankings better court times and easier access to clientele. Being new to the profession, I had to work my way up, but it was a tough pill for me to swallow. I had been an executive chef, the highest-ranking person in the kitchen, and now I was supposed to roll over and defer to pretty much everyone else at the club. When I complained about it, Nancy advised me to continue working on my certifications.

Every few months, people would go to a regional testing center to demonstrate their skills and take a written exam. I signed up to take the test for the professional license at a facility in South Jersey.

Walking in, I saw that it was a smallish group of maybe ten to fifteen people. The Instructor-level certification had been a much larger group; the further up the ranks you progressed, the more people got weeded out. I looked over my fellow test takers and saw a guy in his mid-forties, with brown hair and lively blue eyes. He looked like he might be a fun companion for the day, so I walked over and set my things down next to him.

"Paul Tharp," the gentleman said, extending his hand.

"John Wagner. Nice to meet you."

As the twelve of us took turns demonstrating our skills and teaching techniques, there were quite a few breaks where Paul and I were able to get to know each other. The guy was definitely a talker. I found out that Paul had already been a PTR Professional for almost a decade, that he was there to renew his license, and that he worked full-time for an organization out of Philadelphia, the Arthur Ashe Youth Tennis Association.

"We work with at-risk groups of youth—you know, the kids who would ordinarily find themselves unsupervised on the streets of Philly and Camden. Our programs in the summer are mostly recreational, with staff members at local courts coaching kids and also doing some basic reading activities," Paul explained. "Then in the winter months, we have a large facility in Manayunk, right outside Philadelphia, where we do after-school groups. Kids get help with their homework in addition to tennis lessons before heading home to their parents. Again, our goal is to keep the kids engaged in healthy activities and teach them skills they can use, both on and off the courts."

That sounded amazing and exactly what I had been thinking about when I planned to provide tennis lessons for the kids of Long Branch.

"You know, Paul, I started doing this because my daughter and her tennis team were a group of kids in similar situations to what you're talking about. Now Long Branch isn't Camden, certainly, but these kids definitely need activities to keep them out of trouble. I'm so glad to hear that programs like this exist."

"John, if you'd like to come down and see what we do, we're always on the lookout for like-minded individuals. I know Philly is a drive for you, but I'd love to show you around," he said, handing me his card.

Going back to work at the Atlantic Club the day after passing the test was harder than I anticipated. Every person who pulled into the parking lot in their luxury vehicle, then grabbed their oversized racket bag with the latest, greatest gear inside irked me. Working in the restaurant business, I had also catered to the whims of the wealthy patrons and, truth be told, it was starting to make me sick. I thought about my own childhood and how amazing it would have been to have a place I could have gone every day to escape the woods and the brutality. That could have changed everything for me. How many more kids like me were there in those hills who could have benefitted from a program like Arthur Ashe? Maybe it was time to start working for the working class.

I made arrangements with Paul to tour his facility in Philly on my day off. I wore my coaching attire, hoping that after the tour we'd be able to hit around some. I was finding that I didn't go many places without wearing a warm-up suit and sneakers. It was almost comical to think that I had spent the last twenty years in starched, ironed whites, and now I got to tool around town in sweatpants.

The facility blew away any preconceived notions about what tennis courts could look like. I was expecting something similar to the club, a domed building with a couple of changing rooms and an observation deck. While Ashe had those things, it also had an entire wing of classrooms with little tables, sofas, and books. There was a completely different feel about the place, an air of importance I hadn't anticipated. Purpose-driven is probably the best way to describe it; every person walking around, every child hitting balls, every coach shouting instructions all hummed with a greater purpose than mere tennis lessons.

"So now that you've seen what we do here, you want to head down onto the courts and play with some of our kids?" Paul asked.

"Absolutely. I was hoping you'd ask," I said.

"I could tell you wanted to hit. Not everyone brings a racket bag for a facility tour." He chuckled.

We walked down onto the immaculate courts. I pulled out my favorite racket and walked over to the side the students were on. The kids smiled at me but never lost their focus on their instructor. While I watched, they took turns running the drill. Ultimately, they were just hitting forehands, but the way the coach laid it out for them was interesting. There were brightly colored rubber spots at various locations on the court. Each kid would hit a forehand at the baseline, run to the service line, hit another shot, and then approach the net to hit a volley. When they finished, the students would run to the other side of the net, collect three balls, put them back in the instructor's bin, and return to their place in line. The transitions were smooth, the kids were constantly in motion, and there was very little downtime. The whole thing ran seamlessly. I got in line with the students and ran through the drill with them twice. After the second run-through, Paul motioned for me to come to the other side of the net where the instructor was.

"Here, you feed them some balls," Paul said.

Moving into coaching position, I picked up a handful of balls and took a deep breath. The instructor stepped off to the side, and I continued the lesson exactly as I had observed. After a couple of rounds, I began to feel more at ease and my instincts took over. The kids took my directions without question, and soon I forgot we were being watched. We kept playing until I heard a whistle cut through the noise.

"Thank you, four o'clock stars! Please grab your gear and head to the locker rooms to change. Your scholar session begins in fifteen minutes," came a voice on a loudspeaker.

The students responded immediately. Their discipline was impressive. I hadn't seen such willing regimentation since the military. As they filed out, I approached Paul and the coach.

"Hi, I'm Lisa Tharp," the instructor said, wiping her hands on a towel. "You did well out there."

"Pleased to meet you, Lisa. Are you two related?"

"Yes, John. This is my wife, Lisa." Paul laughed. "Neither of us normally instructs directly anymore, but we wanted to test you out together."

"I didn't realize this was a test." I shifted uncomfortably. "I hope I passed."

Paul patted me on the back. "You did great. Let's move into the office and talk this thing through."

They were looking for regional supervisors for the summer program. They employed a head instructor and a few support staff at each court. Supervisors had to have a basic knowledge of tennis and some level of PTR certification. The rest of the crew would be akin to camp counselors. The regional supervisor wouldn't have just one court program to look after; he would drive from location to location over the course of the day and check in with each court. If anything came up that was out of the ordinary or they were running low on supplies, the supervisor would communicate to the headquarters in Philly. The pay was decent—not quite the same hourly rate as I would make in private lessons, but it was a consistent nine-to-five job, something I had never had before. The only issue with it was the location. The area I would be supervising was in Camden, which was roughly an hour's commute from home. If I had to go to the headquarters, it would be closer to an hour and a half each way.

This job was so close to what I had envisioned for Long Branch, I couldn't pass it up. A program that would help keep kids off the streets and out of trouble, while at the same time introducing them to the game I loved? It was almost too good to be true. At the very least, I would be able to see what they were doing for a summer and then try to replicate it in my own neighborhood. Paul encouraged me to approach the Long Branch recreation department and try to get a satellite program going. We wouldn't be able to use the Arthur Ashe name there, as they didn't have funding for another program, but we would have access to their leadership.

It took about an hour to settle on which sites I would supervise, how many courts was a realistic number to oversee, and how many staff members would be reporting to me. We agreed upon a salary for the summer months, with a plan to reconnect toward the end of the program to figure out what I could do for the winter. Being no stranger to seasonal employment, I knew how dangerous it was to give up my gig at the Atlantic Club, which provided year-round steady employment, to work for a nonprofit a few months out of the year. But there was only one thing for me to consider, really: the kids. For the first time in my life, I would be doing something to help the community and be a part of something bigger than myself. There was absolutely no two ways about it; being regional supervisor for Arthur Ashe was definitely the direction for me.

REDEMPTION SONG

I FINALLY UNDERSTOOD why Nancy was able to keep the same job all of these years. In addition to the stability it had provided for the family, doing something for the greater good just felt right. It was almost intoxicating. The sense of working for something larger than yourself could drive you out of bed early in the morning. I found myself the happiest I had been in years, maybe ever. The only thing holding me back was how isolated I felt from the family. Lauren was away at school in Delaware, so her visits were few and far between, and they seemed to be over as quickly as they began. Jon-boy was in his first year of high school. He was a drummer in the marching band and showed some real promise. In addition, he had shocked everyone in the family when he decided to go out for the boy's tennis team. Nancy was everywhere—super involved in her church, driving Jonathan around town to hang with his skate friends or to a band rehearsal or a concert. It felt like we were all moving in different directions, living in our own busy worlds.

Even though Lauren wasn't on the tennis team anymore, I had kept in touch with some of the girls and their parents who wanted to pursue private lessons. While we waited for school to let out for the summer and for the sessions at Ashe to start up, I kept myself busy attending meetings with Ashe organizers, making sure the sites in South Jersey were clean and ready, while also doing some afternoon lessons in Long Branch. Since the courts at the high school were occupied by the tennis team, I had to get creative. The city had built a new park near the projects in the middle of Long Branch, complete with a baseball diamond, basketball courts, a playground and two tennis courts with a practice wall behind them. That's where I would meet Meliza and Sarah, the two young ladies I taught after school a couple of days per week.

Some afternoons it would be just the three of us hitting at the park, with their parents dropping them off and picking them up. As summer approached, the park grew busier with basketball and the occasional softball or baseball game. Soon a security guard began working at the small storage building near the basketball courts. He would sign out equipment and was also responsible for locking up each evening as dusk approached and the courts were closing. One night as I was loading up my car, he approached me in the parking lot.

"Hey, mister, you know you could lock your balls up in the back if you wanted to. We got a whole room for storage and only a couple of basketballs and bases for the field back there."

"Oh, uh, thanks. I think I'll hold on to the stuff, though. I use it all the time, not just here. What did you say your name was?"

"They call me Six Nine—started in high school on the basketball court." He smiled and shrugged. The guy was massive, and his name reflected his size.

"That's cool. My name is John. You know, Six Nine, I was wondering how you got this job here. I want to talk to someone about a summer tennis program at these courts."

"I work for the recreation department. My boss's name is Timmy, but his boss is Mr. Kyle. He runs everything over at the office."

I thanked him and resumed packing up the trunk. It was already too late in the day to expect them to be open, but I intended to visit the main office first thing the next morning. We had a tennis program to design.

The director of the recreation department, Kyle Jennings, was a warm and welcoming man. He surprised me by inviting me to sit down in his office right when I arrived. I was anticipating making an appointment and having to come back another day, so I have to admit that I was anxious at being put on the spot. His demeanor was so calm that just being in his presence relaxed me. Before I knew it, I was animatedly describing the program I had envisioned for the past several years.

"The children of this town are at a disadvantage, Mr. Jennings. The annual average income is low, lower than low, and most children are being raised either in a single-parent environment or in a home where both of their parents need to work in order to make ends meet. What they are left with is hours upon hours of unsupervised, unstructured time, especially in the summer and in the after-school hours. I know the town runs a summer program—both of my children attended it—but they spend most of their time cooped up inside, playing board games and working on art projects. I was raised in the South, and even when we had nothing, we had the ability to go outside and play.

"None of this is news to you, but I came here today to help solve this problem. I am a professionally trained and certified tennis instructor, and I work for the Arthur Ashe Association out of Philadelphia. We are dedicated to innovative youth tennis and education programs that assist children in finding healthy alternatives to life on the streets, namely through participation in our tennis programs. I don't know exactly how we can structure it to work here in Long Branch, but I was hoping you could help with that," I concluded, looking at him expectantly.

His face cracked wide open in a big toothy grin. "Mr. Wagner, I like it. I like your passion, enthusiasm, and ideas for this town's youth. I will have to look at the budget—I'm not sure what we can do on such short notice—but I give you my word I will do my best to see what can be done for this summer. Thanks for coming in. You really got my wheels turning this morning."

Even if the program didn't get off the ground, I knew that I had done my part. Speaking about my vision was easy once I got started. My excitement was palpable; I hoped it was also contagious. The children had been spoken for and now their fate was in someone else's hands.

It took a few weeks of going about my business, checking on the courts in Camden, meeting my site instructors, and doing my afternoon lessons before I heard back from Long Branch Rec. They were in. They were going to be able to fund a six-week program, with six hours of lessons, three two-hour sessions for different age groups. They could afford to pay me to supervise and have three on-site instructors. I would have to take a drug test, which was laughable when I realized I would actually be able to pass, and they mentioned they had conducted a background check. They hadn't asked me if I had a criminal record, and I wasn't going to be the one to bring it up. Aside from that, the only catch was that I needed to find my own staff.

Meliza was going to graduate that year and had become a good player under my instruction. She was looking for summer work and I knew she would be a good fit. Meliza was a good kid, but she didn't have the leadership skills or personality to run the whole site. I needed charisma. I needed spunk. I needed Lauren. She was due home from college in a few days, and already had several jobs lined up for the summer. She was planning to work at two restaurants to earn her spending money for the following year at school. The good news was that she was planning to work nights, which meant that her days were still wide open. If I had the two girls to run the camp, then all I needed was a support person. Someone to help pick up balls and keep the kids in line while they were waiting their turn. Jon-boy was good for that spot. At sixteen, he was old enough to work for the city and could benefit from the structure of a job.

With my crew assembled in both locations, we were all set for a fantastic season. It was hard to believe that my vision was about to be realized. Opening day was unlike any other kickoff I had ever had. I thought restaurants were busy, but I had failed to recognize the enthusiasm and energy that would come when your customers were children. There were kids everywhere. Every site I stopped by to check on in Camden had at least twenty kids present and accounted for. They came from every nook and cranny in the city and were completely unprepared for play. They treated rackets like they were baseball bats, and instead of trying to keep the ball inside the lines, they swung for the fences and cheered when they hit home runs. At each site we had to designate someone to chase down all the balls as they sailed over the fences to ensure we would have enough left to play the following day. As I watched the kids learn how to hold a racket properly and saw their disappointment when they learned the goal was to keep the ball inside the park, I couldn't help but fondly remember teaching Jonathan those same lessons.

I decided to check in on Long Branch around three o'clock. By then, they should've been halfway through their day. With just a few weeks to advertise, I wasn't sure how many kids they would have or how many people would be interested. I called Lauren, and she answered on the fifth ring, breathless.

"Hey, Dad. What's up?" she asked quickly.

"Just checking in. You busy?"

"You have no idea. Dad, there are forty kids here right now. And they're all over the map. I have six-year-olds and sixteen-year-olds, all ready to play at the same time, and only two courts."

Forty kids? That blew away any expectations I had for the camp. I knew that our town needed the program, but I guess I had underestimated how many people would take us up on our offer. We wrapped up our conversation so Lauren could get back to the kids, with the intention of talking that night about how we could best structure the days to make the program more efficient after her waitressing job. I was starting to see that the reason Ashe functioned so well was the careful planning and preparation during the winter months. The Long Branch program lacked that foresight, so we would need to get creative to catch up.

When Lauren walked in the back door at ten that night, exhaustion rolled off her. As she took her shoes off, she launched into her ideas for the Long Branch program. She was planning to split them into groups by age and ability so each session would have a better flow. The youngest kids would come first and the age groups would progress until the four o'clock session, which would be for the high school kids. As she talked, I realized how proud of her I was. The kid was growing into a beautiful and intelligent adult, capable of handling multiple jobs while acing college. I had always known she would be great, but it was amazing to see her blossoming right before my eyes.

"Dad, did you hear me? Why aren't you listening?" she demanded.

Smiling, I grabbed her and pulled her in for a hug, "I'm listening, kid. You did good today. Real good."

She smiled crookedly and hugged me back. "This is going to be a helluva summer."

Being with the kids each day was the best part of that summer. There was this incredible balance between interacting with Paul and Lisa at the Ashe headquarters and then getting to spend the rest of the day with our students. Don't get me wrong, it was exhausting work, and at the end of the day I fell asleep easily. Rewarding work and giving back to communities that were desperately in need suited me. A lot of the guilt and resentment I had harbored found release in this work, while being so busy kept my mind from wandering.

As the weeks passed, we all fell into a working rhythm. I would spend Monday through Thursday down at the Ashe sites, with periodic check-ins on Long Branch. On Friday I would spend the day in Long Branch, checking in on Camden as needed. Lauren, Meliza, and Jonathan were doing a great job. They were doing so well, in fact, that the high school tennis coach started sending her players to the four o'clock session. It was a great way for them to hit together before the official practice season started. In the earlier classes, we had plenty of kids whose parents brought them each day, but we also had some students who came directly from the projects next door on their own. They would be there when we set up in the morning and wouldn't leave until we closed up for the night. The benefits for the kids of Long Branch looked to be exactly what we had hoped.

It was a Wednesday morning when my phone rang; I was on site in Camden.

"Dad. This is really, really bad." Lauren was frantic. "I don't know what I am supposed to do. There's blood everywhere, and there's kids here!"

"Whoa, slow down, kid. What blood?" I asked, covering my other ear so I could hear her better.

"Jonathan and I are here to set up for the day, and we got the equipment out of the hut and were bringing it back to the courts. I saw David and TyKing playing around on the baseball bleachers. When they saw us pull up, they came running and told me there was something on the courts. I told Jonathan to stay with them so I could check it out. There's a pool of blood, a bloody condom, a little girl's T-shirt, and a broken charm necklace. Dad, I'm really scared."

"Okay. You can do this," I told her. "Keep the kids on the basketball courts with Jonathan. Call the rec office and let them know what's going on, but first you have to call the police. I'm getting in the car now and will be there soon."

Down in Camden, we had encountered problems with drug addicts using the courts to shoot up, get drunk, and do God knows what else. We would often have to spend the first fifteen minutes each morning sweeping up vials and used needles to make sure the courts were safe for the kids to use. While Long Branch had never experienced that, this seemed to be much, much worse than a couple of baggies littering the courts. If Lauren's description was accurate, something very bad had gone down in that park the night before.

It took me an hour and a half to get to the courts. I figured the place would be crawling with cops and lessons would be cancelled for the day. Lauren could handle this situation, but she could be really sensitive so I was hoping that she could keep it together for the kids. As I rounded the corner, I was shocked at the scene before me. Or should I say, the lack of a scene before me. The Long Branch Rec public works pickup truck was there, and I could see Timmy and his crew out on the courts. I didn't see a single flashing light or police officer anywhere.

"What's going on?" I asked as I walked up, Lauren and Jonathan were standing under the gazebo with their arms crossed.

"The cops didn't do anything," Lauren said, dejected. "They walked around a bit and just told us that it was probably a prostitute on her period."

"But what about the necklace and the little girl's T-shirt?"

"Yeah, I don't know. They just told us it wasn't a crime scene. They didn't take any pictures or evidence. We were instructed to clean it up and move on. That's what Timmy and his guys are working on now. Jonathan and I walked around the fields and the creek behind the courts ourselves to look, but we didn't see anything, so I guess there's nothing else we can do."

We opened the courts for the late afternoon tennis session. Our little guys, David and TyKing, hung around all day, waiting for lessons to start. The crew clearly needed a pick-me-up, so I bought McDonald's for everyone. Watching Lauren and Jonathan eat, I realized that they had never experienced anything like this before. While I may have exposed them to things that were beyond their years and maturity levels while I was using, they had never seen violence like this. They also had never been let down by the authorities before. Cops were still the glossy superheroes they saw on TV. You called them when you had a problem and they made things better. Today they had learned that wasn't always true. Police officers were people just like everyone else. Sometimes they got it right, but often enough, they got it wrong.

DREAM ON

ASHE WAS A well-oiled machine that only required periodic check-ins with headquarters. I spent most of my days doing exactly what I loved, teaching the kids. Parents, teachers, and coaches are never supposed to have favorites, but let's be honest, we all do. My favorite court was located in downtown Camden. The instructors were big guys, which was helpful for clearing out the homeless in the morning. I'd ride up with coffee for the crew, and we'd set to sweeping the courts, picking up any paraphernalia that was littered around the playground, and then set up drills for the kids.

Teaching for a few hours in the morning allowed me to clear my head and gave me an unprecedented clarity of purpose. By the time I headed in to headquarters, I was already bursting with ideas to share with Paul and Lisa. Today, the idea was a tournament. Held at each site, it would be a culminating activity and give the students something to focus on. When I told Paul my idea, he laughed. Of course there was going to be a tournament. Only the next best part was that the winners from each site would be invited and bussed to Ashe in Philadelphia to compete in a grand end-of-season tournament. The purpose was twofold. There was the obvious culmination of a season's worth of lessons, but the other reason was much more intriguing. Because many students came from families where tennis wasn't a sport that was often played or even seen on TV, holding a tournament and awarding students for their progress was a way to show the parents that their child had actually learned a skill. And more than that, it praised the students for their determination and rewarded them for their efforts.

The last week of the program was dedicated to the tournaments. Lauren organized a tournament for Long Branch; each day was a different exposition. One day was a ground-stroke demo. The next, the students had the opportunity to show off their serve. By the middle of the week, the courts were crowded with parents and siblings, eager to witness their children compete for the title of champion within their respective age brackets. As I watched the kids' excitement grow, I realized that there was one distinct group of supporters missing: TyKing's family.

The child had spent more time on the court than any of the other students. He was always waiting for us to arrive in the morning and the last to leave at the end of the day. Most days, he didn't even leave when we left. He would simply walk over to the basketball courts and work his way into a group of kids playing. He was, by far, the best student in the ten-year-old class, and there would be no one here to cheer for him when he won. This realization took away from the spirit of the moment and reminded me that sometimes, no matter how hard we try, there are simply some things that sheer effort cannot overcome. We would continue to try and lift this boy up, of course, but without any support at home, chances were that he would fall victim to his surroundings.

With enthusiasm and genuine excitement, the students showcased the skills they had harnessed over the six-week summer programs. In the grand scheme of things, six weeks was nothing but a drop in the bucket of time, but the children could soak up so much in a few short weeks. The students took turns playing one another, keeping score, and filling the role of linesmen. As the parents watched, their children acted with maturity and displayed real skills. By the time we began awarding certificates and trophies, everyone was on their feet. Seeing the pride and joy on the students' faces as they accepted their awards was a life-changing moment. Our hard work had been worth it, and it was clear that this program really did mean something to both the kids and their parents. Six weeks each year was simply not going to be enough; the kids deserved more than that.

Just as I began to wonder what we were to do next, Ashe revealed that it had one more trick up its sleeve for the end of the season. All of the students and some of their parents would be taking a trip to New York City. The US Open was played in Flushing, Queens, each summer, beginning the last week in August. The final Grand Slam tournament of the professional tennis season was kicked off with a unique event: Arthur Ashe Kids Day. The US Open would be the first tennis match I would get to attend, and I was so excited. I pushed Paul to throw some tickets at the Long Branch program and, before long, everyone was buzzing with the excitement.

On the morning of the trip, I woke early. Coming down the stairs, I heard the shower running; Lauren was awake, too. After we finished getting ready, we stopped at Dunkin' Donuts to get coffee and some doughnuts for the kids. The forty kids and most of their parents were all scheduled to meet us at six in the morning in the parking lot of the Senior Citizens Center on Second Avenue. It was five-thirty when we got there, and when I saw the massive group assembled by the bus, I couldn't help but chuckle. Every single one of the kids and their chaperones was there and ready to board the bus. The excitement was infectious, and as Lauren and I got out of the car, they clapped and cheered.

I directed everyone to board the bus and told the driver we were ready to leave.

"Wait!" Lauren exclaimed, "We aren't ready yet."

As I watched, Lauren pulled out a large manila envelope. Inside was a roster, signed permission slips, and the tickets from Ashe. She walked down the aisle checking off groups of parents and their children. As she did so, she handed each adult a paperclipped, numbered stack of tickets. There were a handful of older students whose parents were not planning to attend, which we had okayed in advance. Lauren assigned those kids to groups that had a parent with them and gave the tickets to the adult in charge.

"All right, all chaperones, when I call your name, please call out your cell phone number, in case we need to reach you throughout the day."

One by one, the adults all complied, and Lauren wrote down the numbers on her roster.

"Thank you for your help! Let's go to New York City!" she cried as she gave the bus driver a thumbs-up.

As she slid into the seat across from me, I thought about how this program seemed to have benefitted more than just the kids and their families. Lauren had truly embraced her role of site supervisor and grown into a mature adult. The level of organization that she displayed could have only come from one place: her mother. I forgot my underwear some days, so she definitely hadn't gotten that from me. It took me seeing her through the eyes of the parents on the trip to comprehend the changes that had taken place in her over the course of her first year at college and that summer. Sometimes the things that are right in front of us are the hardest to see.

The grounds at Billie Jean King National Tennis Center were massive. As we approached the bus parking area, you could see the large globe fountain and remnants of the World's Fair towers in the distance. There were crowds of people spilling out of the main gate and pouring over the pedestrian walkways and entrance bridge. The energy levels soared as we exited the bus and gathered into our small groups for the day. The chatter of the kids grew louder as we began to mingle into the throngs of people making their way inside the grounds. As we reached the crest of the bridge and saw the walkway turn right toward the main entrance, a hush descended on my group; they were awestruck.

Like many other aspects of the game of tennis, attending an elite event such as the U.S. Open was previously out of reach for the children of Long Branch. While some may have attended a local sporting event before, for many this was their first stadium experience. In addition to the main Ashe stadium, there were two other large courts, the Grandstand and Louis Armstrong Stadium. Topping that were the field courts; I counted sixteen. On a given day of match play, you could catch one or two of the top players in the stadiums and then a bunch of less-attended side matches on the field courts. This Kids Day event was special because it was more of an exposition than actual match play. The big stars would all be involved in the day's main event, a large show at Ashe Stadium, and would also be playing and practicing on the side courts, as match play for the Open was scheduled to officially begin the next day. On some of the side courts, there were competitions and games that the kids could play while rubbing elbows with mega stars.

Around the outside of Ashe Stadium were shops, info booths, and food courts. There was enough to keep everyone occupied for a few hours, and before I knew what had happened, I noticed the crowds had started to thin out. Checking my watch, I realized that the main show was going to begin any minute. As I made my way through the turnstiles and onto the escalators to the upper level, I took in the sweeping view around me. The grounds were immaculately kept, and the globe fountain reflected the sun at a perfect angle. It was a great day for tennis.

I joined Lauren and the kids just in time for the event to kick off. There were games, jokes, skits, and musical performances for our viewing pleasure, and please us they did. The first people to hit the court were Andre Agassi, James Blake, and the Williams sisters. The kids all cheered, and even I was awestruck. Agassi had been my favorite player for years, and to get to watch him live was a real treat. The students were much more interested in the Williams sisters, and as those two hit

Coach John and the Long Branch Recreation Tennis Program—2005

back and forth on the court, the stadium came alive. The normal hush that fell over a tennis match just didn't fit in at Kids Day. The players and the crowd existed on a different plane; the cheering grew louder and the players hit harder, until one couldn't coax the other to rise any higher. The symbiosis was inspiring.

As the last musician took the stage, I reflected on how far we had come. Kids who had never held a racket before this summer were in the greatest tennis stadium in America, watching elite stars play for their entertainment. Lauren was a bona-fide instructor, complete with management skills ready to take responsibility for fifty people on a field trip to the busiest city in the world. And me, I had done this for them. I had an idea and a vision for what this program could be, and I had made it a reality. I hadn't taken the easy way out and I had done something that benefitted people other than myself; I was proud.

CARRY ON WAYWARD SON

IT STARTED OFF innocently enough. Tennis was everything that I had hoped for, and I was able to find employment for most of the year. I worked for Ashe and Long Branch Rec in the summer and did private lessons in some of the wealthier towns on the outdoor courts during the summer and fall. I covered winter coaching the Long Branch kids one day a week at a local racket club that cut the regular fees for us. Lauren had finished college and was working as a special education teacher in New York. Jon was pretty much done with high school and had his sights set on New York City for college. Nancy, well, I wasn't exactly sure what she was up to, but I knew she was busy.

For so much of my life, especially my sober life, Nancy and the kids were all around me. They'd come to my restaurants for dinner— hell, they worked with me a lot of the time. With tennis, both kids worked with me for years, but they had moved on from that. If I had to explain the place for Amelia in my life, it would have to be to fill some sort of void, but I'm jumping ahead.

I had taken a gig at a new local restaurant, just for the winter; some cleaning and prep work during the morning hours to pass time and make a little money. The Avenue was in a brand new shopping area in downtown Long Branch that was designed for the summer tourists. After work, I would often stop in the shops and chat with the store owners and also try to drum up some tennis lessons for when the weather turned. One store's name was Nirvana. It was a high-end clothing shop, but it was the name that made me go in. It called to my inner hippie, reminded me of my years practicing yoga and my letters with Swami Sivananda in the Bahamas. I shopped around, looking at clothes for Nancy, when a clerk stopped by to see how I was making out. After a few minutes of exchanging pleasantries, I began to shift gears and explained that I was a tennis instructor. The shop girl, who was probably about Lauren's age, rang me up and expressed an interest in hitting with me, specifically in taking lessons. I gave her my phone number and told her to give me a call.

The next few months passed quickly. The girl from Nirvana, Amelia, became a regular on the courts. She took instruction well and before long was assisting me with the kids in the Long Branch program on Sunday nights. It was perfect; she was capable of supervising the kids and making sure the courts were in order so I could focus on the instruction. She lacked the technical ability to coach, but I was confident that if we spent enough time on the basics, she would be able to play at a much higher level.

Getting to know her, I found out that Amelia's father was not in the picture; she lived with her mother, who had been her primary caregiver for most of her life. Money was always tight for them, and Amelia didn't have the opportunity to attend college. She was absolutely desperate to rise above her working-class roots and seemed willing to put in the work in order to get there. Honestly, she reminded me of Tara, a kid looking for a way out, in need of some guidance.

As we spent more and more time together; Nancy began to get anxious about our relationship. Who was this girl? Why was I spending so much time riding around town with her? I knew there was more to her attitude toward Amelia than met the eye. Maybe she was actually worried less about the time spent with Amelia and more about the lack of time that she and I had been spending together. And that was a real issue for us; we didn't really have anything in common now that the kids had basically left home. There weren't any games to attend, recitals to see, or plays to watch. There was only us and our history, which spanned volumes. Last but not least was the money problem: we didn't have any. Not to say we were broke, but putting Lauren through school had certainly tightened the budget, and now Jon was heading to a private college. Pair that with my seasonal employment and affection for expensive things, and we had a recipe for a precarious financial situation.

One afternoon, after wrapping up a lesson with Amelia, we were driving down Broadway in my old blue Saab, when I spotted a deep jade-green Jaguar sitting on the edge of the lot at Premier Motors.

"Oh God, wow. Isn't that beautiful?" I exclaimed as I slowed to admire the Jag.

"It's really pretty," Amelia agreed.

"I would do almost anything for a car like that," I mumbled.

"Why don't we go look at it?" Amelia asked.

Turned out the car was listed at a really good price, only $10,000 more than my Saab was worth. The more I sat in it and felt the smooth leather under my fingers, the more I wanted it. The dashboard had this gorgeous blondewood inlay, and the car responded to voice commands. It could tell you the temperature or adjust settings on command. I had never ridden in anything like it.

The question came to me across a wave of emotion. "Why don't you get it?"

I deserved to have something nice. I worked hard, day in and day out. Nancy had her jewelry, Lauren got college, Jon-boy had the half-pipe we had built him in the backyard; wasn't it time I got something out of working and staying clean? I knew I didn't have the cash, but if I traded the Saab, there had to be some way to make the car affordable. I got them to come down $2,000 on the price, with a balance of $8,000 after trading in the Saab. I pulled out my American Express and handed it over. Watching the owner walk away with my card, I glanced over at Amelia. Her eyes were wild; she was excited.

Nancy had stopped yelling at me years ago. If I had been expecting a battle over the car, I was going to be disappointed. She asked me how much it cost and how I had paid for it. I told her I used my Amex and that it was a really good deal. She set her lips in a line and responded in short clipped phrases. She was pissed but, truthfully, I didn't much care. I deserved that car and wasn't going to be made to feel guilty for finally doing something for myself.

Driving around in that car was more fun than had I anticipated. People watched me as I drove past them, and I absolutely loved answering questions about it. It was like becoming a member of an elite club that had previously denied me access. For service, I stopped going to Premier and started going to the Jaguar dealership. Walking around in there was fun; seeing the cars on the showroom floor and people-watching the other owners only reinforced my satisfaction. The bills were almost double at the dealership what they would have been at Premier, but I was unfazed. I loved that car.

Somewhere in the midst of that new car smell, Amelia and I crossed a line. Our teacher-student relationship morphed, and for the first time in my life, I was on the cheating end of an affair. Acting as a father figure or mentor to younger women wasn't new for me, but somehow this was different from my relationships with Tara or Meliza. Maybe it was just that she was willing to make our relationship more, whereas none of the other young women were interested. Another variable was Amelia's age. She was twenty-six, and Tara had been at most nineteen. Somehow those few years made a difference. My behavior was impulsive, reckless even, but it was intoxicating being with someone with whom I shared no responsibilities. We never had to talk about money or bills; there was only fun and adventures waiting to be had.

As my midlife crisis deepened, I felt more and more disconnected from the family man I had once been. My obligations didn't matter anymore. I was having fun living life on my own terms. I didn't think about the implications of what I was doing—I just acted. Each day I'd wake up excited for what that day had in store. I'd spend my time riding around, teaching lessons here and there, and hanging out with Amelia. The darkest part of my day was when I'd come home at night and be faced with the double life I was leading. It was exhausting, truth be told, trying to fend off questions and keep up the illusion that everything was normal.

As the summer breeze faded and the tennis programs closed up for the year, the familiar nagging, depressive feeling began creeping in. It was going to get cold, and I would get bored. Without tennis as an excuse, seeing Amelia was becoming more difficult to pull off. With the lies came guilt, and with the guilt, the glow began to dull. Instead of looking forward to the time we would spend having lunch or driving around town, I began to dread my phone. Every time it'd ring, I would tense up, hoping, praying that the caller ID would read someone else's name. If I didn't answer, the calls would become more frequent, the demands more insistent. As I was trying to pump the brakes, Amelia was pushing the gas pedal straight into the floor.

The situation with Amelia was bad. She was calling night and day, and Nancy had drawn a line in the sand; she didn't want me spending any more time with her. The harder I pushed Amelia away, the closer she tried to pull herself in. She threatened to show up at the house. The more I wanted the relationship to end, the clearer all I stood to lose became.

I had to get away from it; there had to be a way for the situation to cool off and for Amelia to find something or someone else to focus on. I decided to do something drastic. I needed to go somewhere where winter didn't exist, somewhere far away from this crisis I had created. As I watched the beach houses in Deal close up for the winter season, I realized that all of these people went somewhere when it was cold, and that somewhere was south.

Since my mother's death, I hadn't been back to Florida, or really even thought much about it. Her passing had seemed to close that chapter of my life permanently, but now I needed somewhere to go where I could still teach lessons and get away from Amelia. Mentally, I created a list of all of the people I knew who might still live down there. My brother, Tony, and his daughter were still down there, but I wasn't sure what they were up to; I had been pretty self-absorbed in recent years. The only other person I could really think of easily was Francis, one of the purveyors I had become friendly with at Redhead's. His wife had passed away, and to escape the constant reminders of his life with her, Francis had moved to Florida. Connecting with him might just be my way out.

I had to sell the family on the move without it looking suspicious. Nancy was all for me having steady work throughout the off-season; with Jonathan's tuition bills looming, she was relatively easy to convince. Jon didn't seem very interested when I explained it all to him; he didn't really want much to do with me. Not that I could blame him. The summer session at Long Branch Rec had been rocky this year, as he was finishing his last season as an assistant coach and was working directly with Amelia on a daily basis. I don't think he liked her to begin with; even before we began our affair, he didn't take direction from her well. Anyway, he was glad to be rid of me.

Lauren didn't respond as positively as I'd hoped. Always one with an inquisitive mind, she had a ton of questions. Unfortunately, I lacked the answers. Where would I live? How long would I stay? Where would I work? How would I get down there? Were her parents getting divorced, again? As she questioned me, I would only be able to get out of town if I went to see her first. She had been begging me to come and see her new school and had come up with some crazy plan that involved me doing a cooking activity with her students. She wanted me to wear my chef uniform, as she had been doing a unit with her students and had them all excited to meet a real-life chef. I promised her I would come up and leave from the city for Florida, instead of from Long Branch.

Pulling up to her school in Chelsea, I parked the Jag around the corner. It was loaded up with all my tennis equipment and two additional duffel bags of clothing. It was a gorgeous November day and I was enjoying the fresh air. I let a full breath fill my lungs as I walked up to the front door and saw Lauren, waiting for me by the security desk.

"Looking good, Dad," she commented, as she reached out to hug me.

"Same to you, kid," I said, kissing the top of her head.

"Let's go see the kids. And remember, Dad, if you get uncomfortable or nervous with them, just say you need to go to the bathroom and take a break," she instructed.

Lauren's classroom was around a corner and down the hall. As we turned into her corridor, I was struck by the amount of equipment in the halls. There were walkers, wheelchairs, and all sorts of other gadgets lining the walls. She opened the door to her classroom and I tried my best to keep my composure. The children were seated around a U-shaped table, looking up at me from underneath their very own chef hats. Each student in the room had a severe disability. Lauren had told me this before I agreed to come, but looking at their sweet, innocent faces and realizing that the majority of them were seated in wheelchairs was almost too much for me to bear.

"Boys and girls, meet Chef John. He is here with us today to make our fall recipe this week, pumpkin cheesecake!" Lauren began.

Hearing her voice and seeing the enthusiasm erupt not only from the students but also from the many classroom aides brought me out of my head and back into reality.

"Who's ready to make some cheesecake?" I asked.

Over the course of the next hour, we mixed, we poured, and we measured out the ingredients for the cheesecake. I watched as the students used computers to talk to one another, in order to overcome their speech disabilities, answer questions, and ask for a turn. They definitely had physical disabilities, but I could see why Lauren was drawn to them. Their smiles and excitement were infectious, just like the kids we coached. Cooking with them was a true gift, a fantastic break from the twisted reality I had been living for the past few months. As the students got ready to have lunch and the aides cleaned up the classroom, I motioned to Lauren that I had to go. She hugged me tightly as she said goodbye, careful not to look at me too long so she wouldn't cry in front of the kids.

"Come back soon," she said.

As I sat in my car in my chef uniform, with all of my belongings loaded into the backseat, ready to head to Florida, it hit me how screwed up everything was, how screwed up I was. Somewhere over the last year I had lost sight of what was important, that the work I did was for the kids. It wasn't about a fast car or a fat bank account, it was about the pure, unadulterated joy that came from teaching children. If I hadn't been sure before, I was now. I had to move past this mess and get back to the basics of the tennis program.

RUNAWAY

I ARRIVED IN Florida mostly unscathed, save for a few speeding tickets I got along the way. I tucked the tickets above the visor and decided to worry about them once I got settled. Francis recommended an apartment complex for me to look into. He and the owner were friends, or at least friendly, and he was able to get me a pretty good deal on a furnished unit. I had brought some of my inheritance money from my mother with me to cover rent and security. I hated dipping into that fund, but I knew I'd be able to put it back once work picked up.

While I was getting situated, my phone rang incessantly, and the caller ID seemed to be screaming her name over and over. Amelia was not going to let up. Part of me liked that she couldn't seem to let me go, but the rest of me knew that she was dangerous. I decided that answering her call and telling her I'd left for Florida should put a damper on things, that she would have to understand that, at least geographically, I was off-limits and that she should move on.

"Easier said than done" seemed to be the current driving force in my life. I lasted just a week in Florida before Amelia arrived. Her argument was compelling; here, no one knew us. We could experiment with our relationship and really see if we were a good match. I had already moved out of the house I shared with my wife; why not truly give us a chance?

Finding work proved more difficult than I had anticipated. All of the outdoor courts seemed to have a resident tennis pro, as did most of the clubs. As the hours and days ticked by and I still didn't have a job, I became increasingly desperate.

Whenever I stopped to think, which was far too often for my liking, I was faced with the facts that I was living in an apartment in Florida, with Amelia, without work, and in an ever-expanding lie. Lying had been my specialty when I was using, but sober I was finding it more and more difficult to field calls from Nancy and Lauren. Fixing the work situation was beyond my reach, as was the mess of my relationship with Amelia. The only thing I could control was my sobriety.

It started with cigarettes, just to take the edge off, to give my hands something to do. If I couldn't calm my mind, I could at least keep my hands occupied. That wasn't enough, though. My mind was the true source of the anxiety and the best way to calm a racing mind was smoking a little pot. Francis smoked, so getting some was no problem. He brought over what he had, a meager little stash, and rolled us up a joint. As we smoked, he put on some music. Sweet relief! In less than five minutes, I went from a high-strung ball of nerves to some semblance of my former self. Relaxed, we started to talk through the work situation and I realized I had been going about this all wrong. I was free in Florida. I didn't have any responsibilities. I had enough cash to make it through the winter. What I really needed to do was relax a bit and take my mind off regular life.

With a new game plan, I started to feel better. I went out to the courts each day and hit around with Amelia. Occasionally, Francis would come by, too. Under the warmth of the Florida sun, life was almost easy, easier than it had been in years, decades, or maybe ever. Once I relaxed, the fun we were having enticed others to approach us. With a couple mixed doubles matches, I began to make friends in the industry, explaining that I was in town for the winter, looking for some seasonal work. There didn't seem to be much to go around, was the general consensus, but I did manage to pick up a few random lessons as a substitute for one of the local pros who had injured his shoulder.

As the weeks passed, the money in my reserves was beginning to run low. I still had my credit cards, but I had already started to fall behind on some of the bills. If we were going to stay in Florida, I would need to find something steady. As much as I loved tennis, I needed to have money coming in, and if I couldn't make a buck on the courts, I would need to shift my focus slightly. I started looking for work in one of the many restaurants in town, but I didn't want to be an executive chef; I didn't want the kind of responsibility that came with that. All I really needed was something simple, like a line cook or a prep guy, similar to my job at the Avenue. It was the hot season for Florida tourism, and with my résumé and experience, it seemed like I would be able to have my pick of jobs.

"What are you really doing down there?" Lauren demanded one day, over the phone.

"Uh, what do you mean?" I asked. I was too high for this conversation.

"I mean, do you just, like, live in Florida now? Mom told me you found a job working as line cook. I don't get it. I thought you moved there to coach tennis for the winter. You could be a cook up here, if that's what you wanted to do."

I shook my head, trying to get the fog to clear. She wasn't wrong. I motioned to Amelia to be quiet as I made my way across the room toward the door to the parking lot. I probably shouldn't have picked up. I just hadn't anticipated this kind of phone call.

"Kid, I have to do something. I'm not finding any lessons down here, and I'm running out of money," I explained, my tone soothing.

"Dad! You are there to make money, not spend it. You were going to make it through the winter, get money to pay for Jonathan's school, and then get back here to work for Ashe for the summer and run Long Branch. This sounds like more than that, like you're planning to stay down there. What's down there for you?"

I didn't know how to answer. When all the pieces were laid out that way, my getting a job at a new restaurant did seem like a change to the story I had told when I was leaving New Jersey. That was apparent even to me, in a time when not much made sense.

"Look, I obviously don't know what's going on down there—that's clear," Lauren snarled. "But if you're leaving us, you should probably tell someone. Hiding in Florida isn't going to last forever. You can't just expect us to all wait for you indefinitely. Figure it out soon, or you're going to lose us."

I accepted the job at a restaurant down the street, running the hot table. I made sure all the sides were prepped and served according to the recipes of the head cook. It was a mindless job that paid little more than minimum wage, but it was something to do. Without the distractions from Francis and Amelia, the kitchen provided a place to think. I needed to figure out what I was going to do, but truly I didn't know where to start. My day-to-day life was fun and light, but it had the stink of a lie on it; it wasn't real, and we all knew that. How could I go home, though? Florida was supposed to free me from Amelia, but it had done just the opposite and driven us closer together. To leave would only bring a much larger problem much closer to home.

Mulling this over, I drove into the apartment complex. There were a couple extra cars in the lot close to my unit, but I didn't really think that much of it. As I opened the door to the apartment, I saw three guys in the living room. The one closest to me had a video camera in his hand. The second was Francis, smoking a joint and sitting in the corner. The third guy was having sex with Amelia while the others looked on.

"What is this?" I asked, eyes wide in disbelief.

"John," Francis said, "come hit this. And please, man, be quiet!"

My mind was reeling. I was experiencing so many emotions at once. The scene before me was eerily similar to the times I had walked in and interrupted MaryAnn with a slew of other guys. There was a major difference here, though; I didn't actually care who was having sex with Amelia. I cared about her that little.

I walked outside the frame of the camera and sat next to Francis. I took the joint out of his hand and took a long pull. Exhaling, my mind settled on the conclusion it had known was there all along. This girl was trouble and clearly didn't love me, nor did I love her. Getting away from her would be the absolute best choice I could make.

It would've been great to be able to just say, "Hey, guys, I'm outta here. I have to go home. My real life is waiting for me, and hanging around with you two has been real fun, but enough is enough."

Unfortunately, that just wasn't how this was going to go, and I knew that going in. I presented my case that I needed to get back home. I blamed Lauren, I blamed Nancy, I passed blame all around, but I just couldn't bring myself to say the words that would have released me. I needed to go home because I didn't want to do this anymore; I was done with this game and wanted to straighten my shit out. Without saying it to them that way, I was prolonging this painful existence and continuing to dig myself deeper into a hole. Somehow, I managed to get my message across and the main point that I was leaving, alone. With Amelia bringing in some money from her amateur porn, she was less clingy, almost indifferent to my choice. I took the opportunity to get out of town before she changed her mind.

BACK IN BLACK

NOT RESPONDING TO several tickets was actually kind of a big deal. Unbeknownst to me, my license had been revoked while I was busy joyriding around Florida. Working in Philadelphia and Camden and living in Long Branch was not going to work out if I was unable to drive, and losing that job was not an option. I was on thin ice at home with Nancy. She was finally beginning to come to the realization that not everything I had been saying was adding up. The whole not being able to drive thing was the most concerning for her, or maybe it was that paired with the fact that I had almost no money left in my savings. All I was sure of was that losing Ashe would cost me more than just a job; it would bring more attention to my current situation than I was comfortable with.

As a sort of compromise, I decided to try and find an apartment close to the courts in Camden. There was a direct train to Philadelphia from Camden, so I'd be able to make it back and forth without having to drive. Because Camden was such a poor area, I could get a really nice place for not a lot of money. The only real issue was coming up with the deposit, since I was pretty much tapped out. Bank of America always mailed me offers about cash advances, so I took out a small loan, just enough to cover the expenses for the apartment.

With a place to live and a lot I could leave the car in, I was lined up for the summer's activities. Nancy liked the apartment, too, and seemed to be excited about the prospect of spending occasional weekends in a home away from home. This place came with a few pieces of furniture left by the previous tenant, but mostly it was a blank slate. The house with Nancy had been fun to furnish over the years, but everything there had to have a purpose. When we picked out carpet, it had to be durable enough to stand up to teenage boys, and when we furnished the living room, we had to make sure the couches were dark to hide stains caused by the kids. The new apartment could truly be a reflection of my personal style. I bought a few small glass tables to put by the large picture window and then began collecting houseplants. I found a nice rattan circular chair with a large red cushion that looked perfect for meditation, not that I did much of that, but if I wanted to start up again, that would be the place to do it. I kept the rest of the living room sparse, as the apartment was loft-style and had an open, airy feel to it.

In addition to the furnishings, I allowed myself to get a few decorative items. The store that had the rattan meditation chair also sold Tibetan artwork. Little by little, I filled my apartment with images of Ohms and Buddha. The more I shopped, the more my apartment began to resemble some sort of yoga studio. I dubbed it the Zen Den and found myself looking forward to the prospect of living here. Unlike my move to Florida, this felt like coming home. Here, I could be myself. Maybe it was foolish, but I hoped that if I tried to be my authentic self as often as possible, things would start to fall back into place.

Without much to do until tennis started, it was a little boring hanging around Camden. I didn't have many friends and really couldn't go anywhere, anyway. Smoking would entertain me and keep me occupied for a few hours, but inevitably the subtle high would wear off and I'd still be alone. From the apartment window, I could see the Jaguar parked in the lot. You know, it's possible that a normal person would have been able to look out the window at his car and resist the temptation to go and get in it. For me, on the other hand, that was just too tall an order. I at least had to turn it on every couple of days and drive a couple of blocks. I didn't want it to sit too long; it was used to being driven every single day. And my suspension was only for six months. It wasn't worth letting the car fall apart over a short-term restriction.

The Long Branch Rec program had begun sending out the flyers for the summer tennis program, but this year would be different. Without the ability to drive, I couldn't float back and forth between the courts. There was also the issue of securing a coach with Jonathan off at school. Kyle wanted me to meet with a couple of former Long Branch High School students who had expressed interest in coaching. Taking the train was too much for me to stomach, so I drove up to Long Branch. Nancy couldn't know I was driving—she would be too angry that I was risking further time without a license—so I told her Kyle was picking me up at the train station. I would just have to keep a low profile and stash the car somewhere when I went to the house.

The plan worked perfectly. I drove up, parked the car at a grocery store near the train station, and had Kyle pick me up. After meeting with the kids, it was clear that they could be assistant coaches, but none of them had the experience necessary to run the courts themselves. If we were in a tough spot, they would suffice, but it would be better to keep looking for someone else. That could wait until I was back in Camden, but I wanted to spend some time with Nancy. I had Kyle drop me off at the house.

While I waited for Nancy to get home from work, I began to remember how boring it was in this town. There was never anything to do, nowhere to go to spend your time, and no one I really wanted to see. By the time she got home, I had worked myself up pretty good, pacing around the house and smoking cigarettes. I started to feel a little off, maybe dizzy and slightly queasy, just not right somehow.

"John, when was the last time you ate anything?" Nancy asked as I tried to shake the fog that had settled over me.

"Uh, I don't know. I guess I forgot to eat today," I replied.

"Huh, okay, that's probably what's got you feeling like this. Want a sandwich or something?"

"Sure, I guess a sandwich would be all right. Then could you drive me to train station?"

I don't know if she was disappointed that I wouldn't be staying or not. I really couldn't tell much of anything; the sandwich wasn't helping me feel any better. I needed to get home. We went through the motions of looking up the train schedule, though it wasn't going to be necessary, and eventually she dropped me off at the station. I waited for her to leave and then walked over to my car.

"License, insurance, and registration, please," the officer said as he leaned into the passenger side window.

"Just a minute, officer," I mumbled, reaching into the glove compartment.

"Do you know why I pulled you over?"

I did. I was so ridiculously dizzy that I had been weaving all over the turnpike, struggling to keep the car on the road. I blinked hard, trying to get the world to stop swimming around before me, to focus on the task at hand. I pulled my insurance card and registration out and handed them to the officer. I also pulled out an old expired license that I had been using for ID. This was going to be bad.

As he went back to his car, where he would discover that none of my documents were current, I began to wonder what was going to happen. Getting pulled over wasn't new, but doing so on a suspended license was. The law and its enforcement had never been a specialty of mine, but even a novice knew that this was not going to end well.

He issued me several tickets and a mandatory court appearance to sort this all out. In addition, I clearly wasn't allowed to drive my car home. They towed the car and I was driven to the local precinct. The biggest issue I had was that, in order to get my car out of impound, someone else would have to drive it for me. I couldn't call Nancy. She would freak at finding the truth out about my little train charade, and I really didn't know anyone else in the area. I took a taxi home from the police station and went to lie down immediately. After a couple of hours, I awoke to the buzzing of my phone.

"Hey, I'm at the station," Amelia said. "Which building are you at again?"

"The Victor Lofts, right across the street from the aquarium," I explained.

"Okay, be right over."

With no one else to call, Amelia was my only option. We hadn't spoken since I moved back from Florida, but I had heard from Francis that she left shortly after me and moved back in with her mother. I went to the bathroom and washed my face. My color had come back and my eyes were clear; I was feeling better. There would be fees to get my car out of impound and I also needed money for a taxi to the station. Considering it was a good twenty-five miles away, that wouldn't be cheap. We'd have to stop at the bank on our way; I needed another cash advance.

Once she got down there, she never really left. Amelia became a fixture at the apartment. Since getting back from Florida, she hadn't found work for herself. With nothing tying her to her mother's house, she decided to stay with me. It wasn't what I wanted to happen, exactly, but I also hadn't done anything to prevent it. Calling her to help me out with the car had been an open invitation.

WATCHING THE WHEELS

ULTIMATELY, MY DRIVING infractions caught up with me. Repeatedly driving without a license and getting caught pisses people off. The judge hearing my case was less than amused as I explained that I needed to use my car to get to and from work and really had no other options for transportation. I received a lecture on mass transit and respecting the laws of the state in which I chose to reside, and I was ready to take my slap on the wrist.

"Based on your blatant disregard for the laws of the state of New Jersey, paired with your disobedience of the sanctions placed upon you for failure to comply with the verdicts of this court, you are sentenced to thirty days in your county correctional institute."

The judge banged her gavel and walked out of the courtroom. Hold the phone, jail time, for speeding tickets? I was incredulous. There was no way I could go to jail for a traffic violation. I was sixty years old! Sixty-year-old men couldn't hang in jail with the kids.

I wasn't under arrest, so I would have to turn myself in. The benefit was that I could make arrangements to go in whenever I wanted, though it highlighted that I didn't really have anyone to make arrangements with. All I would be missing out on were secretive days spent in the apartment. Worrying about Ashe could wait a couple of months until I got everything sorted out.

The Monmouth County Jail was filled with low-level offenders and seemed to be much more mellow than Trenton State Penitentiary. I didn't have to worry about my safety on a daily basis. With most people in for only short stints, there wasn't the opportunity for gangs to form. The greatest danger came from the unpredictability that comes with mental illness. It did take a special kind of stupid or a real lunatic to do the sorts of things that I had been doing, and many of the others had been through similar ordeals to end up in county jail.

The longer I spent inside, the more I saw that I was much further out there than I had realized. Normal people don't engage in the sort of reckless behavior that I was exhibiting. They followed routines, they went to work every day, they came home at night, they ate the same things. Me, I didn't even have a state I lived in regularly. In jail, eating three square meals a day, with fruits and the occasional vegetable, it was crystal clear how poorly I had been caring for myself on the outside. Since I wasn't smoking paired with a balanced diet and somewhat regular sleep hours, my mind was slowly beginning to clear.

With that lucidity, I took my time writing letters. Every two or three days, without fail, I would get a letter from Lauren. She was the only one writing to me, and her letters were a source of hope, a beacon of light that shone into an otherwise dark existence. As I read her letters, it was glaringly obvious that she was the only one writing because she was getting close to being the only one I had left. I knew Amelia was with me out of convenience and probably for the money, and I had hung Nancy out to dry too many times. If I was going to straighten myself out, I would need to start with her. She knew I was doing things that weren't right, but she didn't comprehend the depth of my betrayal, and I wasn't sure what would happen if she ever found out.

Twenty-seven days into my thirty-day sentence, I was released. Nancy picked me up and took me back to the house. Being home was nice, but I felt like an alien. Any time my phone buzzed, I jumped, anxious that it would be Amelia and that Nancy would ask who it was and I'd have to lie. I don't know when home stopped feeling like home, but it definitely had. My clothes were in the dresser, my coats in the closet, my extra rackets in the sports closet under the stairs. But it felt different without either of the kids. There wasn't anyone there except me and Nancy, and she was at work during the day. I was alone, trapped without my car, without a way to get out.

I took the train down to Camden, and Amelia met me at the station in my car. We drove back to my apartment and parked in the lot. Walking into the apartment, it struck me that this didn't feel like home either. I had created a situation where no matter where I went, I felt lost.

It was easy to fall back into our routine, smoking in the evenings and sometimes in the mornings, spending lazy days putzing around the apartment. I quickly lost any clarity or focus I had gained in jail. Finding motivation to get up and go was hard, harder for me than before. I was quite comfortable in that space, wasting time, almost waiting for something to force me out of this cycle. Amelia drove me to and from tennis in Camden, and in Long Branch, I just let the program run itself. The general malaise was hard to shake; nothing really held my interest anymore.

In August, I stopped showing up to work all together. I didn't feel like the program needed me. I called to check in with the site supervisors every once in a blue moon, but I just didn't care anymore. We had worked to put good people in place, and over the years the necessity of my job had shrunk. With everyone thinking that I must be at one of the other sites, no one seemed to notice. The central office in Philly must have gotten a hint, though, because my checks just stopped coming after the summer session, when they usually continued through the fall while we transitioned the students to after-school programs. Without any income, it was hard to support our habits, but I had stopped worrying about credit card debt months before. I charged everything we needed: food, gas, and a few pieces of jewelry here and there for Amelia. I couldn't charge pot, or rent, so I continued to take out cash advances. I can't be sure that Amelia had any idea that the money we spent wasn't actually mine. For all I knew, she thought I had a bottomless bank account.

It had been a while since I had seen Lauren. She had been busy working summer school through August and then the new school year started up almost immediately. My birthday was in September, and she told me she wanted to come down and have lunch with me. While I loved to see her no matter what, this would pose some challenges. With Amelia living in the apartment, I made sure that whenever I saw Nancy, I went to her. Lauren was pretty sharp, and if she visited here, she'd pick up on things that were out of place or didn't belong to a sixty-year-old man. We would have to eat out, and I would have to keep her from coming inside.

When she arrived, I was waiting out in front of the apartment building. She needed to use the bathroom, but luckily the building had a ladies room in the lobby. I waited for her to come out, thinking about how precarious my current state was. All it would take would be for her to demand to go upstairs, and everything would be revealed. And what if Nancy wanted to come down for a weekend and I couldn't talk her out of it?

"What is this?" Lauren asked, handing me a flyer from the mailroom. While I had been lost in thought, she had come out of the bathroom and wandered around the lobby.

"Oh, uh, that's the flyer I put out to see if I could drum up some private lessons in the area," I replied.

"Huh, it looks good. Who made this for you?"

I couldn't use a computer and we both knew it; I didn't even own one. For years, she had written my menus and updated my résumé, so creating an advertising flyer was well beyond my skills. Thinking quickly, I made up something about one of the coaches at Ashe headquarters helping me out with it. She looked straight at me, almost into me, and I could tell she didn't buy it. I don't know why exactly, but this particular lie seemed too transparent to fly.

"Let's grab lunch?" I asked changing the subject. "There's this great soul food place I want to take you to."

Thankfully, she let it drop and we made our way to the car. We stopped to pick up lunch and then drove to the riverbank so we could picnic. It was a pretty nice day out, but a chill had settled into my bones. This day was harder than I anticipated. She knew there was something off with me and just couldn't put her finger on it. As we ate, sitting under a willow tree, I could feel her watching me, trying to figure out how to broach the subject of my strange behavior.

"Dad, do you work for Arthur Ashe anymore?" she inquired.

"Why do you ask that?" I replied, stalling.

"You just seem weird, not like yourself. Your hair is really long and you look thin, almost gaunt. Whenever we talk, work never ever seems to come up. It used to be that I couldn't get you to shut up about tennis, who was hitting well, who wasn't, who won the tournament, and on and on." She paused and looked at me expectantly.

This was a turning point. Either I would tell the truth or continue the lies. "Well, I worked there all summer, and right now I'm taking a little break. I haven't quit and I haven't been fired. I'm just trying to figure it out."

She nodded and looked out at the river. "I'm worried about you."

The truth was, I was worried about me, too. I had started to feel sick again, similar to the day I got pulled over, and nothing seemed to make it better. The feeling was different from my heart attack. It wasn't overwhelming; it was more of a constant state of lightheadedness. Food tasted like ash in my mouth and, as a result, my desire to eat was practically nonexistent. The trouble was that it was a vicious circle. I would wake up without an appetite, making me feel weak, and definitely not like cooking, so I would lie back down, which would only result in my feeling worse. Around and around the days went, one running into another and everything smearing together.

DEAD MAN, DEAD MAN

"JOHN!" NANCY EXCLAIMED, brightening as the door swung open. "I didn't realize you were coming home today!"

I was standing on the front porch of the house; I had rung the bell and waited for Nancy to answer before going in. Walking past her, I entered the living room with my duffel bag in hand.

"Yeah, I'm home. I don't want to go back to Camden anymore. I just want to be here. I need to smoke a cigarette, though."

She let me walk back outside without really saying much in response. I had woken that morning feeling worse than I'd ever felt, with a dull headache that seemed to permeate my entire being. The thought that I might be dying, and dying as a result of karma paying me back for my reckless behavior, had spread over me slowly, but once the idea was planted, it quickly took root. Going home was my desperate plea to the universe to make me better, to get me out of this funk once and for all. As I took a drag of my cigarette, I tried to think about how to explain this change of heart, this return of the prodigal son, and telling more lies was not the answer. The truth wasn't an option either, but somewhere in that gray area between reality and perception, I was hoping to pull something out that would free me from my entrapment.

Walking back inside, Nancy asked, "How did you get here?"

I still wasn't supposed to be driving, but that had never stopped me. "Route 66," came my reply.

Even to my ears, the answer wasn't right. I tried again. "Took the train on Route 66. Stopped at the weigh station." Wrong again. My mouth opened and closed like a fish out of water. The words that were coming out were not the ones that were forming in my brain. Something was wrong.

"Are you drunk?" Nancy asked me. Stumbling, she led me to the sofa. I sat down next to Nancy and started to cry—nothing was making sense.

She sniffed my breath. "You don't smell like alcohol. If you're not drunk, I don't understand what you're saying."

"Route 66," was all I could get out.

Nancy helped me walk out to her car and she drove me to the hospital. I couldn't seem to get it together, and the more I struggled, the more upset I became.

"Take deep breaths. Breathe in—good. Now out—good," Nancy coached.

As we began the walk from the parking lot into the hospital, I pulled back, resisting. My heart attack was my last hospital stay, and going back was not the homecoming I had hoped for. Gently but firmly, Nancy led me inside, and under the glare of the fluorescent lights, with the smell of antiseptic in the air, I remembered how much I loved her. How whenever I truly needed someone, it was always Nancy who came to my rescue.

"Mr. Wagner, can you tell me the date today?" the doctor asked.

"Uh, leaves, the leaves fall," I tried.

"Okay. Mr. Wagner, it is fall, but what is the date?"

"Red leaves, no, the leaves are red."

In and out the doctors came with endless questions, none of which I could answer. These weren't tough questions; I just couldn't get my mouth to say the right words. It was confusing—what was happening?—and before long they moved me upstairs to a private room. I didn't want a private room; I wanted to go home. I had finally come home. Why couldn't I just stay there? With the doctors and their questions came tests, needles, and IVs. I didn't want any of that either. Without the ability to speak, I tried communicating in a universal language, body language. Every line they stuck in me, I pulled out; every time they dressed me in a hospital gown, I got up and put on my jeans. They took my things and put them in a closet; I took them out and laid them on the bed.

Lauren, her boyfriend, Jay, and Jonathan came down the following day. With their arrival, I was faced with seeing myself through their reactions. Both Jonathan and Jay couldn't meet my eyes and had trouble attempting conversation with me. Lauren's brow was furrowed with concern. I knew then that what the doctors were saying must be at least somewhat serious. But I couldn't ask what was happening or tell the kids I was okay. Where had my sharp tongue and quick wit gone?

As the male nurse came in to attempt to put in yet another IV line, I stood. With my family there, my confidence surged; they would help me straighten this out and get me home. Pushing past the nurse and the orderly that followed him in, I struggled to get my balance.

"Dad!" Lauren yelled, "You have to sit down! You need this medicine they are going to give you."

"Mr. Wagner, please relax, or we will have to sedate you again," the nurse barked.

Lauren looked over to Jay, Jonathan, and Nancy, who had slowly backed out of the room, and then back to me. "Dad, look at me. You have had a stroke. Your brain isn't getting what it needs in order to work properly. Everything is scrambled." Her eyes filled with tears as she explained.

I stopped struggling long enough for the orderly to push me back onto the bed. He reached for the restraints, and Lauren put her hand up. "Don't, he doesn't need them. He will leave it all in, won't you, Dad?"

Her eyes pleaded with me to cooperate. I had been powerless to her requests for years by this point. Settling back onto the pillows, I nodded. The orderly shook his head but listened to her. With a little difficulty, they got the IV started again and this time I didn't pull out the line. I tried to think about what she had said. A stroke? Lauren sat on the edge of the bed and squeezed my hand.

Doctors tried to explain what had happened to me, but their words made little sense. Mostly, they explained things to Nancy, who passed the info along to the kids. She also tried to tell me what was happening, but it was as though I was missing some critical connection. The words she said would make it three quarters of the way to a complete thought and just get lost. Speaking was equally challenging. I would form a thought, and by the time my mouth moved, what I hoped to say was completely different. Everyone seemed to agree on one thing, that I would need to go somewhere to get help to get back to normal: rehab.

A rehabilitation center had helped me tremendously when I recovered from abusing drugs and alcohol, but this time, the sort of facility I was going to be sent to would be for a different kind of therapy. Speech, occupational, and physical therapy were my prescription, and I was to live there while they worked to get me back to normal. There was no way I was doing that. I had spent such a long time away from home—in Florida, then jail, and then in Camden—that I simply would not agree to go away again. I had to get home and get it all back together, and I knew that Nancy would help me with it, and it would all be okay. As the days passed in the hospital, I was able to answer yes and no questions more easily and could choose correct answers when given multiple choices. With my comprehension skills returning, albeit slowly, they couldn't deem me incompetent and force me into the rehab. They needed my consent, and that wasn't something I would give.

Back at home, I struggled to do the little things. Speech was near impossible, as well as the normal daily activities like bathing and dressing. My body was uncoordinated and seemed to have a mind of its own. If I tried to lift my left leg to put on my pants, both legs would give out and I would slide to the floor. Walking from room to room also posed a bit of a problem as my depth perception wasn't quite right. I would reach out to steady myself on the doorframe and miss, hurtling forward and stumbling to the floor. To say this was frustrating would be a drastic understatement. Truth be told, it was downright depressing. I couldn't do things for myself, and I couldn't tell people what I needed. Always an emotional kind of guy, post stroke, I found that my emotions ran wild, like that of a hormonal teenage girl. After attempting to explain to Lauren what I wanted to eat and her not getting it, I would begin to sob uncontrollably, making the words even harder to find.

To cheer me up, Lauren and Jay stayed at the house for the weekend, and she brought with her a couple of pieces of paper with a bunch of pictures on them. She had made it at work with the help of her students' speech therapists. The first one had all different kinds of food on it so that I could point to what I wanted and then practice saying the words. The next piece had clothes on it, so I could ask for a sweater or say I wanted to change my shoes. As she went through her stack, I saw there was one with pictures of faces, the different emotions.

Stopping her, I pointed to the crying face and said, "Sad, Lauren, sad."

She looked back at me, "Me too, Dad. I'm sad, too. Listen to me, though. They told me that if you have any ability to speak, you could be able to get it all back. They compared the brain to a filing cabinet and said that all of our words are in organized drawers and that when we want to speak, we pull out a drawer, say, for food items, and are able to describe what we want without even thinking about it. It's like somebody knocked over your cabinet and threw your words all over the floor. When you go to look for a word, it isn't where you expect it to be, and other words are in that place instead. If we use these boards, it will help your brain reorganize and put the words back in their right drawers."

That made sense, but I wasn't sure it would work. I took the boards out of her hands and found the one with dinner food on it. "Spaghetti," I said.

"Sure, we can make spaghetti," she said excitedly. "Jay, can you run to the store for us?"

With the fixings for spaghetti and meatballs on the counter, we went through the motions of making sauce. Following the steps to make the recipe was harder than I thought it would be, but it was manageable with my family there to help me. As I stood at the stove and stirred, I felt like maybe, just maybe, I would be able get it all back.

"Dad!" Lauren yelled, alarmed. "Your hand is on that pot! It's burning hot!"

It took me a minute to grasp her meaning, and by the time I looked down, she was already there pulling my hand off the pot. There was an angry red burn running up my left arm. Nancy quickly grabbed ice out of the freezer and passed it to me to put on the burn. Everyone was moving around me, but I just stood there, looking at my arm. I hadn't felt anything—no sensation at all.

"John, uncurl your fist. Relax that hand," Nancy instructed, trying to pull my fingers away from the ball they were clenched in.

I couldn't do what she wanted, no matter how hard I tried. Crying, Lauren ran up the stairs to her childhood bedroom and I heard the door slam. I took the ice pack from Nancy, put it on my numb arm, and tried to walk up the stairs. Holding the railing and the ice pack proved difficult, but I did make it up the stairs. I banged on the bedroom door and Lauren opened it, tears streaming down her face. I tried to lean against her wall and misjudged the distance, falling backwards and sliding to the floor. We sat there together, both of us crying, not wanting to believe that this might very well be my new normal.

My recovery slowed, and almost reversed, over the next two days. My extremities grew more and more rigid, and my limited vocabulary disappeared. The numbness and tingling sensation that had settled into my left hand had spread to my other arm and begun to travel to my feet. As I tried to communicate to my family what was happening, I found all I could do was moan. At the end of the second day, Nancy took me back to the hospital.

Doctors came and ran tests, took blood, gave me my medications, and scratched their heads. The scans showed no new brain damage, no plausible reason why my condition should be growing worse instead of better. Typically, stroke patients only improve or remain constant. Getting worse didn't add up if I hadn't had any new stroke activity.

Finally, someone found a lead in my blood work. The levels of lithium in my bloodstream were high, dangerously high, and my kidney function seemed to be diminished. Since my stroke, I no longer had control over my medication for my bipolar disorder, and was given them either by the doctor or at home by Nancy. Following the prescribed dose, which had been written fifteen years prior in the drug rehab facility, I was getting a full 1500 mg of lithium a day, in three 500 mg pills. Over the years, I had gotten into the habit of taking a pill as needed. If I didn't feel like I needed the middle one or the last one, I would skip it, starting over the following morning. Since my stroke, my meds were being doled out exactly as prescribed, and apparently my kidneys just couldn't handle that high of a dose anymore. Each day the level of lithium in my system had continued to climb, reaching near catastrophic levels.

As soon as the lithium was stopped, my hand tremors and muscle tightness began to ease and my speech improved. The effects of the stroke were still there, but my balance and coordination returned almost immediately. This time, when I was discharged, the biggest issues were about what kinds of medications I could take based on the kidney damage I had sustained. Taking a simple Tylenol could put me back in the hospital, so most medications were going to be off-limits. This applied to the lithium as well; I would have to find a way to manage my bipolar disorder without the aide of medicine. I was simply too fragile for the doctor to prescribe anything that would help. The work of my recovery would still be pretty serious, but at least I could speak in simple phrases and think for myself. Nancy would be able to go back to work, and I wouldn't need round-the-clock supervision.

DON'T SPEAK

I HAD ALWAYS had a pretty minimal filter when it came to speaking my mind. Unfortunately, my stroke exacerbated that. As my ability to speak returned, I started saying things to Nancy and the kids that would have been better left unsaid. It started small, with things like, "When we left Florida . . ." to which Nancy would ask, "When who left Florida, John?" I couldn't pick up the signals she sent with her tone of voice and her facial expressions. Sometimes I answered the questions with responses like, "What about Florida?" and other times I told the truth: "Me and Amelia."

At first, it was easy to chalk these slips up to my stroke and my crossed wires, but it was enough to get Nancy thinking. She also started going through my finances, in order to help pay my bills. This was troublesome for a couple reasons. She saw that I didn't have any money left. There were also bills for jewelry that wasn't hers, the cost of Amelia's tuition for her massage therapy school, and probably a dozen other charges I couldn't explain.

Nancy didn't tell me before she went down to my apartment. Though even if she had, I don't know that I would have thought to tell Amelia to get out, nor do I know if she would have listened. I hadn't thought about her very much in the weeks since my stroke, though she called occasionally. I rarely answered her and, when I did, she didn't get the attention she was used to.

When Nancy came home after driving to Camden, finding Amelia living in my apartment and kicking her out, I wish there had been a fight. A woman who is fighting for you is a woman who is passionate about being with you, who would do anything to keep you. As Nancy told me that she had found out about Amelia, there wasn't a fire in her eyes—there were only facts. I had screwed around, she knew, and she was done. I wasn't a worthy opponent for her by that point, anyway. The more upset I got, the harder it was to speak, so for Nancy, who could verbally assault people in high places and cut them down to size, I was a waste of breath.

Because Nancy had always been better than I deserved, she stayed true to form, even during that time that would have brought a regular woman crashing down. She took me to and from doctor's appointments, made sure I ate regularly, and quietly went about the business of getting me ready to move back to Camden, alone. She was so nice about kicking me out that I didn't really understand the severity of what was happening until she dropped me off in Camden and drove off to meet her friends.

Alone, looking around that apartment, my Zen Den no longer seemed so cool and peaceful. It looked pathetic, like a college dorm room, haphazardly thrown together with pieces of furniture that were never truly meant to be lived on. I had assembled a room full of things that were meaningless, disconnected from the actual life I had lived for sixty years. There weren't pictures of the kids, or of me and Nancy, or even of me and Amelia; it was simply a lifeless collection of things that could have belonged to anyone.

The depression settled in quite quickly. It was plain to see how incapacitated I still was when I tried to go to the grocery store for the first time by myself. I didn't know what to get or where anything was, so I left with bread, milk, and cheese. Back in my apartment, I struggled to make cheese sandwiches and change the channel with my remote. Showering was difficult; I constantly forgot what I had already washed and ended up washing myself multiple times before I was convinced I was clean.

I tried calling Lauren, and then Nancy, and even Amelia, but none of them wanted to speak to me. Lauren was hurt that I had lied, that I hadn't been able to stop the affair before it got to the point of no return. She would speak to me briefly, but as soon as I would try and talk about how lonely I was or how hard things were, the conversation would turn nasty, with her telling me that I was getting what I deserved. Nancy wouldn't really entertain any length of conversation. When I would try to tell her that Amelia hadn't mattered, that it was meaningless, she would balk. It didn't matter to her how little Amelia meant to me—the betrayal meant something more to her. Her lack of interest in talking with me about it made it quite clear that she was over me. And Amelia—well, when Nancy threw her out of the apartment, there had been some talk about the fact that I was broke, credit cards maxed, savings gone. Without the money, Amelia didn't want anything to do with an old man. I was really and truly alone.

Unchecked and unmedicated for the first time since rehab, I was left to my own devices for self-regulation. With no one who cared about me checking in, I began to self-destruct. I didn't eat, I didn't drink, and most days I didn't get out of bed. Cooking for myself was out of the question, as was going to the store. There wasn't any motivation to do anything at all. I kept calling Lauren, hoping that she would find some way to forgive me and just let me talk.

"Dad, this is the fourth time today that you've called me. Is there something you need?"

"Yes, I need someone to talk to. I was just thinking about when I was a kid living in the woods and how lonely I felt."

She exhaled deeply. "Okay, listen. I have a job and a boyfriend and a life. And I know that you screwed everything up and you're upset about it, but I cannot be the only person you talk to each day. I can't be everything for you. Why don't you go for a walk and talk to some people in town?"

"Because I don't know anyone here!" I snapped, "I want to go home, where I know people and they know me."

"Where is home, Dad? You left Mom. You can't go back there."

"I know. I know I can't go back to the house. But get me an apartment there, near the house. Long Branch has been my home for thirty years. That's where I belong."

"Fine, I'll look into it and try to figure something out, but no guarantees, okay?" she replied. "I love you. Now, don't call me again until tomorrow. I will call you on my way home from school in the afternoon."

"Promise?" I asked.

"Only if you promise to eat something."

And so we began to create a new routine. We found safe topics to talk about, mostly about what I ate or what Lauren and Jay would be cooking for dinner. She would call me on her walk home from school, talk about the weather, and food, and every once in while we would discuss plans for my move back to Long Branch. It was only twenty minutes or so each day, but it was something I could count on. I waited for 3:15 every day and started my day when my phone rang.

I didn't own very much, so packing up my stuff and getting it to Long Branch wasn't difficult. Nancy had helped find a place in town that I could afford and that was a safe arm's length away from the house. It was a garden apartment but had full windows in most of the rooms. Going from living in a loft to a basement was definitely a big change, but it almost felt appropriate, like my penance for all the things I had done wrong. And with a closer proximity to Nancy, maybe I'd be able to win her back with a little effort.

Being back in town was a vast improvement. Running errands, I would bump into old friends. Even the guys at 7-Eleven were happy to see me every day. They urged me to keep coming in to get coffee and visit with them. Little by little, I carved out a new life for myself. The difference between who I was before and after the stroke was staggering. Given a choice, I probably would have asked to be taken out back and shot, just to avoid the embarrassment of becoming old, feeble, and poor. Living life fast and on the edge, I was constantly aware that death could be waiting just around the corner. What hadn't occurred to me was what could happen if I didn't actually die. Becoming a shadow of the man I once had been was a fate worse than death. Looking at myself day in and day out, I was unable to reconcile the image in front of me with the person who used to be there.

The one bonus to my deteriorated state was that I was officially enough of a mess to qualify for Social Security Disability. A steady check would be coming in for the first time in a long time, though it was barely enough to cover my rent and cable bills. After wreaking havoc on my credit cards and savings, there wasn't anything that could be done other than to file for bankruptcy. I wasn't young like I had been the last time I ran up a huge bill. There was no way I could work my way out of a

$150,000 hole. Luckily, the lawyer Nancy connected me with thought I would be able to keep my car. It was quite literally the only declarable asset I had and since it had been charged on a credit card, and all of my debt was being lumped together, at least the Jag would get to stay with me.

Nancy would come by the apartment every once in a while with something for me to sign, either a form for the lawyer handling my bankruptcy or something for the Monmouth County Office of Social Services for my disability checks. She would slide a stack of papers across the kitchen table and tell me where to sign. As we were repeating this procedure for the third or fourth time since my move back to Long Branch, she stopped me as I grabbed for the last stack of papers in a manila folder.

"John, wait. I need to tell you about these," she said, placing her hand on my arm.

Looking up at her, I knew what was in front of me without needing to read it.

"Divorce papers?" I asked.

She nodded her head.

I exhaled and reminded myself we had been through this before and I had still gotten her back. It was crucial that I didn't freak out.

"Okay, no problem. I'll sign them," I said, pulling them out and grabbing my pen.

"Thank you for not fighting me," she replied.

I worked my way through the pile and tried not to think about what each page probably said. Dissolution of our marriage, bankruptcy, infidelity—you name it, it was all in there. To say I had this coming would be an understatement, but that didn't change the fact that it hurt. Everything I had done seemed like it had been done by another person. I don't know if it was the stroke that caused that separation in my memory or if it was a defense mechanism, but sitting there at the table with Nancy, it was really difficult for me to wrap my head around what had happened to us. I certainly couldn't put my finger on the event that triggered us coming to this place. I just knew that, somehow, here we were and that I had hurt her again.

At Lauren's behest I called Kyle Jennings to try and get a sense of where I stood with Long Branch Rec. Despite all of the things that had fallen apart, Long Branch had stayed pretty well-insulated from my transgressions. After meeting with Kyle, I learned that the program had lost some of its steam from last summer, but overall it would be fine with a little extra attention. Since I really had nothing else to focus on, I began to put myself back together with the help of the tennis program.

I started small with the once-a-week indoor winter program. I would work all week on getting sleep and eating regularly enough to feel good for a few hours on Sunday night. No matter how awful I felt on a given day, I pulled it together for the kids. That first winter back, Lauren would drive down with Jay and help me out with the coaching and organizational details. Between the three of us, we were able to bring back the enthusiasm to the program, and within a few weeks we had over forty students showing up for lessons.

An added bonus was the real opportunity to get to know Lauren's boyfriend, Jay. He was the complete opposite of any other guy she had brought home before, in the best ways possible. He was bright, hardworking, and supportive of her. Watching them together, I hoped they would be a more stable pair than any relationship I had ever been in.

Seeing my family often, paired with the daily phone calls, I was able to get out of bed and put myself together most days. I would be lying if I said I was truly motivated to keep living life, but somehow I managed to make it to tomorrow every day. Daily life was lonely, and I felt no higher purpose for my actions, but I just kept going through the motions, praying that one day I'd wake up and feel normal again.

CAT'S IN THE CRADLE

AS THE PASSING months grew into years, the world was moving on without me. Nancy had found someone else, Lauren and Jay were getting married, and Jonathan was getting ready to finish college. If I didn't do something to reconnect with them soon, I felt like I would lose them all. After my bankruptcy cleared, I was allowed to keep my car and the small amount of cash that I had left from my inheritance from my mom; that was it. Social Security covered all my bills, and any little money I made coaching tennis was either spending money or money in the bank. It was pretty clear by this point that I wasn't one to hang on to cash. Saving for a rainy day didn't make sense when you were constantly in the middle of a monsoon of your own making.

"Hey, Dad. How are you today?" Lauren asked to open our typical afternoon conversation.

"I'm fine, and bored." I exhaled forcefully. "I gotta get out of this room. It's like being back in prison."

"Your apartment is warm, dry, clean, and spacious. It's hardly a prison. What did you eat today?"

"Cheese sandwich. Coffee. Listen, I don't want to talk about that. I want to go on vacation. With you and Mom and Jonathan. I'll pay for it."

"Haha, that's hilarious, Dad. With what money? And no offense, but Mom wouldn't go anywhere with you." She laughed.

She wasn't trying to be mean. She was right.

"Okay, well, thanks for your input. I'm gonna go by the house today and see what your mom says about a trip to Italy. I don't know why you think she'd say no; she lets me come to Christmas and stuff. We could go this spring, while Jon-boy is still in school."

"Okay, whatever you want to do. You should probably call her first; she gets angry when you just show up over there." She paused. "Italy would be pretty cool."

I had one. I would have to work to get Jonathan and Nancy. Lauren had always been the easy sell, but I thought I could do it. If I could get them all together again, there would be a real chance for our family to reconnect. And I'd be out of that room for a while, which was incentive enough to keep trying.

I tried phone calls, driving by, and even stopping at the hospital to see her. Nancy was not going on any trip with me anywhere. She seemed to be happy in her new relationship and wasn't interested in putting that in jeopardy for a trip. While I believed her, there must have been at least a small part of her that was worried I would be able to win her back if we went on this trip. While that was a disappointment, there was one victory to come out of it: Jonathan was willing to go with me.

The summer that he worked with Amelia had put serious strain on an already distant relationship. He had a front-row seat to my infidelity and had suspected right from the start that something was wrong, probably even before I knew. Once he had been proven correct, he hadn't wanted anything to do with me. It's not that he was mean or rude, or even aggressive; he just didn't call, or really even return calls. At Christmas and Thanksgiving, he was cordial, sometimes even friendly, but never forgiving. The distance between us wasn't his fault, and I knew that. I had never put the time or energy into our father-and-son relationship; relating to him had always been too hard for me. No one had ever shown me how to be a father, and a son was so very different from a daughter.

Nancy agreed to drive Jonathan and me to the airport, and Lauren would meet us there; she was coming straight from school for the start of spring break with one of her teaching friends, Dacia. Lauren had traveled with her before, but this time Dacia coming was also sort of a buffer. If there was a stranger with us, she hoped we would behave better.

It had been a few years since I'd been on an airplane, and the flight to Europe was longer than any of our excursions to Mexico or the Caribbean. Security took too long, the seats seemed smaller, and while I expected horrible food, I didn't realize there wouldn't be any food at all. Luckily, we had stopped in the airport to grab a bite before boarding the plane, so that would tide us over. Sleep eluded me in the nights before our trip, so it was a blessing when I finally nodded off a few minutes after takeoff.

When I woke a few hours later, I looked around the cabin and tried to focus my eyes. Taking off my glasses, I rubbed the sleep away and cleared my throat. The interior of the plane came into focus and I saw that I was seated on the aisle next to Lauren with Jonathan on the other side of her. They were both absorbed in their electronics with earplugs in and brightly lit screens in front of them. I couldn't help but feel a little joy spring up deep inside at the thought of getting to spend an entire week with these two.

In Rome, we checked into our rooms, one for the girls and one for the boys, and agreed to meet in a half hour to go find something to eat. While I brushed my hair and washed my face, it began to dawn on me that somehow I had gotten to

Italy, on vacation, with my kids. It was lucky that I had made it this far and that, somehow, I had been given this opportunity to make memories with them—happy memories. As I walked downstairs I made a choice that, no matter what, I would not waste this trip; I would enjoy this time that we had been given.

Lauren booked the flights and hotels, arranged for the car, and made sure we all had current passports, but my God, the girl had packed our itinerary. I don't think she realized it, but my big activity each day was making a cheese sandwich or driving to the store to buy the materials to make said cheese sandwich. Walking three miles just to see the Trevi Fountain to start the day was going to be a challenge. I really didn't care what we were looking at or where we were going. After all, I wasn't there to sightsee; all I wanted was to spend time with my family.

For a guy who had never been to Europe, I was spoiled that week with the sights and sounds of Italy. We visited the Colosseum—or what is left of it—took in the Sistene Chapel, and heard the Pope give an address on Palm Sunday in the Vatican. And while the dynamics between us weren't perfect, we had found a way to relate to each other. With every place we visited and each meal we ate sitting together, we grew a little bit closer. The most amazing part of the trip was that Jon-boy could have been our paid tour guide. When we would approach a church, his pace would quicken, and he'd excitedly begin describing the style of architecture and then launch into a seminar on the artists featured inside and what was special about their work. While I had always wanted him to be a lawyer, it was really special to get to see how much he had learned while majoring in art history. He had shifted his focus a few times while in school, but who was I to talk about that? I had declared a major one semester before graduation. It seemed like he and I maybe had more in common than either of us had considered before.

John, Lauren, and Jonathan in Vatican City

Italian food was traditionally my specialty, my all'Amatriciana and vodka sauces had opened many doors for me. Getting to experience true Italian cuisine was something I had always dreamt about. I don't know what they were doing to the cows in Italy, but the fresh mozzarella just didn't compare to anything I'd ever tasted before. Caprese salad was how we began most every meal in Rome, and I just couldn't get enough. At every restaurant we visited, we loaded up on traditional favorites. From creamy rich risotto to prosciutto-wrapped melons, we were treated to exquisite traditional execution. If we did nothing else on the entire trip but eat, we would have been satisfied.

It's true, with every vacation when it comes time to return home, there is a sense of disappointment that the adventure is over. That something you have been looking forward to has come and gone. I knew the moment the plane touched down in Newark that I would never get another experience with my family like the time we spent in Italy, and I was beyond grateful that we got to spend that time together before Lauren's wedding. While it was bittersweet that our trip was over, we had memories to keep forever and a huge milestone on the horizon.

BOLD AS LOVE

IT HAD SEEMED a long way off, but the wedding crept up on us. The few weeks leading up to the event were busy, and I got to see Nancy a lot more than usual. She took me to get fitted for my tuxedo and also to pick it up the night before we drove up to the hotel for the rehearsal dinner. Other than the trip to Italy, this would be the longest stay away from my apartment since my stroke. Being in my element, I was able to prepare for big events with weeks of hard work, but staying in a hotel would definitely be a challenge. Lauren, Jay, Jonathan, Tony, and Nancy would provide a support system, so I hoped for the best.

The rehearsal dinner was at a restaurant, The Melting Pot, right on the Hudson River. There were views of the New York City skyline as we approached, and it was a beautiful sight to behold. With the Empire State Building in the background, it really began to sink in what we were doing here. My baby was getting married. She had found herself a good man, one who genuinely loved her and cared about her and seemed as though he would be able to take care of her, if and when she ever needed someone to. As we walked into the party, I tried to calm my emotions. I didn't want to walk in crying. I took a deep breath, and as I exhaled I felt a hand clamp down on my shoulder. I turned toward it, and there was Tony, his daughter, and granddaughter. He looked much different from the last time I had seen him, but the twinkle in his eye was the same. I grinned from ear to ear and reached around to hug him. This was going to be okay.

We spent the rest of the night with Lauren and Jay, their closest friends, and both sides of their family. I sat with Tony and his family and had an absolutely great time catching up with them. As the night went on, I found myself more at ease than I had expected, and when I laughed, the sound I heard was genuine. How long had it been since I really laughed or had something to laugh about? I didn't know that answer, but I knew that it had been too long.

Getting back to the hotel for the night, I was spent. I said good night to Lauren, Nancy, Jon-boy, and Tony and went up to bed. Sleep, which was usually so elusive, found me easily that night. I woke early, before the sun came up and all my nervous energy crept back in. If I fell back to sleep, I might miss something or be late, so I stayed awake and waited for the rest of the hotel to wake up. There wasn't any smoking allowed in the hotel room, so I rode the elevator down to the lobby and wandered around the parking lot while I smoked a cigarette. I saw another red-tipped glow in the early morning dark, and slowly walked in that direction. Leaning against the railing, and looking toward Manhattan was my brother.

"Couldn't sleep?" I asked.

"I don't ever sleep anymore." He laughed. His Southern accent was thick; his voice sounded more like my mother's than I remembered.

"Me neither," I replied.

We stood and smoked together as the sun rose over the skyline, heading into the lobby to find ourselves some coffee a little after six. There was a lot of time before I needed to be anywhere, so I spent most of the morning putzing around the hotel with Tony and his family. We ate breakfast at the restaurant downstairs and, with a full belly, another wave of exhaustion hit me. Heading upstairs, I decided to stop by Lauren's room to see what she and the girls were up to. I knocked and Dacia opened the door.

"Lauren, your dad is here. Come in, John. Nice to see you," she chattered.

Lauren wasn't in her gown just yet, but her hair and makeup were done and she was close to getting ready to start taking pictures. I could feel how wound-up she was from across the room. I walked over and planted a kiss on the top of her head.

"I'm going to go take a shower and get dressed. You already look great, kid. Don't worry about everything so much."

"I do? Thanks. I'm so anxious, and the day is already flying by," she said. "I just don't want to miss anything."

"You won't. You'll be there for all of it. I'll see you in a bit."

As I started to leave the room, I saw Nancy and Jonathan coming down the hall.

"Oh good, there you are," Nancy said. "Jonathan wants to get his hair cut, and I have to be with Lauren, so I can't take him. Jay made him an appointment with his hairdresser across town. Can you drive him over for me?"

"Uh, sure I can."

At least now I had something to do to pass the time. I gave Jon-boy a ride to get his haircut and blew a few hours hanging around with him. When he came out of the store and met me back at the car, the guy looked slick. His usual shaggy mop had been replaced by a short cut, combed back and gelled into place. I chuckled when I realized how much like me he really looked.

"Looking good, kid. Let's get dressed and get your sister married."

We got back to the hotel just in time to put on our tuxedos and head down to the bridal suite for picture-taking. Lauren seemed to have calmed down a little by this point, and she greeted us both warmly as we came in. My God, was she beautiful. The dress she and Nancy had picked out was gorgeous, all lace from head to toe, with a corset top that laced up the back. Her hair was curled and the top pinned back, so her neckline was open but also soft. She was going to stun them when she walked in.

We pulled up in front of the venue in our limousine right on time. As the driver started to open the door, Lauren yelled, "Wait! I'm not ready. I need one more song."

He shut the door, and we waited another few minutes while she pulled herself together. As the song ended, she looked up at me.

"Let's do this, Dad."

The bridal party walked in to Pachelbel's "Canon in D," played by the harpist. Lauren and I entered last, after the rest of the party was in place. I heard the beginning chords of Wagner's wedding march, "Here Comes the Bride," and stuck out my elbow. The big oak doors swung open into the sunlit room, and the wedding guests stood and turned toward us. Lauren grabbed my elbow and exhaled deeply. She looked up at me before turning to face her groom, and I swear, in that moment, she was the most beautiful thing I had ever seen. I walked her down the aisle, kissed her on the cheek, and took my seat next to Nancy in the front row. We watched together as our firstborn exchanged vows with her love. There really isn't a way to put into words what that moment feels like; it's almost as though every emotion and every feeling ever experienced in the whole world comes crashing in together and, like a wave, washes over you. I knew at that moment that, despite all of my mistakes, all of the things I had gotten wrong, I had been right for her. Nancy and I had gotten her here and now she would do the rest.

Lauren and John walking down the aisle

Jonathan and John Wagner, father and son
at Lauren and Jay's wedding ceremony

Post-wedding, the glow faded—well for me, at least, it faded quickly—and I was back to my room in the basement alone. I devoted my better, more lucid moments to coaching tennis. In the afternoons, my kids would trickle in here and there after school for a few lessons. Summer was right around the corner, and it would bring its usual busyness and buzz. The depressing part was that I looked forward to summer tennis all year long, and it was always over in six weeks, right after it began. Then came fall and the prospect of a cold winter that grew longer with each passing year.

When we'd speak on the phone, Lauren would try to keep me focused on the present, helping me to enjoy each summer day as it passed; there would be plenty of time to be depressed about the winter—no need to worry about it in advance. Taking that advice was key in making the most out of my favorite time of year and made me a better coach for the students. I was correct, though; tennis was over pretty much as quickly as it started. Falling back into the spring routine, I'd hit around on nice days and make myself available for lessons after school. It was the day-to-day routine that kept me going, making it possible to keep my chin up.

Since Nancy and I had split up, the family started to do its own things for the holidays. Jonathan tended to stay up in the city and work through Thanksgiving, coming home just for Christmas. Lauren went to spend Turkey Day with Jay's family, which left me on my own. The second year of that routine, Lauren told me that she wasn't able to really enjoy herself that year while knowing that I was sitting home alone, so her in-laws invited me to come to their house in Pennsylvania. Because I hadn't ever been out there before, Lauren didn't trust me to find my way to their house on my own. So I was to pull myself together and take the train to Hoboken, where she and Jay would pick me up and then drive back to her in-laws' house.

Instead of a week to prepare, I started two weeks before. My "good" clothes had been in the closet since the wedding the spring before, so I pulled them out and made sure they were aired out and clean. Unfortunately, my sport coat had started looking a little threadbare, but without any money, I knew I couldn't get a new one. My loafers were still in good shape, though the tread was worn down. I was almost always cold these days, and Lauren warned me they tended to keep the house on the cooler side. I went through my sweaters, looking for one that didn't have too many moth holes and settled on a yellow merino wool crewneck. I also pulled out a few button-downs and washed my jeans. Packing proved difficult when I realized I didn't have a duffel bag that wasn't filled with tennis rackets.

Lauren was nervous that I wouldn't make it to the train station on time, or that I would miss the connection, or that I'd get off at the wrong stop. Her anxiety rubbed off on me and I'd spent all night lying in bed thinking about the train. How would I get there? Lauren said I should take a taxi, but that cost money I didn't have. I could drive, but then I'd have to leave my car in the parking lot for a couple days and I didn't have the sticker for the commuter lot at the station in Long Branch. Maybe the car could stay in the lot near the hospital or in the grocery store parking lot, and I could walk across the street to catch the train. By the time I came up with that plan, drifting off to sleep would have been possible, but what if I didn't wake up in time and missed my train, ruining the whole weekend. I opted to stay awake and just drive over early.

I parked at the grocery store and then walked over to catch the train. I made it with thirty minutes to spare, so I sat, shivering, on the train platform with my Macy's bag full of clothes. I was the first to board and found myself a comfortable seat next to the window. All I had to do was sit, watch the world go by, and get off when the train stopped in Hoboken. As the stations came and went, I drifted off to a fitful sleep, waking with a start each time the conductor strode through the cabin, shouting the name of each station stop.

There was a miserable, chilly drizzle coming down as I exited the train. Scanning the line of cars for Lauren and Jay, I began to make my way toward his familiar gray Audi. Lauren popped out of the car and rushed to help me with my bag. It was always funny to see her do that, as if I hadn't just managed the bag perfectly well by myself for the past three hours. It must have made her feel useful to be able to help me, or she wouldn't have done it so often, so I let her take the bag and usher me into the back seat.

"Great job, Dad!" she cheered as she shut her car door. "You made it right on time. We should be in Pennsylvania just in time for a late dinner."

"Good, I'm starving," I replied, realizing that I hadn't eaten anything all day.

"I figured as much." Lauren shook her head and handed me a cheese sandwich, a banana, and a bottle of water.

Reaching for the food, I could only laugh. Of course, she had brought me something to eat; she always mothered me. "When are you going to have kids and stop practicing on me?" I asked.

"There's time for that, but not yet. Besides, I don't know how I would be able to take care of you and a baby." She laughed, dismissing me.

As Jay drove around the corner toward the highway, the light turned yellow and we slowed to a stop. Sitting at the intersection, we chatted about the drive and our plans for when we got there. Despite the weather and the holiday traffic we were bound to face, everyone seemed to be in good spirits.

The light turned green, and as we were about to move forward, Jay yelled, "This idiot is going to hit me!"

Coming toward us from the opposite direction, an old SUV was veering into our lane as it skidded through the intersection. We were boxed in and couldn't move to avoid the impact, so instead we braced ourselves. The truck bumped into the front driver side and smashed its way down the side of Jay's car door. As it came to a stop and we all looked around to determine if everyone was okay, I realized with a sinking feeling that our weekend was about to take on a very different tone from the jovial one we had started out with. We pulled over to the side of the road and waited for the police to arrive.

If there was ever a lucky car accident, this was it. As a result of getting hit, Lauren realized she had forgotten a bag of food at home and we were still close enough to their apartment that she walked back to get it. When she got there, she discovered in their haste to pick me up they had left without closing the front door to their apartment. If we had gone to Pennsylvania as planned, there was a very real chance that they would have gotten robbed over the holidays. The second stroke of luck came when we realized that Jay's car was still totally driveable. It wasn't pretty, but all the damage was cosmetic. With a little less wind in our sails, we once again set out for Thanksgiving with Jay's parents.

The weekend was better than I had expected, especially after our rocky start. I don't know what I had been so nervous about; they really were nice people and made every effort to make sure that I was comfortable. The room I slept in was clean, with a bathroom attached, and the Thanksgiving Day food was well done. It's funny how wrapped up in our own traditions we'd become; it hadn't really occurred to me that there were other items people ate on Thanksgiving aside from what we served each year. I missed the mashed potatoes the most, but Lauren made our macaroni and cheese and baked an apple pie, so between those two things and a delicious deep-fried bird, I was satisfied. The best part of the whole experience was getting to see that, while our nuclear family may have fallen apart a bit, Lauren was still enveloped in a loving family environment. She and Jay had dated long enough that she looked like she belonged here with his family around the holiday table, and while I knew there must be the same pangs of sadness that I felt when I thought our own family traditions, she was happy. Her happiness was all that really mattered to me anymore, and seeing her safe and loved put me at ease.

WHIPPING POST

IT WASN'T QUICK. My deterioration began with my stroke, or maybe even with my heart attack, and continued on a slow track that led me to the worst summer of my life. All through the winter, my skin crawled and itched, and I began to have strange pains in my abdomen that I couldn't shake, no matter what I ate or drank. I had been mostly left to my own devices since Lauren announced that she was pregnant. She came occasionally, taking me to the grocery store to buy food I wouldn't eat or taking me to lunch so I could get out of the house, but her attention was decidedly elsewhere.

I tried to keep up appearances and show up for tennis, but the pain in my side was too much; it was truly debilitating. I barely ate, so I knew the size of my belly couldn't be because I was getting fat. Day after day, it continued to grow, swelling like one of those pictures you see of starving children in some third world country. If I did get up and make it to the courts, I would find a comfortable seat in the shade of the only tree and give my instructions from there. The parents understood there really wasn't anything else I could do. I had been teaching these kids for so many years; they knew that if I needed to be seated, it must be for a good reason.

What was usually the best six weeks of my entire year stretched past me with painful new additions to my repertoire of daily problems. The idea of doing basic everyday tasks was so daunting that I simply didn't do them. I didn't wash my laundry; I just took out new clothes each day. I didn't cook dinner; I just ate a piece of whatever was closest to me. It occurred to me that I might be dying, that maybe this was truly it for me, once and for all, and then I'd remember that the baby was coming, that I had to see that baby born, and I'd drag myself out of bed to drink a glass of water.

Lauren called every day, but most days I didn't answer. I couldn't bear the questions, but more than that, I couldn't give her the answers she wanted to hear. No, I didn't feel better. No, I hadn't eaten anything. And no, I didn't know how tennis went, because I couldn't get there. Rather than lie, which took a lot of mental energy, I'd just smile at the phone and let it ring. Her calling was enough to remind me that I still had a purpose, a person who loved and needed me. Soon enough, the baby would come and she would have someone else to take care of, and I could rest.

Tennis was in its last week when Nancy called me. Lauren and Jay were headed to the hospital; our grandchild was going to make her appearance any day now. Lauren was to be induced, as the baby didn't seem to be interested in coming out on her own. She offered to drive me up to Lauren's house to wait. I really felt awful, but this was the moment I had been waiting for; all I had to do was get to her house and I would see Lauren become a mom, my mission fulfilled. I told her to pick me up in an hour and that I would do my best to be ready.

When I got into the car, Nancy looked great. Her tanned skin and healthy excitement was a stark contrast to the way I felt. We made some small talk, but as we drove, I felt myself feeling worse and worse. I asked Nancy for a tissue, and as she handed it across the seat, she really looked at me, probably for the first time in a long time, and realized I wasn't well. I'm sure it was frustrating for her to have to be bogged down with me on what was supposed to be one of the happiest experiences of her life, but she did well to keep that to herself. We made it up to Lauren's house, and I stayed in the backyard while she checked in with Jay to see how things were progressing.

The update wasn't great. Things were slow going and Lauren had been in labor for two days already without much progress. We decided to go to the hospital, hoping that seeing our faces might help. By this point, it was clear that I was really not well, and more than the normal not well I had been feeling for most of the summer. My nose was like a faucet and I had the chills despite the August heat. Walking into the air-conditioned hospital air didn't help things, and by the time we made our way up to Lauren's room, I was visibly shaking. Nancy went in ahead of me and I followed closely behind. As soon I got in, I searched for a tissue and found one next the hospital bed Lauren was in. I blew my nose and threw the tissue into the garbage can by the bed, turning to give Lauren a hug.

"Hey, Daddy," she said, sticking her hand out to mine. "You're not feeling good?"

"Oh baby, I feel awful, though not as awful as you probably feel," I said, trying to joke.

"Yeah, I'm definitely not the most comfortable I've ever been in my life," she replied. "I hate to say this, but if you're sick, you really can't be here. The baby will be brand-new and super susceptible to germs."

"I just spoke with the doctor, John. He says we have to go if you're not well," Nancy chimed in.

The thought never crossed my mind that I would be a danger to the baby. It made sense, of course, but in my deteriorated state, I had a hard time thinking about anyone but myself, let alone someone who wasn't here yet.

"Uh, okay. I guess I should go back home then," I said, beginning to realize what this meant.

I would miss it, the birth of the baby, the moment that I had been clinging to for months as my motivation to take another breath, eat another forkful of tasteless food, and drink another jug of water.

Lauren squeezed my hand. "Listen, once she is here, she will be here for the long haul, so it's okay if you aren't here for the first day. You can be there for the seventh day and the fourteenth day and the hundredth day."

I smiled at her, knowing that was what she needed to see. A hundred days from now was too long, was what I was thinking, but the idea was a good one. I kissed her hand and said goodbye, and Nancy drove me to the train station. She promised to let me know as soon as the baby was born. I thanked her for trying to let me be a part of this and went into the station to buy my ticket home.

My phone was ringing again. In my subconscious, I could hear the ring and felt it pull me closer to the surface. Blindly sticking my hand out into the folds of the bed sheets, I fumbled around until I located the source of the noise. Lauren. I cleared my throat and attempted to sit up.

"Hello," was all I could manage.

"Hey, Dad," she said softly, and I could hear it in her voice—the tension, the anxiety, the buildup that had been present for the previous nine months were gone; there was a relaxed, breathy quality to her voice. "I wanted to let you know that the baby is here."

"Oh, sweetheart, I'm so glad. Is everyone okay? You're okay?"

"Yes, I'm fine. Really tired and probably won't be able to walk for a while, but I'm okay. She's perfect, Dad. Stella is perfect."

She hadn't spoken the baby's name aloud before this, out of superstitious fear that if she dared speak the syllables, someone would be able to take them away from her. Hearing her say it was a signal that the worry had passed, a new chapter had begun, and in it we could speak and move freely. I smiled in spite of the pain that had kept me in bed since getting off the train and catching a taxi back home.

She told me that she had to go, she had to feed the baby, and that as soon as I felt better, I should come see them. I told her, "Of course," and went back to sleep almost immediately.

Reality was that now that the baby was here, the pressure was off. I didn't have to think about what was going to happen; everything had already happened. In my head, I knew that I needed to get up and get on a train to them sooner than later, but I just didn't feel well, and the very last thing I wanted was to get there and be sent home again. Two weeks went by, and I still hadn't made the trip to meet my granddaughter. Lauren was beginning to get upset. I was the only person who hadn't met the baby yet, and that wasn't how it was supposed to be.

On the fifteenth day of Stella's life, I dragged myself out of bed and showered for what seemed like the first time in months. Going into my closet, I realized that the clean clothes I had left were ancient, many ten years old or older. Looking behind the door where I piled the dirty laundry, I realized that the mountain of clothes was about as tall me. That was not good. In the kitchen, there wasn't anything to eat that wasn't growing mold or in a can. I was going to have to get my shit together when I got back.

By some miracle the car started, and I drove it to the train station, parking right in the lot, not caring what happened. I didn't think making the walk from the grocery store was a possibility based on my current state. I made it onto the train and took a seat on the upper deck of the bi-level train. I got off the train in Secaucus and met Lauren at the car. It was funny how different she looked already; she had probably lost twenty pounds since I saw her briefly at the hospital. Getting into the car, I saw my standard travel meal waiting for me. The kid never ceased to amaze me. As I ate my sandwich and drank a bottle of water, my mind started to clear a bit and we made conversation as we drove to her house.

The last baby I held was Jonathan, and that had been over twenty-five years ago. Following instructions, I washed my hands and sat down on the sofa. Lauren covered me with a blanket and then Jay laid the baby on my lap. She was a squirmy pink little thing that really couldn't do anything at all. Even holding her own head was still too hard, so I kept one hand behind her head. Jay took a couple of pictures and Lauren just watched us, always keeping a hand close by in case Stella squirmed out of my arms. It was crazy; while holding her, I couldn't process what was actually happening. It wasn't until Lauren scooped her up and sat down next to us that the full gravity of the moment hit me. The circle had come around, the child had become the adult, and a new generation of the family I'd started with Nancy had begun. All I'd ever hoped for was to do a little better than the generation that came before me. Sitting there on the sofa with my family surrounding me, I felt very far away from that log cabin in the woods.

Stella Mae meets Papa John—August 2015

BOHEMIAN RHAPSODY

FOR YEARS I had wondered what I was still doing here—what was I waiting around for? Meeting my granddaughter, I believed I knew. To truly understand the value of my worth, I needed to witness what the fruits of my labor and love had produced. After watching Lauren with her new baby, I had seen all I needed to see. I had been fighting to survive my entire life, and it felt nice to finally be able to let that guard down.

Getting out of bed had become nearly impossible, and there really wasn't much to get out for. Tennis had finished for the year, and I hadn't worked to set up any fall lessons. I just needed to rest; the summer had been too much this year. My favorite student, Ellie, a young girl in the midst of her high school career, had been playing with me since she was six years old. She called me and asked when we could hit, and I had been putting her off for weeks. Coming out to watch her play a match would mean the world to her, but I couldn't let her know I was coming; I didn't want to end up disappointing her.

Driving to the courts, the pain in my belly soared to a crescendo. It had been a few weeks since I stood, and it took the last of my determination to swing my legs out of the car and approach the fence.

"Coach!" she called, hustling to the fence. "I didn't know you'd be here."

She looked at me eagerly.

"I didn't know I'd be here either. And I can't stay really. I just wanted to, uh, give you this," came my reply, surprising even myself.

Looking down, my favorite Babolat tennis racket was in my hand. I extended it toward her, bridging the gap in the space between us.

"Really?" she asked, in awe. "Are you sure? This is your best racket. You never let anyone use it."

"Yes, Ellie, I'm sure. I don't need it anymore, and you will play with it well. You have all the tools. You can beat any of these girls out here."

"Thank you, Coach. I love it," she said.

I left the racket leaning against the edge of the fence and turned to walk back toward my car. Opening the door and sliding in, I knew I didn't have much time to make it home; I'd have to hurry. Pulling in, my vision began to swim. I stumbled out of the car and made it to my staircase; gripping the rail with both hands, I made my way down the stairs and into the apartment. Lying down on the bed, there wasn't any relief—the pain just shifted to the side.

"Dad? Dad? Are you in here?"

I could hear Lauren, but I couldn't see her. I woke with a start and tried sitting up, my head pounding; I was slick with sweat.

"Here. I'm in here," I managed.

Gingerly, Lauren pushed the door to my bedroom open and looked around.

"Oh, Dad," she whispered. "Oh, no."

"What?" I asked, pushing myself into sitting position.

"You really look awful." Her eyes filled with tears. "Like, this is the worst I've ever seen you."

She reached in to hug me and took in the rest of the room. The mountain of clothes behind my door was spilling out across the floor. My bed only had one sheet on it, which was dirty. I knew it was dirty, but following her gaze, I realized I must not have made it to the bathroom the last time my stomach spasmed. Trying to cover the mess, I pulled my pillow down to cover the spot, bit my lip, and looked at her.

"This is bad?" I questioned, already knowing the answer.

She took a deep breath. "Yes, it's bad. I'm sorry. I should've come sooner."

"Where's the baby?"

"I left her with Jay. You haven't answered the phone in four days. Have you been lying in here for four days?" she asked.

We both knew the answer, so I didn't bother responding. I sat on the edge of the bed and Lauren opened the closet. It was empty.

"I guess it was a good thing I decided to get you some new shirts for your birthday," she said, pulling a gift bag into view, "Sixty-nine years young this week."

I had slept through my birthday? What else had I missed? "I have to eat something," I said, standing up.

"Okay, you get dressed. Here's some new, clean clothes, and we'll go to Richard's for lunch. But, Dad, I'm going to take you to the hospital afterward. You need a doctor."

She looked at me expecting a fight, my typical *I don't need a doctor* routine, but instead, I nodded my consent. She went into my living room to wait while I got dressed. I could hear her opening drawers and cabinets, realizing there wasn't any food in the house. When I came out, she didn't give me a hard time; she just took my arm in hers and led me to the front door.

At Richard's, I discovered I couldn't talk to anyone coherently. Lauren asked for our table and then helped me walk across the room. When the waitress came, Lauren ordered for me. When the food came, she cut it up for me. I put small bites of my BLT sandwich into my mouth and tried to chew. My gums hurt, though, and while I should have been starving, I just didn't have an appetite. We made small talk, discussed the weather, talked about the baby and how big she was getting. I was starting to get dizzy again, so Lauren signaled for the check.

We pulled up into the parking lot outside the emergency room where Nancy worked, where our children had been born, where I'd gone when I had my heart attack and my stroke. There was a chill in the air as I stepped out of the car. Pulling open the cellophane on a new pack, I tried to get out a cigarette. Fumbling for the lighter, Lauren looked at me and shook her head.

"Dad, seriously, I don't think you should smoke that right now. You're really not well, and it's definitely not going to make you feel better. If anything, you'll feel worse, which is hard to imagine, right?"

The wind blew and the cold air sank straight into my bones. I looked around the lot and put the cigarette back into the freshly opened pack. Lauren stuck out her arm, and I turned to face the building.

"Cold today," she muttered. "When you get out of here it will almost be winter."

"Winter for who?" I asked.

Chuckling, she said, "Well, winter for everyone."

"No, not for me. I'm finished with winter."

She led me into the hospital and checked me in. Nancy came down to see me. She was at work that day, and the three of us stood there in the emergency room together, waiting for the doctors to poke and prod me.

"Listen, Dad, I have to go." Lauren looked at me regretfully. "It's time to feed the baby. I will come back and visit you, though. Promise me you won't leave the hospital unless the doctors say you can."

"Baby, I'm not going anywhere. You take care of that baby. Give her and Jay a kiss for me. I love you."

"I love you, too," she said, planting a kiss on my forehead and squeezing my hand.

I watched her walk through the doors and thought about all the things I had accomplished, the love that I had shared, and the stark contrast between where I began my life and where I was now. Despite my transgressions, my faults, and my mistakes, I had fought to make something of myself, to escape the hell that I was born into. My life hadn't been traditional, it hadn't been ordinary, but it had been worth something. I had made a difference in the world. As the sounds and the lights faded out of the room, with Nancy standing by my side, I allowed myself to finally stop fighting. There wasn't anything left for me to do.

My struggle was finally over.

EPILOGUE
ACROSS THE UNIVERSE

WE ROLLED INTO the parking lot one minute before the ceremony was slated to begin. It wasn't the entrance I had hoped for, but it would have to do. Jay, Stella, and I raced across the parking lot, collecting ourselves as we hurried to join the rest of the guests. It was a bright and clear summer morning, and a small crowd had gathered at the entrance of the tennis courts.

"Good morning, Mr. Mayor. Pleasure to meet you," I said, extending my hand.

"Oh, you must be Lauren. The pleasure is all mine," Mayor Schneider responded warmly, shaking my hand. "Great to finally put a face to the voice on the phone."

I smiled and turned to meet the gaze of Kyle Jennings. Looking around, I knew all the people at the ceremony. They had all been part of the tennis program, the program that my father had started to save the kids of Long Branch, the same program that ended up saving him. There were kids, their parents, the high school tennis coach, city councilmen and women, and, of course, my family. We were all there to share a moment that my father never would have dreamed possible sitting on his log in the woods.

I heard Kyle say my name, and I came back to the present moment. The group was looking at me expectantly; it was my turn. I approached Kyle and together we removed the cover that had been blocking the sign. Next to the entrance of the courts, where my father spent the last ten years of his life, was a newly installed sign, which read,

Wagner Courts
Dedicated 2016
In honor of
Coach John Wagner
Passionate Visionary—Lover of the Game
For his work with the Long Branch Youth Tennis Program

One by one, people got up and spoke about what the tennis program meant to them, how my father had changed their lives in the short time they had gotten to know him. As his former students fondly recalled their favorite memories of him, I couldn't help but smile. I wasn't smiling at their stories or because I was proud of what he had accomplished. I smiled because while they had all known a small part of the man I called my dad, I knew the whole man, and my memories of him couldn't be shared in a few minutes at a dedication ceremony; they could fill an entire book. My larger-than-life storyteller was gone, but he will never be forgotten because our connection can never be erased.

When I think about my father and the difference his love has made in my life, I know that all his suffering, struggling, and fighting was worth it. He had his faults and he definitely had some regrets, but through his trials and tribulations, and even in his failures, he taught me the most important lesson of all: you get what you give. If you strive for greatness day in and day out, you will achieve greatness; if you give in to life's temptations, they will distract you from your purpose. I gave him love, and he returned it to me tenfold. So I will keep fighting, and I will keep surviving, because no matter where you come from or how you get where you are, the world will be a better place if we all just give each other a little bit more of ourselves. That is his legacy and what he left behind on those courts for his students: give love, get love, be love.

THE END

Plaque erected by Long Branch Recreation Department

ACKNOWLEDGEMENTS

THIS BOOK HAS been my labor of love. A way for me to continue to connect with the man to whom I owe so much. Since his death, I have gotten to spend time every single day in his presence, just by helping archive his story for future generations. For these extra stolen moments, I will be eternally grateful. I needed this time alone with him to process all that he was, and all that he wasn't. Through writing his painful story and reliving each mistake he made again, I have gained the clarity, perspective, and commitment to not make those same mistakes myself.

First, I'd like to thank my mother. Without her support and steadfast guidance, this story would have had a much different ending. While her role in my life wasn't nearly as glamorous, or probably even as much fun, without her I would not be who I am today. While I learn from my father's mistakes, I strive to be as practical and caring as my mother. Also from my family of origin, I owe a debt of gratitude to my brother, Jonathan. We share genetics, and we share childhood memories, but most of all we share the love that was instilled in us by our parents. Without his blessing, I would never have been able to feel comfortable sharing this story.

Beyond that, my friends and family also deserve a moment in the sun. They have all listened to these stories over the years and they are the ones who made me believe that this story was actually something special. Thank you for your encouragement and enthusiasm. You have lifted me up, time and again. The Inkshares community has also stood behind this project in ways that I never saw coming. They have helped answer questions and bolstered my confidence when it was lacking.

A very special thank you to my sister-in-law, Lisa Levis, who poured her creativity into an amazing cover design. I sent her a blurry, out of focus picture of my father standing in a fountain at the USTA Billie Jean King National Tennis Center, and she was able to extract the true meaning of that moment and created the beautiful artwork you are holding in your hands as we speak.

My acknowledgements would be incomplete without special mention of the man who helped me to achieve this dream and so many others over the years. Thank you to my husband, Jay, for your unconditional love, pureness of heart, and tireless support. Our love has been the greatest blessing I could have ever hoped to receive, and I appreciate you and all that you do that allows me to be me.

And, lastly, to my darling Stella. You have brought me to a new phase in my life, and have made me a mother. The job of raising you is the best one I have ever had, and I hope to instill in you the passion for life and immense amount of love that my father instilled in me.

Thank you for reading.

Cover Inspiration

GRAND PATRONS

Abigail Schmelzer
Adam Laub
Amy Warren
Angela Mourer
Bert Gilbert
Bill O'Neil
Blakely Collier
Bob and Susan Levis
Bridget Sayde
Carl Edwards
Carol Volk
Charlie Palella
Dan Blidner
Danielle Quku Rutnik
Danielle Rainey
Fred Levis

Glenn O. Connor
Jay Levis
Jeffrey Warren
Jessica Madalon
John Liccardo
Katie C. McKenna
Lauren Collier
Michael P O'Neil Jr
Nancy Holford Wagner
Naomi A. Singer
Robert A. Stanton II
Sandra C. ONeil
Stella Levis
Steve Cochran
Sumi Chang
Will Sayde

INKSHARES

INKSHARES is a reader-driven publisher and producer based in Oakland, California. Our books are selected not by a group of editors, but by readers worldwide.

While we've published books by established writers like *Big Fish* author Daniel Wallace and *Star Wars: Rogue One* scribe Gary Whitta, our aim remains surfacing and developing the new author voices of tomorrow.

Previously unknown Inkshares authors have received starred reviews and been featured in the *New York Times*. Their books are on the front tables of Barnes & Noble and hundreds of independents nationwide, and many have been licensed by publishers in other major markets. They are also being adapted by Oscar-winning screenwriters at the biggest studios and networks.

Interested in making your own story a reality? Visit Inkshares.com to start your own project or find other great books.